Behavioral Finance and Wealth Management

Founded in 1807, John Wiley & Sons is the oldest independent publishing company in the United States. With offices in North America, Europe, Australia, and Asia, Wiley is globally committed to developing and marketing print and electronic products and services for our customers' professional and personal knowledge and understanding.

The Wiley Finance series contains books written specifically for finance and investment professionals as well as sophisticated individual investors and their financial advisors. Book topics range from portfolio management to e-commerce, risk management, financial engineering, valuation, and financial instrument analysis, as well as much more.

For a list of available titles, please visit our web site at www.Wiley Finance.com.

Behavioral Finance and Wealth Management

How to Build Optimal Portfolios That Account for Investor Biases

MICHAEL M. POMPIAN

WILEY

John Wiley & Sons, Inc.

Published by John Wiley & Sons, Inc., Hoboken, New Jersey.
Published simultaneously in Canada.

For general information on our other products and services or for technical
support, please contact our Customer Care Department within the United
States at (800) 762-2974, outside the United States at (317) 572-3993, or fax
(317) 572-4002.

Wiley also publishes its books in a variety of electronic formats. Some content
that appears in print may not be available in electronic books. For more information about Wiley products, visit our web site at www.wiley.com.

Library of Congress Cataloging-in-Publication Data:

Pompian, Michael, 1963–
  Behavioral finance and wealth management : building optimal portfolios that
account for investor biases / Michael Pompian.
      p. cm. — (Wiley finance series)
    Includes bibliographical references and index.
    ISBN-13 978-0-471-74517-4 (cloth)
    ISBN-10 0-471-74517-0 (cloth)
    1. Investments—Psychological aspects.   2. Investments—Decision making.
I. Title.   II. Series
  HG4515.15.P66   2006
  332.601'9—dc22   2005027756

Printed in the United States of America.

10 9 8 7 6 5 4 3 2 1

This book is dedicated to my wife, Angela. I couldn't have done this without her.

Contents

PART THREE
Case Studies

PART FOUR
Special Topics in Practical Application of Behavioral Finance

Preface

If successful, this book will change your idea about what an optimal investment portfolio is. It is intended to be a guide both to understanding irrational investor behavior and to creating individual investors' portfolios that account for these irrational behaviors. In this book, an optimal portfolio lies on the efficient frontier, but it may move up or down that frontier depending on the individual needs and preferences of each investor. When applying behavior finance to real-world investment programs, an optimal portfolio is one with which an investor can comfortably live, so that he or she has the ability to adhere to his or her investment program, while at the same time reach long-term financial goals.

Given the run-up in stock prices in the late 1990s and the subsequent popping of the technology bubble, understanding irrational investor behavior is as important as it has ever been. This is true not only for the markets in general but most especially for individual investors. This book will be used primarily by financial advisors, but it can also be effectively used by sophisticated individual investors who wish to become more introspective about their own behaviors and to truly try to understand how to create a portfolio that works for them. The book is not intended to sit on the polished mahogany bookcases of successful advisors as a showpiece: It is a guidebook to be used and implemented in the pursuit of building better portfolios.

The reality of today's advisor-investor relationship demands a better understanding of individual investors' behavioral biases and an awareness of these biases when structuring investment portfolios. Advisors need to focus more acutely on why their clients make the decisions they do and whether behaviors need to be modified or adapted to. If advisors can successfully accomplish this difficult task, the relationship will be strengthened considerably, and advisors can enjoy the loyalty of clients who end the search for a new advisor.

In the past 250 years, many schools of economic and social thought have been developed, some of which have come and gone, while others are still very relevant today. We will explore some of these ideas to give some perspective on where behavioral finance is today. In the past 25 years, the interest in behavioral finance as a discipline has not only emerged but rather exploded onto the scene, with many articles written by very prestigious authors in prestigious publications. We will review some of the key people who have shaped the current body of behavioral finance thinking and review work done by them. And then the intent is to take the study of behavioral finance to another level: developing a common understanding (definition) of behavioral biases in terms that advisors and investors can understand and demonstrating how biases are to be used in practice through the use of case studies—a "how-to" of behavioral finance. We will also explore some of the new frontiers of behavioral finance, things not even discussed by today's advisors that may be common knowledge in 25 years.

A CHALLENGING ENVIRONMENT

Investment advisors have never had a more challenging environment to work in. Many advisors thought they had found nirvana in the late 1990s, only to find themselves in quicksand in 2001 and 2002. And in today's low-return environment, advisors are continuously peppered with vexing questions from their clients:

"Why is this fund not up as much as that fund?"
"The market has not done well the past quarter—what should we do?"
"Why is asset allocation so important?"
"Why are we investing in alternative investments?"
"Why aren't we investing in alternative investments?"
"Why don't we take the same approach to investing in college money and retirement money?"
"Why don't we buy fewer stocks so we can get better returns?"

Advisors need a handbook that can help them deal with the behavioral and emotional sides of investing so that they can help their clients understand why they have trouble sticking to a long-term program of investing.

WHY THIS BOOK?

This book was conceived only after many hours, weeks, and years of re-searching, studying, and applying behavioral finance concepts to real-world investment situations. When I began taking an interest in how portfolios might be adjusted for behavioral biases back in the late 1990s, when the technology bubble was in full force, I sought a book like this one but couldn't find one. I did not set a goal of writing a book at that time; I merely took an interest in the subject and began reading. It wasn't until my wife, who was going through a job transition, came home one night talk-ing about the Myers-Briggs personality type test she took that I began to consider the idea of writing about behavioral finance. My thought process at the time was relatively simple: Doesn't it make sense that people of dif-fering personality types would want to invest differently? I couldn't find any literature on this topic. So, with the help of a colleague on the private wealth committee at NYSSA (the New York Society of Securities Analysts —the local CFA chapter), John Longo, Ph.D., I began my quest to write on the practical application of behavioral finance. Our paper, entitled "A New Paradigm for Practical Application of Behavioral Finance: Correlating Personality Type and Gender with Established Behavioral Biases," was ul-timately published in the *Journal of Wealth Management* in the fall of 2003 and, at the time, was one of the most popular articles in that issue. Several articles later, I am now writing this book. I am a practitioner at the forefront of the practical application of behavioral finance.

As a wealth manager, I have found the value of understanding the be-havioral biases of clients and have discovered some ways to adjust in-vestment programs for these biases. You will learn about these methods. By writing this book, I hope to spread the knowledge that I have devel-oped and accumulated so that other advisors and clients can benefit from these insights. Up until now, there has not been a book available that has served as a guide for the advisor or sophisticated investor to create port-folios that account for biased investor behavior. My fervent hope is that this book changes that.

WHO SHOULD USE THIS BOOK?

The book was originally intended as a handbook for wealth management practitioners who help clients create and manage investment portfolios.

As the book evolved, it became clear that individual investors could also greatly benefit from it. The following are the target audience for the book:

■ *Traditional Wire-house Financial Advisors.* A substantial portion of the wealth in the United States and abroad is in the very capable hands of traditional wire-house financial advisors. From a historical perspective, these advisors have not traditionally been held to a fiduciary standard, as the client relationship was based primarily on financial planning being "incidental" to the brokerage of investments. In today's modern era, many believe that this will have to change, as "wealth management," "investment advice," and brokerage will merge to become one. And the change is indeed taking place within these hallowed organizations. Thus, it is crucial that financial advisors develop stronger relationships with their clients because advisors will be held to a higher standard of responsibility. Applying behavioral finance will be a critical step in this process as the financial services industry continues to evolve.

■ *Private Bank Advisors and Portfolio Managers.* Private banks, such at U.S. Trust, Bessemer Trust, and the like, have always taken a very solemn, straightlaced approach to client portfolios. Stocks, bonds, and cash were really it for hundreds of years. Lately, many of these banks have added such nontraditional offerings as venture capital, hedge funds, and others to their lineup of investment product offerings. However, many clients, including many extremely wealthy clients, still have the big three—stocks, bonds, and cash—for better or worse. Private banks would be well served to begin to adopt a more progressive approach to serving clients. Bank clients tend to be conservative, but they also tend to be trusting and hands-off clients. This client base represents a vast frontier to which behavioral finance could be applied because these clients either do not recognize that they do not have an appropriate portfolio or tend to recognize only too late that they should have been more or less aggressive with their portfolios. Private banks have developed a great trust with their clients and should leverage this trust to include behavioral finance in these relationships.

■ *Independent Financial Advisors.* Independent registered representatives (wealth managers who are Series 7 registered but who are not affiliated with major stock brokerage firms) have a unique opportunity to apply behavioral finance to their clients. They are typically not part of a vast firm and may have fewer restrictions than their wire-house brethren. These advisors, although subject to regulatory scrutiny, can for the most part create their own ways of serving clients; and with many seeing that great success is growing their business, they can deepen and broaden these relationships by including behavioral finance.

■ *Registered Investment Advisors.* Of all potential advisors that could include behavioral finance as a part of the process of delivering wealth management services, it is my belief that registered investment advisors (RIAs) are well positioned to do so. Why? Because RIAs are typically smaller firms, which have fewer regulations than other advisors. I envision RIAs asking clients, "How do you feel about this portfolio?" "If we changed your allocation to more aggressive, how might your behavior change?" Many other types of advisors cannot and will not ask these types of questions for fear of regulatory or other matters, such as pricing, investment choices, or others.

■ *Consultants and Other Financial Advisors.* Consultants to individual investors, family offices, or other entities that invest for individuals can also greatly benefit from this book. Understanding how and why their clients make investment decisions can greatly impact the investment choices consultants can recommend. When the investor is happy with his or her allocation and feels good about the selection of managers from a psychological perspective, the consultant has done his or her job and will likely keep that client for the long term.

■ *Individual Investors.* For those individual investors who have the ability to look introspectively and assess their behavioral biases, this book is ideal. Many individual investors who choose either to do it themselves or to rely on a financial advisor only for peripheral advice often find themselves unable to separate their emotions from the investment decision-making process. This does not have to be a permanent condition. By reading this book and delving deep into their behaviors, individual investors can indeed learn to modify behaviors and to create portfolios that help them stick to their long-term investment programs and, thus, reach their long-term financial goals.

WHEN TO USE THIS BOOK?

First and foremost, this book is generally intended for those who want to apply behavioral finance to the asset allocation process to create better portfolios for their clients or themselves. This book can be used:

- *When there is an opportunity to create or re-create an asset allocation from scratch.* Advisors know well the pleasure of having only cash to invest for a client. The lack of such baggage as emotional ties to certain investments, tax implications, and a host of other issues that accompany an existing allocation is ideal. The time to apply the principles learned in this book is at the moment that one has the opportunity to invest only cash or to clean house on an existing portfolio.
- *When a life trauma has taken place.* Advisors often encounter a very emotional client who is faced with a critical investment decision during a traumatic time, such as a divorce, a death in the family, or job loss. These are the times that the advisor can add a significant amount of value to the client situation by using the concepts learned in this book.
- *When a concentrated stock position is held.* When a client holds a single stock or other concentrated stock position, emotions typically run high. In my practice, I find it incredibly difficult to get people off the dime and to diversify their single-stock holdings. The reasons are well known: "I know the company, so I feel comfortable holding the stock," "I feel disloyal selling the stock," "My peers will look down on me if I sell any stock," "My grandfather owned this stock, so I will not sell it." The list goes on and on. This is the exact time to employ behavioral finance. Advisors must isolate the biases that are being employed by the client and then work together with the client to relieve the stress caused by these biases. This book is essential in these cases.
- *When retirement age is reached.* When a client enters the retirement phase, behavioral finance becomes critically important. This is so because the portfolio structure can mean the difference between living a comfortable retirement and outliving one's assets. Retirement is typically a time of reassessment and reevaluation and is a great opportunity for the advisor to strengthen and deepen the relationship to include behavioral finance.

■ *When wealth transfer and legacy are being considered.* Many wealthy clients want to leave a legacy. Is there any more emotional an issue than this one? Having a frank discussion about what it possible and what is not possible is difficult and is often fraught with emotional crosscurrents that the advisor would be well advised to stand clear of. However, by including behavioral finance into the discussion and taking an objective, outside-councilor's viewpoint, the client may well be able to draw his or her own conclusion about what direction to take when leaving a legacy.

■ *When a trust is being created.* Creating a trust is also a time of emotion that may bring psychological biases to the surface. Mental accounting comes to mind. If a client says to himself or herself, "Okay, I will have this pot of trust money over here to invest, and that pot of spending money over there to invest," the client may well miss the big picture of overall portfolio management. The practical application of behavioral finance can be of great assistance at these times.

Naturally, there are many more situations not listed here that can arise where this book will be helpful.

PLAN OF THE BOOK

Part One of the book is an introduction to the practical application of behavioral finance. These chapters include an overview of what behavioral finance is at an individual level, a history of behavioral finance, and an introduction to incorporating investor behavior into the asset allocation process for private clients. Part Two of the book is a comprehensive review of some of the most commonly found biases, complete with a general description, technical description, practical application, research review, implications for investors, diagnostic, and advice. Part Three of the book takes the concepts presented in Parts One and Two and pulls them together in the form of case studies that clearly demonstrate how practitioners and investors use behavioral finance in real-world settings with real-world investors. Part Four offers a look at some special topics in the practical application of behavioral finance, with an eye toward the future of what might lie in store for the next phase of the topic.

Acknowledgments

I would like to acknowledge all my colleagues, both present and past, who have contributed to broadening my knowledge not only in the topic of this book but also in wealth management in general. You know who you are. In particular, I would like thank my proofreaders Sarah Rogers and Lin Ruan at Dartmouth College. I would also like to acknowledge all of the behavioral finance academics and professionals who have granted permission for me to use their brilliant work. Finally, I would like to thank my parents and extended family for giving me the support to write this book.

PART One

Introduction to the Practical Application of Behavioral Finance

CHAPTER 1

What Is Behavioral Finance?

People in standard finance are rational. People in behavioral finance are normal.

—Meir Statman, Ph.D., Santa Clara University

To those for whom the role of psychology in finance is self-evident, both as an influence on securities markets fluctuations and as a force guiding individual investors, it is hard to believe that there is actually a debate about the relevance of behavioral finance. Yet many academics and practitioners, residing in the "standard finance" camp, are not convinced that the effects of human emotions and cognitive errors on financial decisions merit a unique category of study. Behavioral finance adherents, however, are 100 percent convinced that an awareness of pertinent psychological biases is crucial to finding success in the investment arena and that such biases warrant rigorous study.

This chapter begins with a review of the prominent researchers in the field of behavioral finance, all of whom support the notion of a distinct behavioral finance discipline, and then reviews the key drivers of the debate between standard finance and behavioral finance. By doing so, a common understanding can be established regarding what is meant by *behavioral finance*, which leads to an understanding of the use of this term as it applies directly to the practice of wealth management. This chapter finishes with a summary of the role of behavioral finance in dealing with private clients and how the practical application of behavioral finance can enhance an advisory relationship.

BEHAVIORAL FINANCE: THE BIG PICTURE

Behavioral finance, commonly defined as the application of psychology to finance, has become a very hot topic, generating new credence with the rupture of the tech-stock bubble in March of 2000. While the term *behavioral finance* is bandied about in books, magazine articles, and investment papers, many people lack a firm understanding of the concepts behind behavioral finance. Additional confusion may arise from a proliferation of topics resembling behavioral finance, at least in name, including behavioral science, investor psychology, cognitive psychology, behavioral economics, experimental economics, and cognitive science. Furthermore, many investor psychology books that have entered the market recently refer to various aspects of behavioral finance but fail to fully define it. This section will try to communicate a more detailed understanding of behavioral finance. First, we will discuss some of the popular authors in the field and review the outstanding work they have done (not an exhaustive list), which will provide a broad overview of the subject. We will then examine the two primary subtopics in behavioral finance: Behavioral Finance Micro and Behavioral Finance Macro. Finally, we will observe the ways in which behavioral finance applies specifically to wealth management, the focus of this book.

Key Figures in the Field

In the past 10 years, some very thoughtful people have contributed exceptionally brilliant work to the field of behavioral finance. Some readers may be familiar with the work *Irrational Exuberance*, by Yale University professor Robert Shiller, Ph.D. Certainly, the title resonates; it is a reference to a now-famous admonition by Federal Reserve chairman Alan Greenspan during his remarks at the Annual Dinner and Francis Boyer Lecture of the American Enterprise Institute for Public Policy Research in Washington, D.C., on December 5, 1996. In his speech, Greenspan acknowledged that the ongoing economic growth spurt had been accompanied by low inflation, generally an indicator of stability. "But," he posed, "how do we know when irrational exuberance has unduly escalated asset values, which then become subject to unexpected and prolonged contractions as they have in Japan over the past decade?"[1] In Shiller's *Irratonal Exuberance,* which hit bookstores only days before the 1990s market peaked, Professor Shiller warned investors that stock prices, by various historical measures, had climbed too high. He cautioned that the "public may be very disappointed with the performance of the stock market in coming years."[2] It was reported that Shiller's editor at Princeton University Press rushed the book to print, perhaps fearing a market crash and wanting to warn investors. Sadly, however, few heeded the alarm. Mr. Greenspan's prediction came true, and the bubble burst. Though the correction came later than the Fed chairman had foreseen, the damage did not match the aftermath of the collapse of the Japanese asset price bubble (the specter Greenspan raised in his speech).

Another high-profile behavioral finance proponent, Professor Richard Thaler, Ph.D., of the University of Chicago Graduate School of Business, penned a classic commentary with Owen Lamont entitled "Can the Market Add and Subtract? Mispricing in Tech Stock Carve-Outs,"[3] also on the general topic of irrational investor behavior set amid the tech bubble. The work related to 3Com Corporation's 1999 spin-off of Palm, Inc. It argued that if investor behavior was indeed rational, then 3Com would have sustained a positive market value for a few months after the Palm spin-off. In actuality, after 3Com distributed shares of Palm to shareholders in March 2000, Palm traded at levels exceeding the inherent value of the shares of the original company. "This would not happen in a rational world," Thaler noted. (Professor Thaler is the editor of *Advances in Behavioral Finance,* which was published in 1993.)

One of the leading authorities on behavioral finance is Professor Hersh Shefrin, Ph.D., a professor of finance at the Leavey School of Business at Santa Clara University in Santa Clara, California. Professor Shefrin's highly successful book *Beyond Greed and Fear: Understanding Behavioral Finance and the Psychology of Investing* (Harvard Business School Press, 2000), also forecast the demise of the asset bubble. Shefrin argued that investors have weighed positive aspects of past events with inappropriate emphasis relative to negative events. He observed that this has created excess optimism in the markets. For Shefrin, the meltdown in 2000 was clearly in the cards. Professor Shefrin is also the author of many additional articles and papers that have contributed significantly to the field of behavioral finance.

Two more academics, Andrei Shleifer, Ph.D., of Harvard University, and Meir Statman, Ph.D., of the Leavey School of Business, Santa Clara University, have also made significant contributions. Professor Shleifer published an excellent book entitled *Inefficient Markets: An Introduction to Behavioral Finance* (Oxford University Press, 2000), which is a must-read for those interested specifically in the efficient market debate. Statman has authored many significant works in the field of behavioral finance, including an early paper entitled "Behavioral Finance: Past Battles and Future Engagements,"[4] which is regarded as another classic in behavioral finance research. His research posed decisive questions: What are the cognitive errors and emotions that influence investors? What are investor aspirations? How can financial advisors and plan sponsors help investors? What is the nature of risk and regret? How do investors form portfolios? How important are tactical asset allocation and strategic asset allocation? What determines stock returns? What are the effects of sentiment? Statman produces insightful answers on all of these points. Professor Statman has won the William F. Sharpe Best Paper Award, a Bernstein Fabozzi/Jacobs Levy Outstanding Article Award, and two Graham and Dodd Awards of Excellence.

Perhaps the greatest realization of behavioral finance as a unique academic and professional discipline is found in the work of Daniel Kahneman and Vernon Smith, who shared the Bank of Sweden Prize in Economic Sciences in Memory of Alfred Nobel 2002. The Nobel Prize organization honored Kahneman for "having integrated insights from psychological research into economic science, especially concerning human judgment and decision-making under uncertainty." Smith similarly "established laboratory experiments as a tool in empirical economic analysis, especially in the study of alternative market mechanisms," garnering the recognition of the committee.[5]

Professor Kahneman (Figure 1.1) found that under conditions of uncertainty, human decisions systematically depart from those predicted by standard economic theory. Kahneman, together with Amos Tversky (deceased in 1996), formulated *prospect theory*. An alternative to standard models, prospect theory provides a better account for observed behavior and is discussed at length in later chapters. Kahneman also discovered that human judgment may take heuristic shortcuts that systematically diverge from basic principles of probability. His work has inspired a new generation of research employing insights from cognitive psychology to enrich financial and economic models.

FIGURE 1.1 Daniel Kahneman
Prize winner in Economic Sciences 2002. © The Nobel
Foundation

Vernon Smith (Figure 1.2) is known for developing standards for laboratory methodology that constitute the foundation for experimental economics. In his own experimental work, he demonstrated the importance of alternative market institutions, for example, the rationale by which a seller's expected revenue depends on the auction technique in use. Smith also performed "wind-tunnel tests" to estimate the implications of alternative market configurations before such conditions are implemented in practice. The deregulation of electricity markets, for example, was one scenario that Smith was able to model in advance. Smith's work has been instrumental in establishing experiments as an essential tool in empirical economic analysis.

FIGURE 1.2   Vernon L. Smith
Prize winner in Economic Sciences 2002. © The Nobel
Foundation.

Behavioral Finance Micro versus Behavioral Finance Macro

As we have observed, behavioral finance models and interprets phenomena ranging from individual investor conduct to market-level outcomes. Therefore, it is a difficult subject to define. For practitioners and investors reading this book, this is a major problem, because our goal is to develop a common vocabulary so that we can apply to our benefit the very valuable body of behavioral finance knowledge. For purposes of this book, we adopt an approach favored by traditional economics textbooks; we break our topic down into two subtopics: Behavioral Finance Micro and Behavioral Finance Macro.

1. Behavioral Finance Micro (BFMI) examines *behaviors or biases of individual investors* that distinguish them from the rational actors envisioned in classical economic theory.
2. Behavioral Finance Macro (BFMA) detects and describe *anomalies* in the efficient market hypothesis that behavioral models may explain.

As wealth management practitioners and investors, our primary focus will be BFMI, the study of individual investor behavior. Specifically, we want to identify relevant psychological biases and investigate their influence on asset allocation decisions so that we can manage the effects of those biases on the investment process.

Each of the two subtopics of behavioral finance corresponds to a distinct set of issues within the standard finance versus behavioral finance discussion. With regard to BFMA, the debate asks: Are markets "efficient," or are they subject to behavioral effects? With regard to BFMI, the debate asks: Are individual investors perfectly rational, or can cognitive and emotional errors impact their financial decisions? These questions are examined in the next section of this chapter; but to set the stage for the discussion, it is critical to understand that much of economic and financial theory is based on the notion that individuals act rationally and consider all available information in the decision-making process. In academic studies, researchers have documented abundant evidence of irrational behavior and repeated errors in judgment by adult human subjects.

Finally, one last thought before moving on. It should be noted that there is an entire body of information available on what the popular press has termed "the psychology of money." This subject involves individuals' relationship with money—how they spend it, how they feel about it, and how they use it. There are many useful books in this area; however, this book will not focus on these topics.

THE TWO GREAT DEBATES OF STANDARD FINANCE VERSUS BEHAVIORAL FINANCE

This section reviews the two basic concepts in standard finance that behavioral finance disputes: rational markets and rational economic man. It also covers the basis on which behavioral finance proponents challenge each tenet and discusses some evidence that has emerged in favor of the behavioral approach.

Overview

On Monday, October 18, 2004, a very significant article appeared in the *Wall Street Journal*. Eugene Fama, one of the pillars of the efficient market school of financial thought, was cited admitting that stock prices could become "somewhat irrational."[6] Imagine a renowned and rabid Boston Red Sox fan proposing that Fenway Park be renamed *Steinbrenner Stadium* (after the colorful New York Yankees owner), and you may begin to grasp the gravity of Fama's concession. The development raised eyebrows and pleased many behavioralists. (Fama's paper "Market Efficiency, Long-Term Returns, and Behavioral Finance" noting this concession at the Social Science Research Network is one of the most popular investment downloads on the web site.) The *Journal* article also featured remarks by Roger Ibbotson, founder of Ibboston Associates: "There is a shift taking place," Ibbotson observed. "People are recognizing that markets are less efficient than we thought."[7]

As Meir Statman eloquently put it, "Standard finance is the body of knowledge built on the pillars of the arbitrage principles of Miller and Modigliani, the portfolio principles of Markowitz, the capital asset pricing theory of Sharpe, Lintner, and Black, and the option-pricing theory of Black, Scholes, and Merton."[8] Standard finance theory is designed to provide mathematically elegant explanations for financial questions that, when posed in real life, are often complicated by imprecise, inelegant conditions. The standard finance approach relies on a set of assumptions that oversimplify reality. For example, embedded within standard finance is the notion of "Homo Economicus," or rational economic man. It prescribes that humans make perfectly rational economic decisions at all times. Standard finance, basically, is built on rules about how investors "should" behave, rather than on principles describing how they actually behave. Behavioral finance attempts to identify and learn from the human psychological phenomena at work in financial markets and within individual investors. Behavioral finance, like standard finance, is ultimately governed by basic precepts and assumptions. However, standard finance grounds its assumptions in idealized financial behavior; behavioral finance grounds its assumptions in observed financial behavior.

Efficient Markets versus Irrational Markets

During the 1970s, the standard finance theory of market efficiency became the model of market behavior accepted by the majority of academics and a good number of professionals. The Efficient Market Hypothesis had matured in the previous decade, stemming from the doctoral dissertation of Eugene Fama. Fama persuasively demonstrated that in a securities market populated by many well-informed investors, investments will be appropriately priced and will reflect all available information. There are three forms of the efficient market hypothesis:

1. The "Weak" form contends that all past market prices and data are fully reflected in securities prices; that is, technical analysis is of little or no value.
2. The "Semistrong" form contends that all publicly available information is fully reflected in securities prices; that is, fundamental analysis is of no value.
3. The "Strong" form contends that all information is fully reflected in securities prices; that is, insider information is of no value.

If a market is efficient, then no amount of information or rigorous analysis can be expected to result in outperformance of a selected benchmark. An *efficient market* can basically be defined as a market wherein large numbers of rational investors act to maximize profits in the direction of individual securities. A key assumption is that relevant information is freely available to all participants. This competition among market participants results in a market wherein, at any given time, prices of individual investments reflect the total effects of all information, including information about events that have already happened, and events that the market expects to take place in the future. In sum, at any given time in an efficient market, the price of a security will match that security's intrinsic value.

At the center of this market efficiency debate are the actual portfolio managers who manage investments. Some of these managers are fervently passive, believing that the market is too efficient to "beat"; some are active managers, believing that the right strategies can consistently generate alpha (*alpha* is performance above a selected benchmark). In reality, active managers beat their benchmarks only roughly 33 percent of the time on average. This may explain why the popularity of exchange traded funds (ETFs) has exploded in the past five years and why venture capitalists are now supporting new ETF companies, many of which are offering a variation on the basic ETF theme.

The implications of the efficient market hypothesis are far-reaching.

Most individuals who trade stocks and bonds do so under the assumption that the securities they are buying (selling) are worth more (less) than the prices that they are paying. If markets are truly efficient and current prices fully reflect all pertinent information, then trading securities in an attempt to surpass a benchmark is a game of luck, not skill.

The market efficiency debate has inspired literally thousands of studies attempting to determine whether specific markets are in fact "efficient." Many studies do indeed point to evidence that supports the efficient market hypothesis. Researchers have documented numerous, persistent anomalies, however, that contradict the efficient market hypothesis. There are three main types of market anomalies: Fundamental Anomalies, Technical Anomalies, and Calendar Anomalies.

Fundamental Anomalies.   Irregularities that emerge when a stock's performance is considered in light of a fundamental assessment of the stock's value are known as *fundamental anomalies*. Many people, for example, are unaware that value investing—one of the most popular and effective investment methods—is based on fundamental anomalies in the efficient market hypothesis. There is a large body of evidence documenting that investors consistently overestimate the prospects of growth companies and underestimate the value of out-of-favor companies.

One example concerns stocks with low price-to-book-value (P/B) ratios. Eugene Fama and Kenneth French performed a study of low price-to-book-value ratios that covered the period between 1963 and 1990.[9] The study considered all equities listed on the New York Stock Exchange (NYSE), the American Stock Exchange (AMEX), and the Nasdaq. The stocks were divided into 10 groups by book/market and were reranked annually. The lowest book/market stocks outperformed the highest book/market stocks 21.4 percent to 8 percent, with each decile performing more poorly than the previously ranked, higher-ratio decile. Fama and French also ranked the deciles by beta and found that the value stocks posed lower risk and that the growth stocks had the highest risk. Another famous value investor, David Dreman, found that for the 25-year period ending in 1994, the lowest 20 percent P/B stocks (quarterly adjustments) significantly outperformed the market; the market, in turn, outperformed the 20 percent highest P/B of the largest 1,500 stocks on Compustat.[10]

Securities with low price-to-sales ratios also often exhibit performance that is fundamentally anomalous. Numerous studies have shown that low P/B is a consistent predictor of future value. In *What Works on Wall Street,* however, James P. O'Shaughnessy demonstrated that stocks with low price-to-sales ratios outperform markets in general and also outperform stocks with high price-to-sales ratios. He believes that the price/sales ratio is the strongest single determinant of excess return.[11]

Low price-to-earnings (P/E) ratio is another attribute that tends to anomalously correlate with outperformance. Numerous studies, including David Dreman's work, have shown that low P/E stocks tend to outperform both high P/E stocks and the market in general.[12]

Ample evidence also indicates that stocks with high dividend yields tend to outperform others. The Dow Dividend Strategy, which has received a great deal of attention recently, counsels purchasing the 10 highest-yielding Dow stocks.

Technical Anomalies.   Another major debate in the investing world revolves around whether past securities prices can be used to predict future securities prices. "Technical analysis" encompasses a number of techniques that attempt to forecast securities prices by studying past prices. Sometimes, technical analysis reveals inconsistencies with respect to the efficient market hypothesis; these are *technical anomalies.* Common technical analysis strategies are based on relative strength and moving averages, as well as on support and resistance. While a full discussion of these strategies would prove too intricate for our purposes, there are many excellent books on the subject of technical analysis. In general, the majority of research-focused technical analysis trading methods (and, therefore, by extension, the weak-form efficient market hypothesis) finds that prices adjust rapidly in response to new stock market information and that technical analysis techniques are not likely to provide any advantage to investors who use them. However, proponents continue to argue the validity of certain technical strategies.

Calendar Anomalies.   One *calendar anomaly* is known as "The January Effect." Historically, stocks in general and small stocks in particular have delivered abnormally high returns during the month of January. Robert Haugen and Philippe Jorion, two researchers on the subject, note that "the January Effect is, perhaps, the best-known example of anomalous behavior in security markets throughout the world."[13] The January Effect is particularly illuminating because it hasn't disappeared, despite being well known for 25 years (according to arbitrage theory, anomalies should disappear as traders attempt to exploit them in advance).

The January Effect is attributed to stocks rebounding following year-end tax selling. Individual stocks depressed near year-end are more likely to be sold for tax-loss harvesting. Some researchers have also begun to identify a "December Effect," which stems both from the requirement that many mutual funds report holdings as well as from investors buying in advance of potential January increases.

Additionally, there is a Turn-of-the-Month Effect. Studies have shown that stocks show higher returns on the last and on the first four days of each month relative to the other days. Frank Russell Company examined returns of the Standard & Poor's (S&P) 500 over a 65-year period and found that U.S. large-cap stocks consistently generate higher returns at the turn of the month.[14] Some believe that this effect is due to end-of-month cash flows (salaries, mortgages, credit cards, etc.). Chris Hensel and William Ziemba found that returns for the turn of the month consistently and significantly exceeded averages during the interval from 1928 through 1993 and "that the total return from the S&P 500 over this sixty-five-year period was received mostly during the turn of the month."[15] The study implies that investors making regular purchases may benefit by scheduling those purchases prior to the turn of the month.

Finally, as of this writing, during the course of its existence, the Dow Jones Industrial Average (DJIA) has never posted a net decline over any year ending in a "five." Of course, this may be purely coincidental.

Validity exists in both the efficient market and the anomalous market theories. In reality, markets are neither perfectly efficient nor completely anomalous. Market efficiency is not black or white but rather, varies by degrees of gray, depending on the market in question. In markets exhibiting substantial inefficiency, savvy investors can strive to outperform less savvy investors. Many believe that large-capitalization stocks, such as GE and Microsoft, tend to be very informative and efficient stocks but that small-capitalization stocks and international stocks are less efficient, creating opportunities for outperformance. Real estate, while traditionally an inefficient market, has become more transparent and, during the time of this writing, could be entering a bubble phase. Finally, the venture capital market, lacking fluid and continuous prices, is considered to be less efficient due to information asymmetries between players.

Rational Economic Man versus Behaviorally Biased Man

Stemming from neoclassical economics, *Homo economicus* is a simple model of human economic behavior, which assumes that principles of perfect self-interest, perfect rationality, and perfect information govern economic decisions by individuals. Like the efficient market hypothesis, Homo economicus is a tenet that economists uphold with varying degrees of stringency. Some have adopted it in a semistrong form; this version does not see rational economic behavior as perfectly predominant but still assumes an abnormally high occurrence of rational economic traits. Other economists support a weak form of Homo economicus, in which the corresponding traits exist but are not strong. All of these versions share the core assumption that humans are "rational maximizers" who are purely self-interested and make perfectly rational economic decisions. Economists like to use the concept of rational economic man for two primary reasons: (1) Homo economicus makes economic analysis relatively simple. Naturally, one might question how useful such a simple model can be. (2) Homo economicus allows economists to quantify their findings, making their work more elegant and easier to digest. If humans are perfectly rational, possessing perfect information and perfect self-interest, then perhaps their behavior can be quantified.

Most criticisms of Homo economicus proceed by challenging the bases for these three underlying assumptions—perfect rationality, perfect self-interest, and perfect information.

1. *Perfect Rationality.* When humans are rational, they have the ability to reason and to make beneficial judgments. However, rationality is not the sole driver of human behavior. In fact, it may not even be the primary driver, as many psychologists believe that the human intellect is actually subservient to human emotion. They contend, therefore, that human behavior is less the product of logic than of subjective impulses, such as fear, love, hate, pleasure, and pain. Humans use their intellect only to achieve or to avoid these emotional outcomes.

2. *Perfect Self-Interest.* Many studies have shown that people are not perfectly self-interested. If they were, philanthropy would not exist. Religions prizing selflessness, sacrifice, and kindness to strangers would also be unlikely to prevail as they have over centuries. Perfect self-interest would preclude people from performing such unselfish deeds as volunteering, helping the needy, or serving in the military. It

would also rule out self-destructive behavior, such as suicide, alcoholism, and substance abuse.

3. *Perfect Information.* Some people may possess perfect or near-perfect information on certain subjects; a doctor or a dentist, one would hope, is impeccably versed in his or her field. It is impossible, however, for every person to enjoy perfect knowledge of every subject. In the world of investing, there is nearly an infinite amount to know and learn; and even the most successful investors don't master all disciplines.

Many economic decisions are made in the absence of perfect information. For instance, some economic theories assume that people adjust their buying habits based on the Federal Reserve's monetary policy. Naturally, some people know exactly where to find the Fed data, how to interpret it, and how to apply it; but many people don't know or care who or what the Federal Reserve is. Considering that this inefficiency affects millions of people, the idea that all financial actors possess perfect information becomes implausible.

Again, as with market efficiency, human rationality rarely manifests in black or white absolutes. It is better modeled across a spectrum of gray. People are neither perfectly rational nor perfectly irrational; they possess diverse combinations of rational and irrational characteristics, and benefit from different degrees of enlightenment with respect to different issues.

THE ROLE OF BEHAVIORAL FINANCE WITH PRIVATE CLIENTS

Private clients can greatly benefit from the application of behavioral finance to their unique situations. Because behavioral finance is a relatively new concept in application to individual investors, investment advisors may feel reluctant to accept its validity. Moreover, advisors may not feel comfortable asking their clients psychological or behavioral questions to ascertain biases, especially at the beginning of the advisory relationship. One of the objectives of this book is to position behavioral finance as a more mainstream aspect of the wealth management relationship, for both advisors and clients.

As behavioral finance is increasingly adopted by practitioners, clients will begin to see the benefits. There is no doubt that an understanding of how investor psychology impacts investment outcomes will generate insights that benefit the advisory relationship. The key result of a behavioral finance–enhanced relationship will be a portfolio to which the advisor can comfortably adhere while fulfilling the client's long-term goals. This result has obvious advantages—advantages that suggest that behavioral finance will continue to play an increasing role in portfolio structure.

HOW PRACTICAL APPLICATION OF BEHAVIORAL FINANCE CAN CREATE A SUCCESSFUL ADVISORY RELATIONSHIP

Wealth management practitioners have different ways of measuring the success of an advisory relationship. Few could argue that every successful relationship shares some fundamental characteristics:

- The advisor understands the client's financial goals.
- The advisor maintains a systematic (consistent) approach to advising the client.
- The advisor delivers what the client expects.
- The relationship benefits both client and advisor.

So, how can behavioral finance help?

Formulating Financial Goals

Experienced financial advisors know that defining financial goals is critical to creating an investment program appropriate for the client. To best define financial goals, it is helpful to understand the psychology and the emotions underlying the decisions behind creating the goals. Upcoming chapters in this book will suggest ways in which advisors can use behavioral finance to discern why investors are setting the goals that they are. Such insights equip the advisor in deepening the bond with the client, producing a better investment outcome and achieving a better advisory relationship.

Maintaining a Consistent Approach

Most successful advisors exercise a consistent approach to delivering wealth management services. Incorporating the benefits of behavioral finance can become part of that discipline and would not mandate large-scale changes in the advisor's methods. Behavioral finance can also add more professionalism and structure to the relationship because advisors can use it in the process for getting to know the client, which precedes the delivery of any actual investment advice. This step will be appreciated by clients, and it will make the relationship more successful.

Delivering What the Client Expects

Perhaps there is no other aspect of the advisory relationship that could benefit more from behavioral finance. Addressing client expectations is essential to a successful relationship; in many unfortunate instances, the advisor doesn't deliver the client's expectations because the advisor doesn't understand the needs of the client. Behavioral finance provides a context in which the advisor can take a step back and attempt to really understand the motivations of the client. Having gotten to the root of the client's expectations, the advisor is then more equipped to help realize them.

Ensuring Mutual Benefits

There is no question that measures taken that result in happier, more satisfied clients will also improve the advisor's practice and work life. Incorporating insights from behavioral finance into the advisory relationship will enhance that relationship, and it will lead to more fruitful results.

It is well known by those in the individual investor advisory business that investment results are not the primary reason that a client seeks a new advisor. The number-one reason that practitioners lose clients is that clients do not feel as though their advisors understand, or attempt to understand, the clients' financial objectives—resulting in poor relationships. The primary benefit that behavioral finance offers is the ability to develop a strong bond between client and advisor. By getting inside the head of the client and developing a comprehensive grasp of his or her motives and fears, the advisor can help the client to better understand why a portfolio is designed the way it is and why it is the "right" portfolio for him or her—regardless of what happens from day to day in the markets.

CHAPTER 2

The History of Behavioral Finance Micro

*Many individuals grew suddenly rich. A golden bait hung
temptingly out before the people, and one after another, they
rushed to the tulip marts, like flies around a honey-pot. . . . At
last, however, the more prudent began to see that this folly
could not last forever.*

—Charles Mackay,
Memoirs of Extraordinary Popular Delusions (1841),
on the tulip bulb mania of the 1630s.

This chapter traces the development of *behavioral finance micro*
(BFMI). There are far too many authors, papers, and disciplines
that touch on various aspects of behavioral finance (behavioral science, investor psychology, cognitive psychology, behavioral economics, experimental economics, and cognitive science) to examine every
formative influence in one chapter. Instead, the emphasis will be on
major milestones of the past 250 years. The focus is, in particular, on
recent developments that have shaped applications of behavioral finance in private-client situations.

HISTORICAL PERSPECTIVE ON THE LINK BETWEEN PSYCHOLOGY AND ECONOMICS

Historical Roots

Investor irrationality has existed as long as the markets themselves have. Perhaps the best-known historical example of irrational investor behavior dates back to the *early modern* or *mercantilist* period during the sixteenth century. A man named Conrad Guestner transported tulip bulbs from Constantinople, introducing them to Holland. Beautiful and difficult to obtain, tulips were a consumer sensation and an instant status symbol for the Dutch elite. Although most early buyers sought the flowers simply because they adored them, speculators soon joined the fray to make a profit. Trading activity escalated, and eventually, tulip bulbs were placed onto the local market exchanges.

The obsession with owning tulips trickled down to the Dutch middle class. People were selling everything they owned—including homes, livestock, and other essentials—so they could acquire tulips, based on the expectation that the bulbs' value would continue to grow. At the peak of the tulip frenzy, a single bulb would have sold for about the equivalent of several tons of grain, a major item of furniture, a team of oxen, or a breeding stock of pigs. Basically, consumers valued tulips about as highly as they valued pricey, indispensable, durable goods. By 1636, tulip bulbs had been established on the Amsterdam stock exchange, as well as exchanges in Rotterdam, Harlem, and other locations in Europe. They became such a prominent commodity that tulip notaries were hired to record transactions, and public laws and regulations developed to oversee the tulip trade. Can you imagine? Later that year, however, the first speculators began to liquidate their tulip holdings. Tulip prices weakened slowly at first and then plunged; within a month, the bulbs lost 90 percent of their value. Many investors, forced to default on their tulip contracts, incurred huge losses. Do we notice any parallels to the economic events of 1929 or 2000 or similar bubbles?

It wasn't until the mid-eighteenth-century onset of the classical period in economics, however, that people began to study the human side of economic decision making, which subsequently laid the groundwork for behavioral finance micro. At this time, the concept of utility was introduced to measure the satisfaction associated with consuming a good or a service. Scholars linked economic utility with human psychology and even morality, giving it a much broader meaning than it would take on later, during neoclassicism, when it survived chiefly as a principle underlying laws of supply and demand.

Many people think that the legendary *Wealth of Nations* (1776) was what made Adam Smith (Figure 2.1) famous; in fact, Smith's crowning composition focused far more on individual psychology than on production of wealth in markets. Published in 1759, *The Theory of Moral Sentiments* described the mental and emotional underpinnings of human interaction, including economic interaction. In Smith's time, some believed that people's behavior could be modeled in completely rational, almost mathematical terms. Others, like Smith, felt that each human was born possessing an intrinsic moral compass, a source of influence superseding externalities like logic or law. Smith argued that this "invisible hand" guided both social and economic conduct. The prospect of "perfectly rational" economic decision making never entered into Smith's analysis. Instead, even when addressing financial matters, *The Theory of Moral Sentiments* focused on elements like pride, shame, insecurity, and egotism:

FIGURE 2.1   Adam Smith

It is the vanity, not the ease, or the pleasure, which interests us. But vanity is always founded upon the belief of our being the object of attention and approbation. The rich man glories in his riches, because he feels that they naturally draw upon him the attention of the world, and that mankind are disposed to go along with him in all those agreeable emotions with which the advantages of his situation so readily inspire him. At the thought of this, his heart seems to swell and dilate itself within him, and he is fonder of his wealth, upon this account, than for all the other advantages it procures him. The poor man, on the contrary, is ashamed of his poverty. He feels that it either places him out of the sight of mankind, or, that if they take any notice of him, they have, however, scarce any fellow-feeling with the misery and distress which he suffers. He is mortified upon both accounts. For though to be overlooked, and to be disapproved of, are things entirely different, yet as obscurity covers us from the daylight of honour and approbation, to feel that we are taken no notice of, necessarily damps the most agreeable hope, and disappoints the most ardent desire, of human nature.[1]

The topic of this passage is money; yet humanity and emotion play huge roles, reflecting the classical-era view on economic reasoning by individuals. Another famous thinker of the time, Jeremy Bentham, wrote extensively on the psychological aspects of economic utility. Bentham asserted that "the principle of utility is that principle which approves or disapproves of every action whatsoever, according to the tendency which it appears to have to augment or diminish the happiness of the party whose interest is in question: or, what is the same thing in other words, to promote or to oppose that happiness."[2] For Bentham, "every action whatsoever" seeks to maximize utility. Happiness, a subjective experience, is the ultimate human concern—rendering impossible any moral or economic calculation entirely devoid of emotion.

Smith, Bentham, and others recognized the role of psychological idiosyncrasies in economic behavior, but their consensus lost ground over the course of the next century. By the 1870s, three famous economists began to introduce the revolutionary neoclassical framework. William Stanley Jevons's *Theory of Political Economy* (1871), Carl Menger's *Principles of Economics* (1871), and Leon Walras's *Elements of Pure Economics* (1874–1877) defined economics as the study of the allocation of scarce resources among competing forces. Neoclassical theory sought equilibrium solutions whereby individuals maximized marginal utility, subject to situational constraints. Regularities in economies derived from the uniform, simultaneous behavior of individuals optimizing their marginal gains; and large-scale economic phenomena could be explained by simply aggregating the behavior of these individuals. Neoclassical economists distanced themselves from psychology, reframing their discipline as a quantitative science that deduced explanations of economic behavior from assumptions regarding the nature of economic agents.

Pursuing a simple model suited to the neoclassical focus on profit maximization, economists of this period conceived "Homo economicus," or rational economic man to serve as a mathematical representation of an individual economic actor. Based on the assumption that individuals make perfectly rational economic decisions, Homo economicus ignores important aspects of human reasoning.

Rational Economic Man

Rational economic man (REM) describes a simple model of human behavior. REM strives to maximize his economic well-being, selecting strategies that are contingent on predetermined, utility-optimizing goals, on the information that REM possesses, and on any other postulated constraints. The amount of utility that REM associates with any given outcome is represented by the output of his algebraic utility function. Basically, REM is an individual who tries to achieve discretely specified goals to the most comprehensive, consistent extent possible while minimizing economic costs. REM's choices are dictated by his utility function. Often, predicting how REM will negotiate complex trade-offs, such as the pursuit of wages versus leisure, simply entails computing a derivative. REM ignores social values, unless adhering to them gives him pleasure (i.e., registers as a term expressed in his utility function).

The validity of Homo economicus has been the subject of much debate since the model's introduction. As was shown in the previous chapter, those who challenge Homo economicus do so by attacking the basic assumptions of perfect information, perfect rationality, and perfect self-interest. Economists Thorstein Veblen, John Maynard Keynes, and many others criticize Homo economicus, contending that no human can be fully informed of "all circumstances and maximize his expected utility by determining his complete, reflexive, transitive, and continuous preferences over alternative bundles of consumption goods at all times."[3] They posit, instead, "bounded rationality," which relaxes the assumptions of standard expected utility theory in order to more realistically represent human economic decision making. Bounded rationality assumes that individuals' choices are rational but subject to limitations of knowledge and cognitive capacity. Bounded rationality is concerned with ways in which final decisions are shaped by the decision-making process itself.

Some psychological researchers argue that Homo economicus disregards inner conflicts that real people face. For instance, Homo economicus does not account for the fact that people have difficulty prioritizing short-term versus long-term goals (e.g., spending versus saving) or reconciling inconsistencies between individual goals and societal values. Such conflicts, these researchers argue, can lead to "irrational" behavior.

MODERN BEHAVIORAL FINANCE

By the early twentieth century, neoclassical economics had largely displaced psychology as an influence in economic discourse. In the 1930s and 1950s, however, a number of important events laid the groundwork for the renaissance of behavioral economics. First, the growing field of *experimental economics* examined theories of individual choice, questioning the theoretical underpinnings of Homo economicus. Some very useful early experiments generated insights that would later inspire key elements of contemporary behavioral finance.

Twentieth-Century Experimental Economics: Modeling Individual Choice

In order to understand why economists began experimenting with actual people to assess the validity of rational economic theories, it is necessary to understand *indifference curves*. The aim of indifference curve analysis is to demonstrate, mathematically, the basis on which a rational consumer substitutes certain quantities of one good for another. One classic example models the effects of a wage adjustment on a worker's allocation of hours to work versus leisure. Indifference curve analysis also incorporates budget lines (constraints), which signify restrictions on consumption that stem from resource scarcity. In the work-versus-leisure model, for example, workers may not allocate any sum exceeding 24 hours per day.

An indifference curve is a line that depicts all of the possible combinations of two goods between which a person is indifferent; that is, consuming any bundle on the indifference curve yields the same level of utility.

Figure 2.2 maps an exemplary indifference curve. This consumer could consume four hours of work and six hours of leisure—or seven hours of work and three hours of leisure—and achieve equal satisfaction.

With this concept in mind, consider an experiment performed by Louis Leon Thurstone in 1931 on individuals' actual indifference curves.[4] Thurstone reported an experiment in which each subject was asked to make a large number of hypothetical choices between commodity bundles consisting of hats and coats, hats and shoes, or shoes and coats. For example, would an individual prefer a bundle consisting of eight hats and eight pairs of shoes or one consisting of six hats and nine pairs of shoes? Thurstone found that it was possible to estimate a curve that fit fairly closely to the data collected for choices involving shoes and coats and other subsets of the experiment. Thurstone concluded that choice data

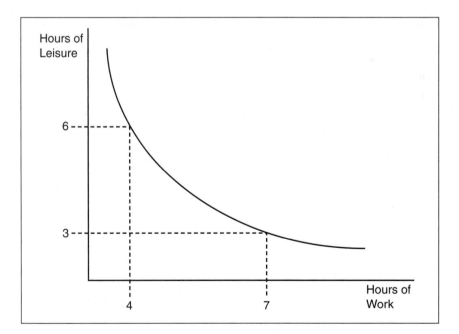

FIGURE 2.2 Indifference Curves Model Consumer Trade-offs

could be adequately represented by indifference curves, and that it was practical to estimate them this way.

Although some researchers felt that Thurston's experiment was too hypothetical, it was still considered important. In the 1940s, two researchers named Stephen W. Rousseas and Albert G. Hart performed some experiments on indifference curves designed to follow up on Thurstone's experiment and to respond to some of the experiment's critics. They constructed what they viewed as a more concrete and realistic choice situation by having subjects select among possible breakfast menus, with each potential breakfast consisting of a specified number of eggs and a specified quantity of bacon strips. They required that "each individual was obliged to eat all of what he chose; i.e., he could not save any part of the offerings for a future time."[5]

In this experiment, individual subjects made only a single choice (repeated subsequently a month later); and, in addition to selecting among available combinations, each was asked to state an ideal combination of bacon and eggs. While this experiment did not ask its subjects to make too many choices of the same type (i.e., different combinations of two goods), thereby averting a common criticism of Thurstone, it left Rousseas and Hart with the problem of trying to aggregate individual choice data collected from multiple individuals. They attempted to ascertain whether choices made by separate individuals stating similar "ideal" breakfast combinations could be pieced together to form consistent indifference curves. This last step presented complications, but overall the project was considered a success and led to further experiments in the same vein.

Also inspired by Thurstone, Frederick Mosteller and Phillip Nogee sought in 1951 to test expected utility theory by experimentally constructing utility curves.[6] Mosteller and Nogee tested subjects' willingness to accept lotteries with given stakes at varying payoff probabilities. They concluded, in general, that it was possible to construct subjects' utility functions experimentally and that the predictions derived from these utility functions were "not so good as might be hoped, but their general direction [was] correct." This is a conclusion that many experimental economists would still affirm, with differing degrees of emphasis.

As these types of experiments continued, various violations of expected utility were beginning to be observed. Perhaps the most famous of violations of expected utility was exposed by another Alfred Nobel Memorial Prize in Economic Sciences winner (1988), Maurice Allais

FIGURE 2.3 Maurice Allais
Prize winner in Economic Sciences 1988. ©
The Nobel Foundation.

(Figure 2.3). Allais made distinguished, pioneering, and highly original contributions in many areas of economic research. Outside of a rather small circle of economists, he is perhaps best known for his studies of risk theory and the so-called Allais paradox. He showed that the theory of maximization of expected utility, which had been accepted for many decades, did not apply to certain empirically realistic decisions under risk and uncertainty. In the Allais paradox, Allais asked subjects to make two hypothetical choices. The first choice was between alternatives "A" and "B," defined as:

A — Certainty of receiving 100 million (francs).
B — Probability .1 of receiving 500 million.
    Probability .89 of receiving 100 million.
    Probability .01 of receiving zero.

The second choice was between alternatives "C" and "D," defined as:

C — Probability .11 of earning 100 million.
    Probability .89 of earning zero.
D — Probability .1 of earning 500 million.
    Probability .9 of earning zero.[7]

It is not difficult to show that an expected utility maximizer who prefers A to B must also prefer C to D. However, Allais reported that A was commonly preferred over B, with D preferred over C. Note that although Allais's choices were hypothetical, the phenomenon he reported has subsequently been reproduced in experiments offering real—albeit much smaller—quantities of money.

As the 1950s concluded and the 1960s progressed, the field of experimental economics expanded, with numerous researchers publishing volumes of data. Their important experiments brought to light new aspects of human economic decision making and drew intellectual attention to the field. Concurrently, two more intellectual disciplines were emerging that would contribute to the genesis of behavioral finance: cognitive psychology and decision theory. Researchers in these subjects would build on concepts learned in experimental economics to further refine the concepts of modern behavioral finance.

Cognitive Psychology

Many scholars of contemporary behavioral finance feel that the field's most direct roots are in cognitive psychology. *Cognitive psychology* is the scientific study of cognition, or the mental processes that are believed to drive human behavior. Research in cognitive psychology investigates a variety of topics, including memory, attention, perception, knowledge representation, reasoning, creativity, and problem solving.

Cognitive psychology is a relatively recent development in the history of psychological research, emerging only in the late 1950s and early 1960s. The term "cognitive psychology" was coined by Ulrich Neisser in 1967, when he published a book with that title. The cognitive approach was actually brought to prominence, however, by Donald Broadbent, who published *Perception and Communication* in 1958.[8] Broadbent promulgated the information-processing archetype of cognition that, to this day, serves as the dominant cognitive psychological model. Broadbent's approach treats mental processes like software running on a computer (the brain). Cognitive psychology commonly describes human thought in terms of input, representation, computation or processing, and output.

As will be discussed later in this chapter, psychologists Amos Tversky and Daniel Kahneman would eventually create a theory—prospect theory—that is viewed as the intellectual foundation of behavioral finance micro. Tversky and Kahneman examined mental processes as they directly relate to decision making under conditions of uncertainty. We will look at this topic now, and then review the groundbreaking work behind prospect theory.

Decision Making under Uncertainty

Each day, people have little difficulty making hundreds of decisions. This is because the best course of action is often obvious and because many decisions do not determine outcomes significant enough to merit a great deal of attention. On occasion, however, many potential decision paths emanate, and the correct course is unclear. Sometimes, our decisions have significant consequences. These situations demand substantial time and effort to try to devise a systematic approach to analyzing various courses of action.

Even in a perfect world, when a decision maker must choose one among a number of possible actions, the ultimate consequences of each, if not every, available action will depend on uncertainties to be resolved in the future. When deciding under uncertainty, there are generally accepted guidelines that a decision maker should follow:

1. Take an inventory of all viable options available for obtaining information, for experimentation, and for action.
2. List the events that may occur.
3. Arrange pertinent information and choices/assumptions.
4. Rank the consequences resulting from the various courses of action.
5. Determine the probability of an uncertain event occurring.

Unfortunately, facing uncertainty, most people cannot and do not systematically describe problems, record all the necessary data, or synthesize information to create rules for making decisions. Instead, most people venture down somewhat more subjective, less ideal paths of reasoning in an attempt to determine the course of action consistent with their basic judgments and preferences. How, then, can decision making be faithfully modeled?

Raiffa. In 1968, in *Decision Analysis: Introductory Lectures on Choices under Uncertainty,*[9] decision theorist Howard Raiffa introduced to the analysis of decisions three approaches that provide a more accurate view of a "real" person's thought process. (1) *Normative* analysis is concerned with the rational solution to the problem at hand. It defines an ideal that actual decisions should strive to approximate. (2) *Descriptive* analysis is concerned with the manner in which real people actually make decisions. (3) *Prescriptive* analysis is concerned with practical advice and tools that might help people achieve results more closely approximating those of normative analysis. Raiffa's contribution laid the foundation for a significant work in the field of behavioral finance micro, an article by Daniel Kahneman and Mark Riepe entitled "Aspects of Investor Psychology: Beliefs, Preferences, and Biases Investment Advisors Should Know About." This work was the first to tie together decision theory and financial advising. According to Kahneman and Riepe, "to advise effectively, advisors must be guided by an accurate picture of the cognitive and emotional weaknesses of investors that relate to making investment decisions: their occasionally faulty assessment of their own interests and true wishes, the relevant facts that they tend to ignore, and the limits of their ability to accept advice and to live with the decisions they make."[10]

Kahnemann and Tversky. At approximately the same time that Howard Raiffa published his work on decision theory, two relatively unknown cognitive psychologists, Amos Tversky and Daniel Kahneman, began research on decision making under uncertainty. This work ultimately produced a very important book published in 1982 entitled *Judgment under Uncertainty: Heuristics and Biases.*[11]

In an interview conducted by a publication called *Current Contents* of ISI in April 1983, Tversky and Kahneman discussed their findings with respect to mainstream investors' thinking:

The research was sparked by the realization that intuitive predictions and judgments under uncertainty do not follow the laws of probability or the principles of statistics. These hypotheses were formulated very early in conversations between us, but it took many years of research and thousands of subject hours to study the role of representativeness, availability, and anchoring, and to explore the biases to which they are prone. The approach to the study of judgment that is reflected in the paper is characterized by (1) a comparison of intuitive judgment to normative principles of probability and statistics, (2) a search for heuristics of judgment and the biases to which they are prone, and (3) an attempt to explore the theoretical and practical implications of the discrepancy between the psychology of judgment and the theory of rational belief.[12]

Essentially, Tversky and Kahneman brought to light the incidence, causes, and effects of human error in economic reasoning. Building on the success of their 1974 paper, the two researchers published in 1979 what is now considered the seminal work in behavioral finance: "Prospect Theory: An Analysis of Decision under Risk." The following is the actual abstract of the paper.

This paper presents a critique of expected utility theory as a descriptive model of decision making under risk, and develops an alternative model, called prospect theory. Choices among risky prospects exhibit several pervasive effects that are inconsistent with the basic tenets of utility theory. In particular, people underweight outcomes that are merely probable in comparison with outcomes that are obtained with certainty. This tendency, called the certainty effect, contributes to risk aversion in choices involving sure gains and to risk seeking in choices involving sure losses. In addition, people generally discard components that are shared by all prospects under consideration. This tendency, called the isolation effect, leads to inconsistent preferences when the same choice is presented in different forms. An alternative theory of choice is developed, in which value is assigned to gains and losses rather than to final assets and in which probabilities are replaced by decision weights. The value function is normally concave for gains, commonly convex for losses, and is generally steeper for losses than for gains. Decision weights are generally lower than the corresponding probabilities, except in the range of low probabilities. Overweighting of low probabilities may contribute to the attractiveness of both insurance and gambling.[13]

Prospect theory, in essence, describes how individuals evaluate gains and losses. The theory names two specific thought processes: editing and evaluation. During the editing state, alternatives are ranked according to a basic "rule of thumb" (heuristic), which contrasts with the elaborate algorithm in the previous section. Then, during the evaluation phase, some reference point that provides a relative basis for appraising gains and losses is designated. A value function, passing through this reference point and assigning a "value" to each positive or negative outcome, is S shaped and asymmetrical in order to reflect loss aversion (i.e., the tendency to feel the impact of losses more than gains). This can also be thought of as risk seeking in domain losses (the reflection effect). Figure 2.4 depicts a value function, as typically diagrammed in prospect theory.

It is important to note that prospect theory also observes how people mentally "frame" predicted outcomes, often in very subjective terms; this accordingly affects expected utility. An exemplary instance of framing is given by the experimental data cited in the 1979 article by Kahneman and Tversky, where they reported that they presented groups of subjects with a number of problems.[14] One group was presented with this problem:

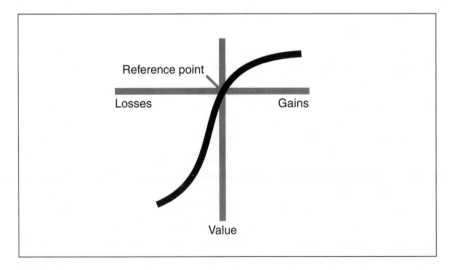

FIGURE 2.4   The Value Function—a Key Tenet of Prospect Theory
Source: The Econometric Society. Reprinted by permission.

1. In addition to whatever you own, you have been given $1,000. You are now asked to choose between:
   A. A sure gain of $500.
   B. A 50 percent chance to gain $1,000 and a 50 percent chance to gain nothing.

Another group of subjects was presented with a different problem:

2. In addition to whatever you own, you have been given $2,000. You are now asked to choose between:
   A. A sure loss of $500.
   B. A 50 percent chance to lose $1,000 and a 50 percent chance to lose nothing.

In the first group, 84 percent of participants chose A. In the second group, the majority, 69 percent, opted for B. The net expected value of the two prospective prizes was, in each instance, identical. However, the phrasing of the question caused the problems to be interpreted differently.

Kahnemann and Riepe.   One of the next significant steps in the evolution of BFMI also involves Daniel Kahneman. Along with Mark Riepe, Kahneman wrote a paper entitled "Aspects of Investor Psychology: Beliefs, Preferences, and Biases Investment Advisors Should Know About."[15] This work leveraged the decision theory work of Howard Raiffa, categorizing behavioral biases on three grounds: (1) *biases of judgment,* (2) *errors of preference,* and (3) biases associated with *living with the consequences of decisions.* Kahneman and Riepe also provide examples of each type of bias in practice.

Biases of judgment include *overconfidence, optimism, hindsight,* and *overreaction to chance events.* Errors of preference include *nonlinear weighting of probabilities;* the tendency of people to *value changes, not states;* the value of *gains and losses as a function;* the *shape and attractiveness of gambles;* the use of *purchase price as a reference point;* *narrow framing;* tendencies related to *repeated gambles and risk policies;* and the adoption of *short* versus *long views.* Living with the consequences of decisions gives rise to *regrets of omission and commission,* and also has implications regarding the relationship between *regret and risk taking.*[16]

One of the reasons that this paper is so important from the practical application perspective is that it was the first scholarly work to really challenge financial advisors to examine their practice from a behavioral standpoint. Moreover, the authors encapsulate their challenge in the form of a detailed "Checklist for Financial Advisors."

PSYCHOGRAPHIC MODELS USED IN BEHAVIORAL FINANCE

Psychographic models are designed to classify individuals according to certain characteristics, tendencies, or behaviors. Psychographic classifications are particularly relevant with regard to individual strategy and risk tolerance. An investor's background and past experiences can play a significant role in decisions made during the asset allocation process. If investors fitting specific psychographic profiles are more likely to exhibit specific investor biases, then practitioners can attempt to recognize the relevant telltale behavioral tendencies before investment decisions are made. Hopefully, resulting considerations would yield better investment outcomes.

Two studies—Barnewall (1987) and Bailard, Biehl, and Kaiser (1986) —apply useful models of investor psychographics.

Barnewall Two-Way Model

One of the oldest and most prevalent psychographic investor models, based on the work of Marilyn MacGruder Barnewall, was intended to help investment advisors interface with clients. Barnewall distinguished between two relatively simple investor types: passive investors and active investors. Barnewall noted:

> "Passive investors" are defined as those investors who have become wealthy passively—for example, by inheritance or by risking the capital of others rather than risking their own capital. Passive investors have a greater need for security than they have tolerance for risk. Occupational groups that tend to have passive investors include corporate executives, lawyers with large regional firms, certified public accountants with large CPA firms,

medical and dental non-surgeons, individuals with inherited wealth, small business owners who inherited the business, politicians, bankers, and journalists. The smaller the economic resources an investor has, the more likely the person is to be a passive investor. The lack of resources gives individuals a higher security need and a lower tolerance for risk. Thus, a large percentage of the middle and lower socioeconomic classes are passive investors as well.

"Active investors" are defined as those individuals who have earned their own wealth in their lifetimes. They have been actively involved in the wealth creation, and they have risked their own capital in achieving their wealth objectives. Active investors have a higher tolerance for risk than they have need for security. Related to their high risk tolerance is the fact that active investors prefer to maintain control of their own investments. If they become involved in an aggressive investment of which they are not in control, their risk tolerance drops quickly. Their tolerance for risk is high because they believe in themselves. They get very involved in their own investments to the point that they gather tremendous amounts of information about the investments and tend to drive their investment managers crazy. By their involvement and control, they feel that they reduce risk to an acceptable level.[17]

Barnewall's work suggests that a simple, noninvasive overview of an investor's personal history and career record could signal potential pitfalls to guard against in establishing an advisory relationship. Her analysis also indicates that a quick, biographic glance at a client could provide an important context for portfolio design.

Bailard, Biehl, and Kaiser Five-Way Model

The Bailard, Biehl, and Kaiser (BB&K) model features some principles of the Barnewall model; but by classifying investor personalities along two axes—level of confidence and method of action—it introduces an additional dimension of analysis. Thomas Bailard, David Biehl, and Ronald Kaiser provided a graphic representation of their model (Figure 2.5) and explain:

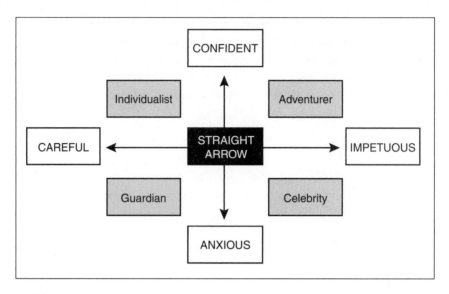

FIGURE 2.5   BB&K Five-Way Model: Graphic Representation
Source: Thomas Bailard, David Biehl, and Ronald Kaiser. *Personal Money Management*, 5th ed. (Chicago: Science Research Associates, 1986).

The first aspect of personality deals with how confidently the investor approaches life, regardless of whether it is his approach to his career, his health, his money. These are important emotional choices, and they are dictated by how confident the investor is about some things or how much he tends to worry about them. The second element deals with whether the investor is methodical, careful, and analytical in his approach to life or whether he is emotional, intuitive, and impetuous. These two elements can be thought of as two "axes" of individual psychology; one axis is called "confident-anxious" and the other is called the "careful-impetuous" axis.[18]

Box 2.1 includes BB&K's descriptions of each of the five investor personality types that the model generates. The authors also suggest approaches to advising each type of client.[19]

In the past five to ten years, there have been some new and exciting developments in the practical application of behavioral finance micro.

The **Adventurer**—People who are willing to put it all on one bet and go for it because they have confidence. They are difficult to advise, because they have their own ideas about investing. They are willing to take risks, and they are volatile clients from an investment counsel point of view.

The **Celebrity**—These people like to be where the action is. They are afraid of being left out. They really do not have their own ideas about investments. They may have their own ideas about other things in life, but not investing. As a result they are the best prey for maximum broker turnover.

The **Individualist**—These people tend to go their own way and are typified by the small business person or an independent professional, such as a lawyer, CPA, or engineer. These are people who are trying to make their own decisions in life, carefully going about things, having a certain degree of confidence about them, but also being careful, methodical, and analytical. These are clients whom everyone is looking for—rational investors with whom the portfolio manager can talk sense.

The **Guardian**—Typically as people get older and begin considering retirement, they approach this personality profile. They are careful and a little bit worried about their money. They recognize that they face a limited earning time span and have to preserve their assets. They are definitely not interested in volatility or excitement. Guardians lack confidence in their ability to forecast the future or to understand where to put money, so they look for guidance.

The **Straight Arrow**—These people are so well balanced, they cannot be placed in any specific quadrant, so they fall near the center. On average this group of clients is the average investor, a relatively balanced composite of each of the other four investor types, and by implication a group willing to be exposed to medium amounts of risk.

BOX 2.1 BB&K Five Investor Personality Types
Source: Thomas Bailard, David Biehl, and Ronald Kaiser. *Personal Money Management*, 5th ed. (Chicago: Science Research Associates, 1986).

Specifically, there is some very thoughtful work being done in the field of brain research that is attempting to demonstrate how the brain works when making financial decisions. Additionally, research is also conducted on how various personality types behave when it comes to making financial decisions. Later in this book, a chapter is devoted to each of several of these new, exciting topics. For now, however, basic strategies for incorporating behavioral finance into the asset allocation decision are introduced in Chapter 3.

Incorporating Investor Behavior into the Asset Allocation Process

If you don't know who you are, the stock market is an expensive place to find out.

—Adam Smith, *The Money Game*

The foundations of behavioral finance micro have been covered, so the discussion turns to the main focus of this book: practical applications for investors and advisors. This chapter establishes a basic framework for integrating behavioral finance insights into portfolio structure.

PRACTICAL APPLICATION OF BEHAVIORAL FINANCE

Almost anyone who knows from experience the challenge of wealth management also knows the potential for less-than-rational decision making in finance. Therefore, many private-client advisors, as well as sophisticated investors, have an incentive to learn coping mechanisms that might curb such systematic miscalculations. The overview of behavioral finance research suggests that this grow ing field is ideally positioned to assist these real-world economic actors. However, only a few of the biases identified in behavioral finance research today are common considerations impacting asset allocation. Why does behavioral finance remain underutilized in the mainstream of wealth management?

First, because no one has ever contextualized it in an appropriately user-friendly manner. Researchers have worked hard to reveal behavioral biases, which are certainly usable; but practitioners would benefit not merely from an academic discourse on discovered biases, but also from lessons on how to go about detecting biases themselves and advising their clients on how best to deal with these biases. Second, once an investor's behavioral biases *have* been identified, advisors lack pragmatic guidelines for tailoring the asset allocation process to reflect the specific bias.

This book intends not only to familiarize financial advisors and investors with 20 of the major biases unearthed in behavioral finance research, but to do so in a lexicon and format that is applicable to asset allocation. This chapter establishes a knowledge base that serves in the following chapters, wherein each of 20 specific biases is reviewed in detail. The central question for advisors when applying behavioral finance biases to the asset allocation decision is: When should advisors attempt to *moderate*, or counteract, biased client reasoning to accommodate a predetermined asset allocation? Conversely, when should advisors *adapt* asset allocation recommendations to help biased clients feel more comfortable with their portfolios?[1]

Furthermore, how extensively should the moderate-or-adapt objective factor into portfolio design? This chapter explores the use of quantitative parameters to indicate the magnitude of the adjustment an advisor might implement in light of a particular bias scenario.

This chapter, which reviews the practical consequences of investor bias in asset allocation decisions, might, with any luck, sow the seeds of a preliminary thought process for establishing an industry-standard methodology for detecting and responding to investor biases. This chapter, first, examines the limitations of typical risk tolerance questionnaires in asset allocation; next, introduces the concept of *best practical allocation*, which in practice is an allocation that is behaviorally adjusted; then identifies clients' behavioral biases and discusses how discovering a bias might shape an asset allocation decision; finally, reviews a quantitative guideline methodology that can be utilized when adjusting asset allocations to account for biases.

Limitations of Risk Tolerance Questionnaires

Today, a dizzying variety of sources supply financial advice. In an attempt to standardize asset allocation processes, financial service firms ask and may, for compliance reasons, require their advisors to administer risk tolerance questionnaires to clients and potential clients prior to drafting any asset allocation. In the absence of any other diagnostic analysis, this methodology is certainly useful and generates important information. However, it is important to recognize the limitations of risk tolerance questionnaires. William Sharpe—Nobel Prize winner, prolific portfolio theorist, capital markets expert, and manager of the Financial Engines advisory firm—discounts the use of risk tolerance questionnaires. He argues that risk tolerance levels, which the tests purport to measure, don't have significant implications for portfolio design.[2] In general, there are a number of factors that restrict the usefulness of risk tolerance questionnaires. Aside from ignoring behavioral issues, an aspect shortly examined, a risk tolerance questionnaire can also generate dramatically different results when administered repeatedly but in slightly varying formats to the same individual. Such imprecision arises primarily from inconsistencies in the wording of questions. Additionally, most risk tolerance questionnaires are administered once and may not be revisited. Risk tolerance can vary directly as a result of changes and events throughout life. Another critical issue with respect to risk tolerance questionnaires is that many advisors interpret their results too literally. For example, some clients might indicate that the maximum loss they would be willing to tolerate in a single year would comprise 20 percent of their total assets. Does that mean that an ideal portfolio would place clients in a position to lose 20 percent? No! Advisors should set portfolio parameters that preclude clients from incurring the maximum specified tolerable loss in any given period. For these reasons, risk tolerance questionnaires provide, at best, broad guidelines for asset allocation and should only be used in concert with other behavioral assessment tools.

From the behavioral finance perspective, in fact, risk tolerance questionnaires may work well for institutional investors but fail regarding psychologically biased individuals. An asset allocation that is generated and executed based on mean-variance optimization can often result in a scenario in which a client demands, in response to short-term market fluctuations and the detriment of the investment plan, that his or her asset allocation be changed. Moving repeatedly in and out of an allocation can cause serious, long-term, negative consequences. Behavioral biases need to be identified before the allocation is executed so that such problems can be avoided.

BEST PRACTICAL ALLOCATION

Practitioners are often vexed by their clients' decision-making processes when it comes to structuring investment portfolios. Why? As noted in the previous section, many advisors, when designing a standard asset allocation program with a client, first administer a risk tolerance questionnaire, then discuss the client's financial goals and constraints, and finally recommend the output of a mean-variance optimization. Less-than-optimal outcomes are often a result of this process because the client's interests and objectives may not be fully accounted for. According to Kahneman and Riepe, financial advising is "a prescriptive activity whose main objective should be to guide investors to make decisions that serve their best interest."[3] Clients' interests may indeed derive from their natural psychological preferences—and these preferences may not be served best by the output of a mean-variance model optimization output. Investors may be better served by moving themselves up or down the efficient frontier, adjusting risk and return levels depending on their behavioral tendencies.

More simply, a client's *best practical allocation* may be a slightly underperforming long-term investment program to which the client can comfortably adhere, warding off an impulse to "change horses" in the middle of the race. In other cases, the best practical allocation might contradict clients' natural psychological tendencies, and these clients may be well served to accept risks in excess of their individual comfort levels in order to maximize expected returns. The remainder of this book develops an understanding of how, exactly, a real client situation might be construed in order to determine a particular allocative approach. In sum, the right allocation is the one that helps the client to attain financial goals while simultaneously providing enough psychological security for the client to sleep at night. The ability to create such optimal portfolios is what advisors and investors should try to gain from this book.

HOW TO IDENTIFY BEHAVIORAL BIASES WITH CLIENTS

Chapters 4 through 23 discuss 20 prominent biases, along with strategies for identifying and applying them in client relationships. In general, biases are diagnosed by means of a specific series of questions. Some bias chapters will contain a list of diagnostic questions to determine susceptibility to each bias. In other chapters, more of a case-study approach is used to determine susceptibility. In either case, as advisors begin to incorporate behavioral analysis into their wealth management practices, they will need to administer diagnostic "tests" with utmost discretion, especially at the outset of a relationship. As they get to know their clients better, advisors reading this book should try to apply what they've learned in order to gain a tentative sense of a client's biases prior to administering any tests. This will improve the quality of advice when taking into account behavioral factors.

HOW TO APPLY BIAS DIAGNOSES WHEN STRUCTURING ASSET ALLOCATIONS

This section has been adapted from an article entitled "Incorporating Behavioral Finance into Your Practice," which I, with my colleague John Longo, originally published in the March 2005 *Journal of Financial Planning*. It sets forth two principles for constructing a best practical allocation in light of client behavioral biases. These principles are not intended as prescriptive absolutes, but rather should be consulted along with other data on risk tolerance, financial goals, asset class preferences, and so on. The principles are general enough to fit almost any client situation; however, exceptions can occur. Later on, some case studies provide a better sense of how these principles are applied in practice.

To review, recall that when considering behavioral biases in asset allocation, financial advisors must first determine whether to moderate or to adapt to "irrational" client preferences. This basically involves weighing the rewards of sustaining a calculated, profit-maximizing allocation against the outcome of potentially affronting the client, whose biases might position them to favor a different portfolio structure entirely. The principles laid out in this section offer guidelines for resolving the puzzle "When to moderate, when to adapt?"

Principle I: Moderate Biases in Less-Wealthy Clients; Adapt to Biases in Wealthier Clients

A client outliving his or her assets constitutes a far graver investment failure than a client's inability to amass the greatest possible fortune. If an allocation performs poorly because it conforms, or adapts, too willingly to a client's biases, then a less-wealthy investor's standard of living could be seriously jeopardized. The most financially secure clients, however, would likely continue to reside in the 99.9th socioeconomic percentile. In other words, if a biased allocation could put a client's way of life at risk, moderating the bias is the best response. If only a highly unlikely event such as a market crash could threaten the client's day-to-day security, then overcoming the potentially suboptimal impact of behavioral bias on portfolio returns becomes a lesser consideration. Adapting is, then, the appropriate course of action.

Principle II: Moderate Cognitive Biases; Adapt to Emotional Biases

Behavioral biases fall into two broad categories, cognitive and emotional, with both varieties yielding irrational judgments. Because cognitive biases stem from faulty reasoning, better information and advice can often correct them. Conversely, because emotional biases originate from impulse or intuition rather than conscious calculations, they are difficult to rectify. Cognitive biases include heuristics (such as anchoring and adjustment), availability, and representativeness biases. Other cognitive biases include ambiguity aversion, self-attribution, and conservatism. Emotional biases include endowment, loss aversion, and self-control. These will be investigated as well as others in much more detail later on.

In some cases, heeding Principles I and II simultaneously yields a blended recommendation. For instance, a less-wealthy client with strong emotional biases should be both adapted to and moderated. Figure 3.1 illustrates this situation. Additionally, these principles reveal that two clients exhibiting the same biases should sometimes be advised differently. (In Chapter 24, the hypothetical cases of Mrs. Adirondack, Mr.

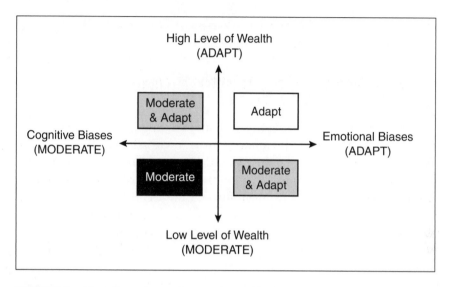

FIGURE 3.1   Visual Depiction of Principles I and II
Reprinted with permission by the Financial Planning Association, *Journal of Financial Planning*, March 2005, M. Pompian and J. Longo, "Incorporating Behavioral Finance into Your Practice." For more information on the Financial Planning Association, please visit www.fpanet.org or call 1-800-322-4237.

Boulder, and the Catskill Family will add clarity to this complex framework, while also illustrating how practitioners can apply Principles I and II to determine the best practical allocation.)

QUANTITATIVE GUIDELINES FOR INCORPORATING BEHAVIORAL FINANCE IN ASSET ALLOCATION

To override the mean-variance optimizer is to depart from the strictly rational portfolio. The following is a recommended method for calculating the magnitude of an acceptable discretionary deviation from default of the mean-variance output allocation. Barring extensive client consultation, a behaviorally adjusted allocation should not stray more than 20 percent from the mean-variance-optimized allocation. The rationale for the 20 percent figure is that most investment policy statements permit discretionary asset class ranges of 10 percent in either direction. For example, if a prototype "balanced" portfolio comprises 60 percent equities and 40 percent fixed-income instruments, a practitioner could make routine discretionary adjustments resulting in a 50 to 70 percent equities composition and a 30 to 50 percent fixed-income composition.

Given here is a basic algorithm for determining how sizable an adjustment could be implemented by an advisor without departing too drastically from the pertinent mean-variance-optimized allocation.

Method for Determining Appropriate Deviations from the Rational Portfolio

1. Subtract each bias-adjusted allocation from the mean-variance output.
2. Divide each mean-variance output by the difference obtained in Step 1. Take the absolute value.
3. Weight each percentage change by the mean-variance output base. Sum to determine bias adjustment factor.

Tables 3.1 and 3.2 show behaviorally modified allocations calculated for two hypothetical investors, Mr. Jones and the Adams Family. Neither client's bias adjustment factor exceeds 20 percent.

SUMMARY OF PART ONE

Congratulations! We have now completed Part One of this book. We introduced the basics of behavioral finance, focusing on the aspects most relevant to individual wealth management. In Chapter 1, we reviewed some of the most important academic scholarship in modern behavioral finance. We also distinguished between micro- and macro-level applications, reviewed the differences characterizing standard versus behavioralist camps, and discussed how incorporating insights from behavioral finance can enhance the private-client advisory relationship.

In Chapter 2, we traced the emergence of the modern behavioral finance discipline, beginning with its roots in the premodern era. We started with a review of the work by Adam Smith and continued our way

TABLE 3.1   Distance from Mean-Variance Output for Mr. Jones

	Mean-Variance Output Recommendation	Behaviorally Adjusted Allocation Recommendation	Variance	Change in Percent (Absolute Value)	Change in Percent (Weighted Average)
Equities	70	75	−5	7%	5%
Fixed income	25	15	10	40%	10%
Cash	5	10	−5	100%	5%
	100	100	Bias Adjustment Factor		= 20%

Reprinted with permission by the Financial Planning Association, *Journal of Financial Planning,* March 2005, Pompian and Longo, "Incorporating Behavioral Finance into Your Practice." For more information on the Financial Planning Association, please visit www.fpanet.org or call 1-800-322-4237.

TABLE 3.2   Distance from Mean-Variance Output for the Adams Family

	Mean-Variance Output Recommendation	Behaviorally Adjusted Allocation Recommendation	Variance	Change in Percent (Absolute Value)	Change in Percent (Weighted Average)
Equities	15	10	5	33%	5%
Fixed income	75	80	−5	7%	5%
Cash	10	10	0	0%	0%
	100	100	Bias Adjustment Factor		= 10%

Reprinted with permission by the Financial Planning Association, *Journal of Financial Planning,* March 2005, Pompian and Longo, "Incorporating Behavioral Finance into Your Practice." For more information on the Financial Planning Association, please visit www.fpanet.org or call 1-800-322-4237.

forward in time to cover Homo economicus and the dawn of the twentieth century. More influences on behavioral finance, which we also examined, included studies in cognitive psychology and decision making under uncertainty. Here, we focused often on the contributions of Kahneman and Tversky, and of Kahneman and Riepe, as well as on psychographic modeling. We also looked at new developments in the practical application of behavioral finance micro.

Chapter 3 dealt with incorporating investor behavior into the asset allocation process. We discussed some of the limitations of risk tolerance questionnaires, introduced the concept of best practical allocation, and looked at methodology for diagnosing behavioral biases in clients. Of critical importance was our discussion of how detecting certain types of biases in particular types of clients might impact asset allocation decisions. The quantitative guidelines laid out for adjusting portfolio structure comprised another key element of Chapter 3. We are now ready to move on to Part Two, which investigates specific investor biases as well as their implications in practice.

Investor Biases Defined and Illustrated

Behavioral biases are defined, abstractly, the same way as systematic errors in judgment. Researchers distinguish a long list of specific biases, applying over 50 of these to individual investor behavior in recent studies. When one considers the derivative and the undiscovered biases awaiting application in personal finance, the list of systematic investor errors seems very long indeed.

More brilliant research seeks to categorize the biases according to some kind of meaningful framework. Some authors refer to biases as heuristics (rules of thumb), while others call them beliefs, judgments, or preferences; still other scholars classify biases along cognitive or emotional lines. This sort of bias taxonomy is helpful—an underlying theory about *why* people operate under bias has not been produced. Instead of a universal theory of investment behavior, behavioral finance research relies on a broad collection of evidence pointing to the ineffectiveness of human decision making in various economic decision-making circumstances.

The classification or categorization of biases, while relevant, is not as important here as are the implications of biased behavior in actual private-client situations. Therefore, no attempt will be made in this book to distinguish elaborately among types of biases, except to note whether a bias is cognitive or emotional. As noted in Chapter 3, this cognitive/ emotional distinction becomes pertinent in the investor case studies, where it helps to determine if an asset allocation should undergo behavioral modification.

The focus will be on gauging the presence or the absence—not the magnitude—of each bias examined; that is, how overconfident someone is will not be decided, but rather if someone is overconfident or not. Furthermore, the discussion is not concerned with how certain biases relate to others, unless to make a practical application point. Finally, it is important to note that the study of behavioral finance is still nascent, and therefore overarching theory of investor behavior should not be a realistic expectation.

OVERVIEW OF THE STRUCTURE OF CHAPTERS 4 THROUGH 23

Each of the following 20 chapters discusses a bias in the same basic format in order to promote greater accessibility. First, each bias is named, categorized as emotional or cognitive, and then generally described and technically described. This is followed by the all-important concrete practical application, where it is demonstrated how each bias has been used or can be used in a practical situation. The practical application portion varies in content, either consisting of an intensive review of applied research or a case study approach. Implications for investors are then delineated. At the end of the practical application section is a research review of work directly applicable to each chapter's topic. A diagnostic test and test results analysis follow, providing a tool to indicate the potential bias of susceptibility. Finally, advice on managing the effects of each bias in order to minimize the effects of biases is offered.

Overconfidence Bias

Too many people overvalue what they are not and undervalue what they are.

—Malcolm S. Forbes

BIAS DESCRIPTION

Bias Name: Overconfidence
Bias Type: Cognitive

General Description.   In its most basic form, *overconfidence* can be summarized as unwarranted faith in one's intuitive reasoning, judgments, and cognitive abilities. The concept of overconfidence derives from a large body of cognitive psychological experiments and surveys in which subjects overestimate both their own predictive abilities and the precision of the information they've been given. People are poorly calibrated in estimating probabilities—events they think are certain to happen are often far less than 100 percent certain to occur. In short, people think they are smarter and have better information than they actually do. For example, they may get a tip from a financial advisor or read something on the Internet, and then they're ready to take action, such as making an investment decision, based on their perceived knowledge advantage.

Technical Description.   Numerous studies have shown that investors are overconfident in their investing abilities. Specifically, the confidence intervals that investors assign to their investment predictions are too narrow. This type of overconfidence can be called *prediction overconfidence*. For example, when estimating the future value of a stock, overconfident investors will incorporate far too little leeway into the range of expected payoffs, predicting something between a 10 percent gain and decline, while history demonstrates much more drastic standard deviations. The implication of this behavior is that investors may underestimate the downside risks to their portfolios (being, naturally, unconcerned with "upside risks"!).

Investors are often also too certain of their judgments. We will refer to this type of overconfidence as *certainty overconfidence*. For example, having resolved that a company is a good investment, people often become blind to the prospect of a loss and then feel surprised or disappointed if the investment performs poorly. This behavior results in the tendency of investors to fall prey to a misguided quest to identify the "next hot stock." Thus, people susceptible to certainty overconfidence often trade too much in their accounts and may hold portfolios that are not diversified enough.

PRACTICAL APPLICATION

Prediction Overconfidence.   Roger Clarke and Meir Statman demonstrated a classic example of prediction overconfidence in 2000 when they surveyed investors on the following question: "In 1896, the Dow Jones Average, which is a price index that does not include dividend reinvestment, was at 40. In 1998, it crossed 9,000. If dividends had been reinvested, what do you think the value of the DJIA would be in 1998? In addition to that guess, also predict a high and low range so that you feel 90 percent confident that your answer is between your high and low guesses."[1] In the survey, few responses reasonably approximated the potential 1998 value of the Dow, and no one estimated a correct confidence interval. (If you are curious, the 1998 value of the Dow Jones Industrial Average [DJIA], under the conditions postulated in the survey, would have been 652,230!)

A classic example of investor prediction overconfidence is the case of the former executive or family legacy stockholder of a publicly traded company such as Johnson & Johnson, ExxonMobile, or DuPont. These investors often refuse to diversify their holdings because they claim "insider knowledge" of, or emotional attachment to, the company. They cannot contextualize these stalwart stocks as risky investments. However, dozens of once-iconic names in U.S. business—AT&T, for example—have declined or vanished.

Certainty Overconfidence.   People display certainty overconfidence in everyday life situations, and that overconfidence carries over into the investment arena. People tend to have too much confidence in the accuracy of their own judgments. As people find out more about a situation, the accuracy of their judgments is not likely to increase, but their confidence does increase, as they fallaciously equate the quantity of information with its quality. In a pertinent study, Baruch Fischoff, Paul Slovic, and Sarah Lichtenstein gave subjects a general knowledge test and then asked them how sure they were of their answer. Subjects reported being 100 percent sure when they were actually only 70 percent to 80 percent correct.[2] A classic example of certainty overconfidence occurred during the technology boom of the late 1990s. Many investors simply loaded up on technology stocks, holding highly concentrated positions, only to see these gains vanish during the meltdown.

Implications for Investors.   Both prediction and certainty overconfidence can lead to making investment mistakes. Box 4.1 lists four behaviors, resulting from overconfidence bias, that can cause harm to an investor's portfolio. Advice on overcoming these behaviors follows the diagnostic test later in the chapter.

RESEARCH REVIEW

Numerous studies analyze the detrimental effects of overconfidence by investors, but the focus here is on one landmark work that covers elements of both prediction and certainty overconfidence. Professors Brad Barber and Terrance Odean, when at the University of California at Davis, studied the 1991–1997 investment transactions of 35,000 households, all holding accounts at a large discount brokerage firm, and they published their results in a 2001 paper, "Boys Will Be Boys: Gender, Overconfidence, and Common Stock Investment."[3] Barber and Odean

1. Overconfident investors overestimate their ability to evaluate a company as a potential investment. As a result, they can become blind to any negative information that might normally indicate a warning sign that either a stock purchase should not take place or a stock that was already purchased should be sold.

2. Overconfident investors can trade excessively as a result of believing that they possess special knowledge that others don't have. Excessive trading behavior has proven to lead to poor returns over time.

3. Because they either don't know, don't understand, or don't heed historical investment performance statistics, overconfident investors can underestimate their downside risks. As a result, they can unexpectedly suffer poor portfolio performance.

4. Overconfident investors hold underdiversified portfolios, thereby taking on more risk without a commensurate change in risk tolerance. Often, overconfident investors don't even know that they are accepting more risk than they would normally tolerate.

BOX 4.1 Overconfidence Bias: Behaviors That Can Cause Investment Mistakes

were primarily interested in the relationship between overconfidence as displayed by both men and women and the impact of overconfidence on portfolio performance.

Overconfident investors overestimate the probability that their personal assessments of a security's value are more accurate than the assessments offered by others. Disproportionate confidence in one's own valuations leads to differences of opinion, which influences trading. Rational investors only trade and purchase information when doing so increases their expected utility. Overconfident investors decrease their expected utilities by trading too much; they hold unrealistic beliefs about how high their returns will be and how precisely these returns can be estimated; and, they expend too many resources obtaining investment information. See Figure 4.1.

Odean and Barber noted that overconfident investors overestimate the precision of their information and thereby the expected gains of trad-

FIGURE 4.1   Trading Is Hazardous to Your Wealth
Reprinted with permission by Blackwell Publishing, *Journal of Finance* (April 2000),
Barber and Odean, "Trading Is Hazardous to Your Wealth."

ing. They may even trade when the true expected net gains are negative. Models of investor overconfidence predict that because men are more overconfident than women, men will trade more and perform worse than women. Both men and women in Barber and Odean's study would have done better, on average, if they had maintained their start-of-the-year portfolios for the entire year.

In general, the stocks that individual investors sell go on to earn greater returns than the stocks with which investors replace them. The stocks men chose to purchase underperformed those they chose to sell by 20 basis points per month. For women, the figure was 17 basis points per month. In the end, Barber and Odean summarized overconfidence as a factor that is "hazardous to your wealth." They concluded that "individuals turn over their common stock investments about 70 percent annually." Mutual funds have similar turnover rates. Yet, those individuals and mutual funds that trade most earn lowest returns. They believe that there is a simple and powerful explanation for the high levels of counterproductive trading in financial markets: overconfidence.[4]

DIAGNOSTIC TESTING

This is a diagnostic test for both prediction overconfidence and certainty overconfidence. If you are an investor, take the test and then interpret the results. If you are an advisor, ask your client to take these tests and then discuss the results with you. After analyzing the test results in the next section, we will offer advice on how to overcome the detrimental effects of overconfidence.

Prediction Overconfidence Bias Test

Question 1: Give high and low estimates for the average weight of an adult male sperm whale (the largest of the toothed whales) in tons. Choose numbers far enough apart to be 90 percent certain that the true answer lies somewhere in between.

Question 2: Give high and low estimates for the distance to the moon in miles. Choose numbers far enough apart to be 90 percent certain that the true answer lies somewhere in between.

Question 3: How easy do you think it was to predict the collapse of the tech stock bubble in March of 2000?
a. Easy.
b. Somewhat easy.
c. Somewhat difficult.
d. Difficult.

Question 4: From 1926 through 2004, the compound annual return for equities was 10.4 percent. In any given year, what returns do you expect on *your* equity investments to produce?
a. Below 10.4 percent.
b. About 10.4 percent.
c. Above 10.4 percent.
d. Well above 10.4 percent.

Certainty Overconfidence Bias Test

Question 5: How much control do you believe you have in picking investments that will outperform the market?
a. Absolutely no control.
b. Little if any control.

    c. Some control.

    d. A fair amount of control.

Question 6: Relative to other drivers on the road, how good a driver are you?

    a. Below average.

    b. Average.

    c. Above average.

    d. Well above average.

Question 7: Suppose you are asked to read this statement: "Capetown is the capital of South Africa." Do you agree or disagree?

Now, how confident are you that you are correct?

    a. 100 percent.

    b. 80 percent.

    c. 60 percent.

    d. 40 percent.

    e. 20 percent.

Question 8: How would you characterize your personal level of investment sophistication?

    a. Unsophisticated.

    b. Somewhat sophisticated.

    c.. Sophisticated.

    d. Very sophisticated.

Prediction Overconfidence Bias Test Results Analysis

Question 1: In actuality, the average weight of a male sperm whale is approximately 40 tons. Respondents specifying too restrictive a weight interval (say, "10 to 20 tons") are likely susceptible to prediction overconfidence. A more inclusive response (say, "20 to 100 tons") is less symptomatic of prediction overconfidence.

Question 2: The actual distance to the moon is 240,000 miles. Again, respondents estimating too narrow a range (say, "100,000 to 200,000 miles") are likely to be susceptible to prediction overconfidence. Respondents naming wider ranges (say, "200,000 to 500,000 miles") may not be susceptible to prediction overconfidence.

Question 3: If the respondent recalled that predicting the rupture of the Internet bubble in March of 2000 seemed easy, then this is likely to indicate prediction overconfidence. Respondents describing the collapse as less predictable are probably less susceptible to prediction overconfidence.

Question 4: Respondents expecting to significantly outperform the long-term market average are likely to be susceptible to prediction overconfidence. Respondents forecasting returns at or below the market average are probably less subject to prediction overconfidence.

Certainty Overconfidence Bias Test Results Analysis

Question 5: Respondents professing greater degrees of control over their investments are likely to be susceptible to certainty overconfidence. Responses claiming little or no control are less symptomatic of certainty overconfidence.

Question 6: The belief that one is an above-average driver correlates positively with certainty overconfidence susceptibility. Respondents describing themselves as average or below-average drivers are less likely to exhibit certainty overconfidence.

Question 7: If the respondent agreed with the statement and reported a high degree of confidence in the response, then susceptibility to certainty overconfidence is likely. If the respondent disagreed with the statement, and did so with 50–100 percent confidence, then susceptibility to certainty overconfidence is less likely. If respondents agree but with low degrees of confidence, then they are unlikely to be susceptible to certainty overconfidence. Confidence in one's knowledge can be assessed, in general, with questions of the following kind:
> Which Australian city has more inhabitants—Sydney or Melbourne?
> How confident are you that your answer is correct? Choose one: 50 percent, 60 percent, 70 percent, 80 percent, 90 percent, 100 percent.
> If you answer 50 percent, then you are guessing. If you answer 100 percent, then you are absolutely sure of your answer.

Two decades of research into this topic have demonstrated that in all cases wherein subjects have reported 100 percent certainty when answering a question like the Australia one, the relative frequency of correct answers has been about 80 percent. Where subjects have reported, on average, that they feel 90 percent certain of their answers, the relative frequency of correct answers has averaged 75 percent. Subjects reporting

80 percent confidence in their answers have been correct about 65 percent of the time, and so on.

Question 8: Respondents describing themselves sophisticated or highly sophisticated investors are likelier than others to exhibit certainty overconfidence. If the respondent chose "somewhat sophisticated" or "unsophisticated," susceptibility is less likely.

ADVICE

Overconfidence is one of the most detrimental biases that an investor can exhibit. This is because underestimating downside risk, trading too frequently and/or trading in pursuit of the "next hot stock," and holding an underdiversified portfolio all pose serious "hazards to your wealth" (to borrow from Barber and Odean's phrasing). Prediction and certainty overconfidence have been discussed and diagnosed separately, but the advice presented here deals with overconfidence in an across-the-board, undifferentiated manner. Investors susceptible to either brand of overconfidence should be mindful of all four of the detrimental behaviors identified in Box 4.1. None of these tendencies, of course, is unavoidable, but each occurs with high relative frequency in overconfident investors.

This advice is organized according to the specific behavior it addresses. All four behaviors are "wealth hazards" resulting frequently from overconfidence.

1. **Unfounded belief in own ability to identify companies as potential investments.** Many overconfident investors claim above-average aptitudes for selecting stocks, but little evidence supports this belief. The Odean study showed that after trading costs (but before taxes), the average investor underperformed the market by approximately 2 percent per year.[5] Many overconfident investors also believe they can pick mutual funds that will deliver superior future performance, yet many tend to trade in and out of mutual funds at the worst possible times because they chase unrealistic expectations. The facts speak for themselves: From 1984 through 1995, the average stock mutual fund posted a yearly return of 12.3 percent, whereas the average investor in a stock mutual fund earned 6.3 percent.[6]

   An advisor whose client claims an affinity for predicting hot stocks should consider asking the investor to review trading records of the past two years and then calculate the performance of the client's trades. More often than not, the trading activity will demonstrate poor performance (if it doesn't, go back further in time).

2. **Excessive trading.** In Odean and Barber's landmark study, "Boys Will Be Boys," the average subject's annual portfolio turnover was 80 percent (slightly less than the 84 percent averaged by mutual funds).[7] The least active quintile of participants, with an average annual turnover of 1 percent, earned 17.5 percent annual returns, outperforming the 16.9 percent garnered by the Standard & Poor's index during this period. The most active 20 percent of investors, however, averaged a *monthly* turnover of over 9 percent, and yet realized pretax returns of only 10 percent annually. The authors of the study do indeed seem justified in labeling trading as hazardous.

When a client's account shows too much trading activity, the best advice is to ask the investor to keep track of each and every investment trade and then to calculate returns. This exercise will demonstrate the detrimental effects of excessive trading. Since overconfidence is a cognitive bias, updated information can often help investors to understand the error of their ways.

3. **Underestimating downside risks.** Overconfident investors, especially those who are prone to prediction overconfidence, tend to underestimate downside risks. They are so confident in their predictions that they do not fully consider the likelihood of incurring losses in their portfolios. For an advisor whose client exhibits this behavior, the best course of action is twofold. First, review trading or other investment holdings for potentially poor performance, and use this evidence to illustrate the hazards of overconfidence. Second, point to academic and practitioner studies that show how volatile the markets are. The investor often will get the picture at this point, acquiring more cautious respect for the vagaries of the markets.

4. **Portfolio underdiversification.** As in the case of the retired executive who can't relinquish a former company's stock, many overconfident investors retain underdiversified portfolios because they do not believe that the securities they traditionally favored will ever perform poorly. The reminder that numerous, once-great companies have fallen is, oftentimes, not enough of a reality check. In this situation, the advisor can recommend various hedging strategies, such as costless collars, puts, and so on. Another useful question at this point is:

"If you didn't own any XYZ stock today, would you buy as much as you own today?" When the answer is "no," room for maneuvering emerges. Tax considerations, such as low cost basis, sometimes factor in; but certain strategies can be employed to manage this cost.

A FINAL WORD ON OVERCONFIDENCE

One general implication of overconfidence bias in any form is that overconfident investors may not be well prepared for the future. For example, most parents of children who are high school aged or younger claim to adhere to some kind of long-term financial plan and thereby express confidence regarding their long-term financial well-being. However, a vast majority of households do not actually save adequately for educational expenses, and an even smaller percentage actually possess any "real" financial plan that addresses such basics as investments, budgeting, insurance, savings, and wills. This is an ominous sign, and these families are likely to feel unhappy and discouraged when they do not meet their financial goals. Overconfidence can breed this type of behavior and invite this type of outcome. Investors need to guard against overconfidence, and financial advisors need to be in tune with the problem. Recognizing and curtailing overconfidence is a key step in establishing the basics of a real financial plan.

Representativeness Bias

Fit no stereotypes. Don't chase the latest management fads. The situation dictates which approach best accomplishes the team's mission.

—Colin Powell

BIAS DESCRIPTION

Bias Name: Representativeness
Bias Type: Cognitive

General Description. In order to derive meaning from life experiences, people have developed an innate propensity for classifying objects and thoughts. When they confront a new phenomenon that is inconsistent with any of their preconstructed classifications, they subject it to those classifications anyway, relying on a rough best-fit approximation to determine which category should house and, thereafter, form the basis for their understanding of the new element. This perceptual framework provides an expedient tool for processing new information by simultaneously incorporating insights gained from (usually) relevant/analogous past experiences. It endows people with a quick response reflex that helps them to survive. Sometimes, however, new stimuli resemble—are *representative* of—familiar elements that have already been classified. In reality, these are drastically different analogues. In such an instance, the classification reflex leads to deception, producing an incorrect understanding of the new element that often persists and biases all our future interactions with that element.

Similarly, people tend to perceive probabilities and odds that resonate with their own preexisting ideas—even when the resulting conclusions drawn are statistically invalid. For example, the "Gambler's Fallacy" refers to the commonly held impression that gambling luck runs in streaks. However, subjective psychological dynamics, not mathematical realities, inspire this perception. Statistically, the streak concept is nonsense. Humans also tend to subscribe to something researchers call "the law of small numbers," which is the assumption that small samples faithfully represent entire populations. No scientific principle, however, underlies or enforces this "law."

Technical Description. Two primary interpretations of *representativeness bias* apply to individual investors.

1. *Base-Rate Neglect.* In base-rate neglect, investors attempt to determine the potential success of, say, an investment in Company A by contextualizing the venture in a familiar, easy-to-understand classification scheme. Such an investor might categorize Company A as a "value stock" and draw conclusions about the risks and rewards that follow from that categorization. This reasoning, however, ignores other unrelated variables that could substantially impact the success of the investment. Investors often embark on this erroneous path because it looks like an alternative to the diligent research actually required when evaluating an investment. To summarize this characterization, some investors tend to rely on *stereotypes* when making investment decisions.
2. *Sample-Size Neglect.* In sample-size neglect, investors, when judging the likelihood of a particular investment outcome, often fail to accurately consider the sample size of the data on which they base their judgments. They incorrectly assume that small sample sizes are *representative* of populations (or "real" data). Some researchers call this phenomenon the "law of small numbers." When people do not initially comprehend a phenomenon reflected in a series of data, they will quickly concoct assumptions about that phenomenon, relying on only a few of the available data points. Individuals prone to sample-size neglect are quick to treat properties reflected in such small samples as properties that accurately describe universal pools of data. The small

sample that the individual has examined, however, may not be representative whatsoever of the data at large.

PRACTICAL APPLICATION

This section presents and analyzes two miniature case studies that demonstrate potential investor susceptibility to each variety of representativeness bias and then conducts a practical application research review.

Miniature Case Study Number 1: Base-Rate Neglect

Case Presentation.   Suppose George, an investor, is looking to add to his portfolio and hears about a potential investment through a friend, Harry, at a local coffee shop. The conversation goes something like this:

GEORGE: Hi, Harry. My portfolio is really suffering right now. I could use a good long-term investment. Any ideas?

HARRY: Well, George, did you hear about the new IPO [initial public offering] pharmaceutical company called PharmaGrowth (PG) that came out last week? PG is a hot new company that should be a great investment. Its president and CEO was a mover and shaker at an Internet company that did great during the tech boom, and she has PharmaGrowth growing by leaps and bounds.

GEORGE: No, I didn't hear about it. Tell me more.

HARRY: Well, the company markets a generic drug sold over the Internet for people with a stomach condition that millions of people have. PG offers online advice on digestion and stomach health, and several Wall Street firms have issued "buy" ratings on the stock.

GEORGE: Wow, sounds like a great investment!

HARRY: Well, I bought some. I think it could do great.

GEORGE: I'll buy some, too.

George proceeds to pull out his cell phone, call his broker, and place an order for 100 shares of PG.

Analysis.   In this example, George displays base-rate neglect representativeness bias by considering this hot IPO is, necessarily, representative of a good long-term investment. Many investors like George believe that IPOs make good long-term investments due to all the up-front hype that surrounds them. In fact, numerous studies have shown that a very low percentage of IPOs actually turn out to be good long-term investments. This common investor misperception is likely due to the fact that investors in hot IPOs usually make money in the first few days after the offering. Over time, however, these stocks tend to trail their IPO prices, often never returning to their original levels.

George ignores the statistics and probabilities by not considering that, in the long run, the PG stock will most likely incur losses rather than gains. This concept can be applied to many investment situations. There is a relatively easy way to analyze how an investor might fall prey to base-rate neglect. For example, what is the probability that person A (Simon, a shy, introverted man) belongs to Group B (stamp collectors) rather than Group C (BMW drivers)? In answering this question, most people typically evaluate the degree to which A (Simon) "represents" B or C; they might conclude that Simon's shyness seems to be more representative of stamp collectors than BMW drivers. This approach neglects base rates, however: Statistically, far more people drive BMWs than collect stamps.

Similarly, George, our hypothetical investor, has effectively been asked: What is the probability that Company A (PharmaGrowth, the hot IPO) belongs to Group B (stocks constituting successful long-term investments) rather than Group C (stocks that will fail as long-term investments)? Again, most individuals approach this problem by attempting to ascertain the extent to which A appears characteristically representative of B or C. In George's judgment, PG possesses the properties of a successful long-term investment rather than a failed one. Investors arriving at this conclusion, however, ignore the base-rate fact that IPOs are more likely to fail than to succeed.

Miniature Case Study Number 2: Sample-Size Neglect

Case Presentation.   Suppose George revisits his favorite coffee shop the following week and this time encounters bowling buddy Jim. Jim raves about his stockbroker, whose firm employs an analyst who appears to have made many recent successful stock picks. The conversation goes something like this:

GEORGE: Hi, Jim, how are you?

JIM: Hi, George. I'm doing great! I've been doing superbly in the market recently.

GEORGE: Really? What's your secret?

JIM: Well, my broker has passed along some great picks made by an analyst at her firm.

GEORGE: Wow, how many of these tips have you gotten?

JIM: My broker gave me three great stock picks over the past month or so. Each stock is up now, by over 10 percent.

GEORGE: That's a great record. My broker seems to give me one bad pick for every good one. It sounds like I need to talk to your broker; she has a much better record!

Analysis: As we'll see in a moment, this conversation exemplifies sample-size neglect representativeness bias. Jim's description has prompted George to arrive at a faulty judgment regarding the success rate of Jim's broker/analyst. George is impressed, but his assessment is based on a very small sample size; the recent, successful picks Jim cites are inevitably only part of the story. George concluded that Jim's broker is successful because Jim's account of the broker's and analyst's performances seems *representative* of the record of a successful team. However, George disproportionately weighs Jim's testimony, and if he were to ask more questions, he might discover that his conclusion draws on too small a sample size. In reality, the analyst that Jim is relying on happens to be one who covers an industry that is popular at the moment, and *every* stock that this analyst covers has enjoyed recent success. Additionally, Jim neglected to mention that last year, this same broker/analyst team made a string of three *losing* recommendations. Therefore, both Jim's and George's brokers are batting 50 percent. George's reasoning demonstrates the pitfalls of sample-size neglect representativeness bias.

Implications for Investors. Both types of representativeness bias can lead to substantial investment mistakes. Box 5.1 lists examples of behaviors, attributable to base-rate neglect and sample-size neglect, respectively, that can cause harm to an investor's portfolio. Advice on these four areas will come later.

RESEARCH REVIEW

In *Judgment under Uncertainty: Heuristics and Biases*, Daniel Kahneman, Paul Slovic, and Amos Tversky apply representativeness bias to the world

EXAMPLES OF THE HARMFUL EFFECTS OF SAMPLE-SIZE NEGLECT FOR INVESTORS

1. Investors can make significant financial errors when they examine a money manager's track record. They peruse the past few quarters or even years and conclude, based on inadequate statistical data, that the fund's performance is the result of skilled allocation and/or security selection.
2. Investors also make similar mistakes when investigating track records of stock analysts. For example, they look at the success of an analyst's past few recommendations, erroneously assessing the analyst's aptitude based on this limited data sample.

EXAMPLES OF THE HARMFUL EFFECTS OF BASE-RATE NEGLECT FOR INVESTORS

1. What is the probability that Company A (ABC, a 75-year-old steel manufacturer that is having some business difficulties) belongs to group B (value stocks that will likely recover) rather than to Group C (companies that will go out of business)? In answering this question, most investors will try to judge the degree to which A is representative of B or C. In this case, some headlines featuring recent bankruptcies by steel companies make ABC Steel appear more representative of the latter categorization, and some investors conclude that they had best unload the stock. They are ignoring, however, the base-rate reality that far more steel companies survive or get acquired than go out of business.
2. What is the probability that AAA-rated Municipal Bond A (issued by an "inner city" and racially divided county) belongs to Group B (risky municipal bonds) rather than to Group C (safe municipal bonds)? In answering this question, most investors will again try to evaluate the extent to which A seems representative of B or C. In this case, Bond A's characteristics may seem representative of Group A (risky bonds) because of the county's "unsafe" reputation; however, this conclusion ignores the base-rate fact that, historically, the default rate of AAA bonds is virtually zero.

BOX 5.1 Harmful Effects of Representativeness Bias

of sports. The concepts brought forward in this book also translate easily to finance.

Abstract. A game of squash can be played either to nine or to fifteen points. If you think you are a better player than your opponent, then which game—the shorter version, or lengthier version—provides you a higher probability of winning? Suppose, instead, that you are the weaker player. Which game is your best bet now? If you believe that you would favor the same game length in either case, then consider this theorem from probability theory: the larger the sample of rounds (i.e., fifteen rounds versus nine rounds), the greater likelihood of achieving the expected outcome (i.e., victory to the stronger player). So, if you believe you are the stronger player, then you should prefer the longer game; believing yourself to be the weaker player should produce a preference for the shorter game. Intuitively, though, victory over an opponent in either a nine-point or fifteen-point match would strike many people as equally representative of one's aptitude at squash. This is an example of sample-size neglect bias.[1]

The concept of permitting the game "to go longer" in order to increase the probability that the stronger player wins can also apply to investing, where it is called *time diversification*, which refers to the idea that investors should spread their assets across ventures operating according to a variety of market cycles, giving their allocations plenty of time to work properly. Time diversification helps reduce the risk that an investor will be caught entering or abandoning a particular investment or category at a disadvantageous point in the economic cycle. It is particularly relevant with regard to highly volatile investments, such as stocks and long-term bonds, whose prices can fluctuate in the short term. Holding onto these assets for longer periods of time can soften the effects of such fluctuations. Conversely, if an investor cannot remain in a volatile investment over a relatively long time period, he or she should avoid the investment. Time diversification is less important when considering relatively stable investments, such as certificates of deposit, money market funds, and short-term bonds.

Time diversification also comes into play when investing or withdrawing large sums of money from a specified niche within an allocation. In general, it is best to move these amounts gradually over time, rather than all at once, to reduce risk. Borrowed from Kenneth Fisher and Meir Statman,[2] Figures 5.1 and 5.2 show a pair of graphic models illustrating expected average annual returns over a 1-year and a 30-year horizon, respectively.

DIAGNOSTIC TESTING

This test will help to determine a client's susceptibility to both base-rate bias and sample-size neglect bias.

Base-Rate Neglect Representativeness Bias Test

Question 1: Jim is an ex-college baseball player. After he graduated from college, Jim became a physical education teacher. Jim has two sons, both of whom are excellent athletes. Which is more likely?
a. Jim coaches a local Little League team.
b. Jim coaches a local Little League team and plays softball with the local softball team.

Sample-Size Neglect Representativeness Bias Test

Question 2: Consider the two sequences of coin-toss results shown (Figure 5.3). Assume that an unbiased coin has been used. Which of the sequences pictured do you think is more likely: A or B?

Test Results Analysis

Question 1: Respondents who chose "b," which is the predictable answer, are likely to suffer from base-rate neglect representativeness bias. It is *possible* that Jim both coaches and plays softball, but it is *more likely* that he only coaches Little League. Figure 5.4 illustrates this.

Question 2: Most people ascertain Sequence A to be more likely, simply because it appears more "random." In fact, both sequences are equally likely because a coin toss generates a 50:50 probability ratio of heads to tails. Therefore, respondents who chose Sequence B may be subject to sample-size neglect representativeness bias (also known in this case as Gambler's Fallacy, or the "Law of Small Numbers"). If

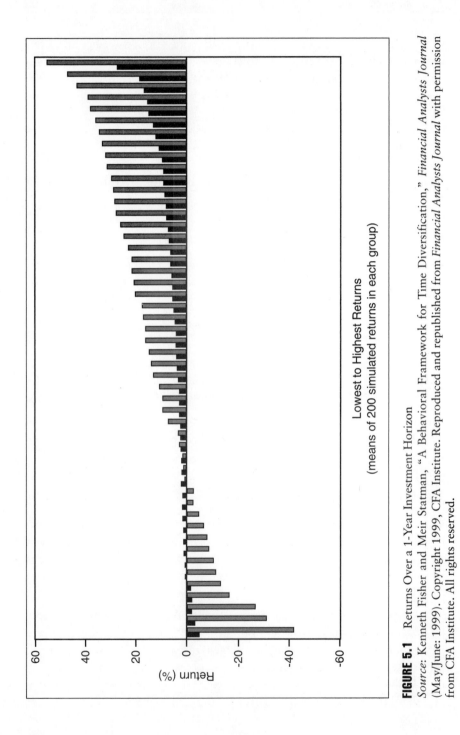

FIGURE 5.1 Returns Over a 1-Year Investment Horizon

Source: Kenneth Fisher and Meir Statman, "A Behavioral Framework for Time Diversification," *Financial Analysts Journal* (May/June 1999). Copyright 1999, CFA Institute. Reproduced and republished from *Financial Analysts Journal* with permission from CFA Institute. All rights reserved.

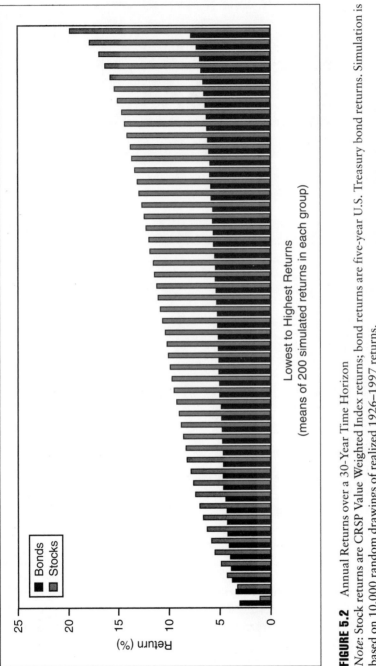

FIGURE 5.2 Annual Returns over a 30-Year Time Horizon

Note: Stock returns are CRSP Value Weighted Index returns; bond returns are five-year U.S. Treasury bond returns. Simulation is based on 10,000 random drawings of realized 1926–1997 returns.

Source: Kenneth Fisher and Meir Statman, "A Behavioral Framework for Time Diversification," *Financial Analysts Journal* (May/June 1999). Copyright 1999, CFA Institute. Reproduced and republished from *Financial Analysts Journal* with permission from CFA Institute. All rights reserved.

FIGURE 5.3 Sample-Size Neglect Diagnostic: Which Sequence of Coin Toss Results Appears Likelier?

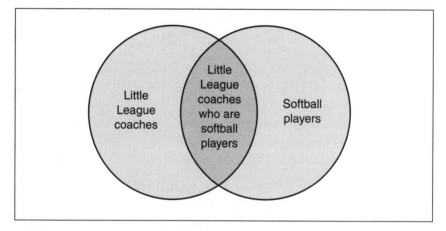

FIGURE 5.4 Softball Players Are Not Necessarily "Representative" of Little League Coaches

six tosses of a fair coin all turn out to be heads, the probability that the next toss will turn up heads is still one-half. However, many people still harbor the notion that in coin tossing, a roughly even ratio of heads to tails should result and that a sequence of consecutive heads signals that a tails is overdue. Again, this is a case of representativeness bias. The law of large numbers when applied to a small sample will produce such biased estimates.

ADVICE

In both sample-size neglect and base-rate neglect, investors ignore the statistically dominant result in order to satisfy their need for patterns. Due to the fact that many examples of representativeniss bias exist, this advice tries to address two especially prevalent errors that representativeness-biased investors often commit. One of these mistakes falls in the base-rate neglect category, while the other exemplifies sample-size neglect.

Advice for Base-Rate Neglect

Earlier in the chapter, a very effective method for dealing with base-rate neglect was presented. When you or a client sense that base-rate neglect might be a problem, stop and perform the following analysis: "What is the probability that Person A (Simon, a shy, introverted man) belongs to Group B (stamp collectors) rather than Group C (BMW drivers)?"

Recalling this example will help you to think through whether you are erroneously assessing a particular situation. It will likely be necessary to go back and do some more research to determine if you have indeed committed an error (i.e., "Are there really more BMW drivers than stamp collectors?"). In the end, however, this process should prove conducive to better investment decisions.

Advice for Sample-Size Neglect

In the earlier example of sample-size neglect (George and Jim), an investor might conclude that a mutual fund manager possesses remarkable skill, based on the fund's performance over just the past three years. Viewed in the context of the thousands of investment managers, a given manager's three-year track record is just as likely an indication that the manager has benefited from luck as it is an indication of skill, right? Consider a study conducted by Vanguard Investments Australia, later released by Morningstar.[3] The five best-performing funds from 1994 to 2003 were analyzed. The results of the study were surprising to say the least:

- Only 16 percent of the top five funds make it to the following year's list.

- The top five funds average 15 percent lower returns the following year.
- The top five funds barely beat (by 0.3 percent) the market the following year.
- Of the top five funds, 21 percent ceased to exist within the following 10 years.

DALBAR, Inc., also conducted the well-known *Quantitative Analysis of Investor Behavior*. Their 2003 study[4] demonstrated that investors tend to buy into a fund immediately following a rapid price appreciation. These points in time also, cyclically, tend to shortly precede a subsequent *decline* in the fund's performance. When prices then fall, investors quickly dump their holdings and search for the next hot fund. The average equity investor earned 2.57 percent average annual return over the period 1984 through 2002. Compare that to a 3.14 percent inflation rate and a 12.22 percent return from the Standard & Poor's 500 in exactly same period. According to the DALBAR study, not only did mutual fund clients fail to keep up with the market, but they actually underperformed it—and lost money to inflation.

There are prudent methods for identifying appropriate long-term investments. Use an asset allocation strategy to guarantee balance and to increase long-term returns among all your investments. Invest in a diversified portfolio to meet your financial goals, and stick with it. These four questions should help you to avoid the futility of chasing returns and to select appropriate, ultimately beneficial investments.

1. How does the fund that you are considering perform relative to similarly sized and similarly styled funds?
2. What is the tenure of the managers and advisors at the fund?
3. Are the managers well known and/or highly regarded?
4. Do the fund's three-, five-, and ten-year returns all exceed market averages?

Finally, remember: Each year is different and brings new leaders and laggards.

CHAPTER 6

Anchoring and Adjustment Bias

To reach a port we must sail, sometimes with the wind, and sometimes against it. But we must not drift or lie at anchor.
—Oliver Wendell Holmes

BIAS DESCRIPTION

Bias Name: Anchoring and Adjustment
Bias Type: Cognitive

General Description.   When required to estimate a value with unknown magnitude, people generally begin by envisioning some initial, default number—an "anchor"—which they then adjust up or down to reflect subsequent information and analysis. The anchor, once fine-tuned and reassessed, matures into a final estimate. Numerous studies demonstrate that regardless of how the initial anchors were chosen, people tend to adjust their anchors insufficiently and produce end approximations that are, consequently, biased. People are generally better at estimating relative comparisons rather than absolute figures, which this example illustrates.

Suppose you are asked whether the population of Canada is greater than or less than 20 million. Obviously, you will answer either above 20 million or below 20 million. If you were then asked to guess an absolute population value, your estimate would probably fall somewhere near 20 million, because you are likely subject to anchoring by your previous response.

Technical Description.   *Anchoring and adjustment* is a psychological heuristic that influences the way people intuit probabilities. Investors exhibiting this bias are often influenced by purchase "points"—or arbitrary price levels or price indexes—and tend to cling to these numbers when facing questions like "Should I buy or sell this security?" or "Is the market overvalued or undervalued right now?" This is especially true when the introduction of new information regarding the security further complicates the situation. Rational investors treat these new pieces of information objectively and do not reflect on purchase prices or target prices in deciding how to act. Anchoring and adjustment bias, however, implies that investors perceive new information through an essentially warped lens. They place undue emphasis on statistically arbitrary, psychologically determined anchor points. Decision making therefore deviates from neoclassically prescribed "rational" norms.

PRACTICAL APPLICATION

This chapter reviews one miniature case study and provides an accompanying analysis and interpretation that will demonstrate investor potential for anchoring and adjustment bias.

Miniature Case Study: Anchoring and Adjustment Bias

Case Presentation.   Suppose Alice owns stock in Corporation ABC. She is a fairly astute investor and has recently discovered some new information about ABC. Her task is to evaluate this information for the purpose of deciding whether she should increase, decrease, or simply maintain her holdings in ABC. Alice bought ABC two years ago at $12, and the stock is now at $15. Several months ago, ABC reached $20 after a surprise announcement of higher-than-expected earnings, at which time Alice contemplated selling the stock but did not. Unfortunately, ABC then dropped to $15 after executives were accused of faulty accounting practices. Today, Alice feels as though she has "lost" 25 percent of the stock's value, and she would prefer to wait and sell her shares in ABC once it returns to its recent $20 high.

Alice has a background in accounting, and she does some research that leads her to conclude that ABC's methods are indeed faulty, but not extremely so. However, Alice cannot entirely gauge the depth of the problem and realizes that holding ABC contains risk, but ABC is also a viable corporate entity with good prospects. Alice must make a decision. On one hand, she has confirmed that ABC does have an accounting problem, and she is unsure of how severe the problem might become. On the other hand, the company has a solid business, and Alice wants to recoup the 25 percent that she feels she lost. What should Alice do?

Analysis. Most investors have been confronted with situations similar to this one. They decide to invest in a stock; the stock goes up and then declines. Investors become conflicted and must evaluate the situation to determine whether to hold onto the stock. A rational investor would examine the company's financial situation; make an objective assessment of its business fundamentals; and then decide to buy, hold, or sell the shares. Conversely, some irrational investors—even after going through the trouble of performing the aforementioned rational analysis—permit cognitive errors to cloud their judgment. Alice, for example, may irrationally disregard the results of her research and "anchor" herself to the $20 figure, refusing to sell unless ABC once again achieves that price. This type of response reflects an irrational behavioral bias and should be avoided.

Implications for Investors. A wide variety of investor behaviors can indicate susceptibility to anchoring and adjustment bias. Box 6.1 highlights some important examples of which investors and advisors should be aware.

RESEARCH REVIEW

Some excellent research into the effects of anchoring and adjustment was performed in 1987 by University of Arizona researchers Gregory Northcraft and Margaret Neale.[1] Their study asked a group of real estate professionals to value a property after being given a proposed selling price quoted by the researchers at the outset of the experiment. The agents were also given 20 minutes to examine the premises before being asked to estimate its worth. Specifically, the study asked each researcher to

1. Investors tend to make general market forecasts that are too close to current levels. For example, if the Dow Jones Industrial Average (DJIA) is at 10,500, investors are likely to forecast the index in a way narrower than what might be suggested by historical fluctuation. For example, an investor subject to anchoring might forecast the DJIA to fall between 10,000 and 11,000 at year-end, versus making an absolute estimate based on historical standard deviation (rational) analysis.

2. Investors (and securities analysts) tend to stick too closely to their original estimates when new information is learned about a company. For example, if an investor determines that next year's earnings estimate is $2.00 per share and the company subsequently falters, the investor may not readjust the $2.00 figure enough to reflect the change because he or she is "anchored" to the $2.00 figure. This is not limited to downside adjustments—the same phenomenon occurs when companies have upside surprises. (At the end of the chapter, we will review a behaviorally based investment strategy leveraging this concept that has proven to be effective at selecting investments.)

3. Investors tend to make a forecast of the percentage that a particular asset class might rise or fall based on the current level of returns. For example, if the DJIA returned 10 percent last year, investors will be anchored on this number when making a forecast about next year.

4. Investors can become anchored on the economic states of certain countries or companies. For example, in the 1980s, Japan was an economic powerhouse, and many investors believed that they would remain so for decades. Unfortunately for some, Japan stagnated for years after the late 1980s. Similarly, IBM was a bellwether stock for decades. Some investors became anchored to the idea that IBM would always be a bellwether. Unfortunately for some, IBM did not last as a bellwether stock.

BOX 6.1 Anchoring and Adjustment Bias: Behaviors That Can Cause Investor Mistakes provide the appraised value of the property, the value of the property should it be put up for sale, the price that a potential buyer should be advised to regard as reasonable, and the minimum offer that the seller should be advised to accept. Table 6.1 summarizes the results with respect to the first two categories—appraised value and salable value (the remaining estimates followed patterns similar to those evidenced here).

During the experiment, the real estate agents were divided into two groups. Each group received a guided tour of the home, a 10-page packet of information describing the home, and a list price for the property. The two trials proceeded identically but with one twist: The first group of agents was quoted a list price higher than that quoted to the second group (for details, please see Table 6.1). When both groups subsequently appraised the property, anchoring and adjustment theory held: *Other things held constant*, the higher proposed list price was determined to have led to higher appraisal estimates. The appraisals, then, did not necessarily reflect the objective characteristics of the property. Rather, they were influenced by the initial values on which the agents "anchored" their estimates.

This study clearly demonstrated that anchoring is a very common bias, applying to many areas of finance and business decision making. Wealth management practitioners need to be keenly aware of this behavior and its effects.

Any time someone fixates on a fact or figures that should not rationally factor in at the anticipated decision juncture, that decision becomes potentially subject to the adverse effects of anchoring. The observations

TABLE 6.1 Estimates by Real Estate Agents in Northcraft and Neale's 1987 Study

Real Estate Agent Group 1	Real Estate Agent Group 2
Given asking price = $119,900	Given asking price = $149,900
Predicted appraisal value = $144,202	Predicted appraisal value = $128,752
Listing price = $117,745	Listing price = $130,981
Purchase price = $111,454	Purchase price = $127,316
Lowest acceptable offer = $111,136	Lowest acceptable offer = $111,136

Reprinted from *Organizational Behavior and Human Decision Processes* 39, no. 1 (1987), Northcroft and Neale, "Experts, amateurs, and real estate: An anchoring-and-adjustment perspective on property pricing decisions," 84–97, copyright 1987 with permission from Elsevier.

recorded in Table 6.1, regarding the real estate study, are anchored by reference points that have no bearing on the future prospects of the property in question. Real-life investors likewise need to guard against the natural human tendency toward anchoring, lest their calculations become similarly swayed.

DIAGNOSTIC TESTING

In this section, we'll outline a hypothetical decision-making problem, and discuss how and why various reactions to this problem may or may not indicate susceptibility to anchoring and adjustment bias.

Anchoring and Adjustment Bias Test

Scenario: Suppose you have decided to sell your house and downsize by acquiring a townhouse that you have been eyeing for several years. You do not feel extreme urgency in selling your house; but the associated taxes are eating into your monthly cash flow, and you want to unload the property as soon as possible. Your real estate agent, whom you have known for many years, prices your home at $900,000—you are shocked. You paid $250,000 for the home only 15 years ago, and the $900,000 figure is almost too thrilling to believe. You place the house on the market and wait a few months, but you don't receive any nibbles. One day, your real estate agent calls, suggesting that the two of you meet right away. When he arrives, he tells you that PharmaGrowth, a company that moved into town eight years ago in conjunction with its much-publicized initial public offering (IPO), has just declared Chapter 11 bankruptcy. Now, 7,500 people are out of work. Your agent has been in meetings all week with his colleagues, and together they estimate that local real estate prices have taken a hit of about 10 percent across the board. Your agent tells you that you must decide the price at which you want to list your home, based on this new information. You tell him that you will think it over and get back to him shortly.

Question: Assume your house is at the mean in terms of quality and salability. What is your likeliest course of action?
1. You decide to keep your home on the market for $900,000.
2. You decide to lower your price by 5 percent, and ask $855,000.
3. You decide to lower your price by 10 percent, and ask $810,000.

4. You decide to lower your price to $800,000 because you want to be sure that you will get a bid on the house.

Test Results Analysis

A tendency toward either of the first two responses probably indicates susceptibility of the subject to anchoring and adjustment bias. Remember that real estate prices here have declined 10 percent. If the subject wants to sell his or her home, he or she clearly must lower the price by 10 percent. Resistance to an adequate adjustment in price can stem, however, from being anchored to the $900,000 figure. Anchoring bias impairs the subject's ability to incorporate updated information. This behavior can have significant impact in the investment arena and should be counseled extensively.

ADVICE

Before delving into specific strategies for dealing with anchoring and adjustment, it's important and, perhaps, uplifting to note that you can actually exploit this bias to your advantage. Understanding anchoring and adjustment can, for example, be a powerful asset when negotiating. Many negotiation experts suggest that the participants communicate radically strict initial positions, arguing that an opponent subject to anchoring can be influenced even when the anchor values are extreme. If one party begins a negotiation by offering a given price or condition, then the other party's subsequent counteroffer will likely reflect that anchor. So, when negotiating, it is wise to start with an offer much less generous than reflects your actual position (beware, however, of overdoing this). When presenting someone with a set of options, state first the options that you would most prefer that the other party select. Conversely, if a rival negotiator makes a first bid, do not assume that this number closely approximates a potential final price.

From the investment perspective, awareness is the best countermeasure to anchoring and adjustment bias. When you are advising clients on the sale of a security, encourage clients to ask themselves: "Am I analyzing the situation rationally, or am I holding out to attain an anchored price?" When making forecasts about the direction or magnitude of markets or individual securities, ask yourself: "Is my estimate rational, or am I anchored to last year's performance figures?" Taking these sorts of actions will undoubtedly root out any anchoring and adjustment bias that might take hold during asset sales or asset reallocation.

Finally, when considering a recommendation by a securities analyst, delve further into the research and ask yourself: "Is this analyst anchored to some previous estimate, or is the analyst putting forth an objective rational response to a change in a company's business fundamentals?" Investment professionals are not immune from the effects of anchoring and adjustment bias. In fact, there is an investment strategy that can leverage this behavior, which will be discussed in the "bonus discussion."

BONUS DISCUSSION: INVESTMENT STRATEGIES THAT LEVERAGE ANCHORING AND ADJUSTMENT BIAS

An awareness of the mechanics of anchoring and adjustment can actually serve as a fundamental tenet of a successful investment strategy. Some finance professionals leverage anchoring and adjustment bias by observing patterns in securities analyst earnings upgrades (downgrades) on various stocks and then purchasing (selling) the stocks in response. The behavioral aspect of this strategy is that it takes advantage of the tendency exhibited by securities analysts to underestimate, both positively and negatively, the magnitudes of earnings fluctuations due to anchoring and adjustment bias.

As previously noted, when issuing upgrades and downgrades, analysts anchor on their initial estimates, which can be exploited. If an analyst is anchored to an earnings estimate and earnings are rising, this is an opportunity for investors to win, as it is likely that the analyst is underestimating the magnitude of the earnings upgrades. Conversely, if an analyst is anchored to an earnings estimate and earnings are falling, this is an opportunity to lose, so it's best to sell immediately on the first earnings downgrade, as it is likely that the analyst is underestimating the magnitude of the earnings downgrades.

In sum, we have learned that we need to be aware of the tendency toward anchoring and adjustment bias and the ill effects it can have on our portfolios. At the same time, we can leverage it to our advantage in certain cases, such as in negotiation and in the investment strategy just reviewed.

CHAPTER 7

Cognitive Dissonance Bias

This above all: to thine own self be true,
And it must follow, as the day the night.

—Polonius to Laertes, in Shakespeare's *Hamlet*

BIAS DESCRIPTION

Bias Name: Cognitive Dissonance
Bias Type: Cognitive

General Description.   When newly acquired information conflicts with preexisting understandings, people often experience mental discomfort—a psychological phenomenon known as cognitive dissonance. *Cognitions*, in psychology, represent attitudes, emotions, beliefs, or values; and *cognitive dissonance* is a state of imbalance that occurs when contradictory cognitions intersect.

The term *cognitive dissonance* encompasses the response that arises as people struggle to harmonize cognitions and thereby relieve their mental discomfort. For example, a consumer might purchase a certain brand of lawn mower, initially believing that it is the best lawn mower available. However, when a new cognition that favors a substitute lawn mower is introduced, representing an imbalance, cognitive dissonance then occurs in an attempt to relieve the discomfort with the notion that perhaps the buyer did not purchase the right lawn mower. People will go to great lengths to convince themselves that the lawn mower they actually bought is better than the one they just learned about, to avoid mental discomfort associated with their initial purchase.

Technical Description. Psychologists conclude that people often perform far-reaching rationalizations in order to synchronize their cognitions and maintain psychological stability. When people modify their behaviors or cognitions to achieve cognitive harmony, however, the modifications that they make are not always rationally in their self-interest. Figure 7.1 illustrates this point.

Any time someone feels compelled to choose between alternatives, some sense of conflict is sure to follow the decision. This is because the selected alternative often poses downsides, while the rejected alternative has redeeming characteristics. These factors challenge the decision maker's confidence in the trade-off he or she has just negotiated. Commitment, which indicates an emotional attachment by an individual to the final decision, always precedes the surfacing of cognitive dissonance. If facts challenge the course to which a subject is emotionally attached, then those facts pose as emotional threats. Most people try to avoid dissonant situations and will even ignore potentially relevant information to avoid psychological conflict. Theorists have identified two different aspects of cognitive dissonance that pertain to decision making.

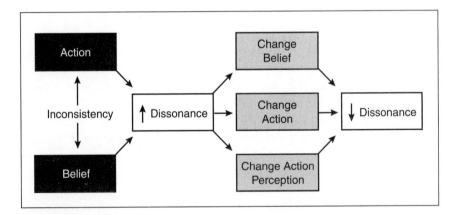

FIGURE 7.1 Cognitive Dissonance Theory
Reprinted from R. H. Rolla, "Cognitive Dissonance Theory," with permission by *Psychology World*. Department of Psychology, University of Missouri—http:// www. umr.edu/~psyworld.

1. *Selective perception.* Subjects suffering from selective perception only register information that appears to affirm a chosen course, thus producing a view of reality that is incomplete and, hence, inaccurate. Unable to objectively understand available evidence, people become increasingly prone to subsequent miscalculations.
2. *Selective decision making.* Selective decision making usually occurs when commitment to an original decision course is high. Selective decision making rationalizes actions that enable a person to adhere to that course, even if at an exorbitant economic cost. Selective decision makers might, for example, continue to invest in a project whose prospects have soured in order to avoid "wasting" the balance of previously sunk funds. Many studies show that people will subjectively reinforce decisions or commitments they have already made.

PRACTICAL APPLICATION

This section reviews the 1957 experiment by renowned psychologist Leon Festinger that gave rise to the first explicit theories about cognitive dissonance.[1]

Overview of Foundational Research in Cognitive Dissonance

Festinger's now-classic experiment asked student subjects to continuously repeat a tedious, meaningless task—minutely repositioning, removing, and returning small pegs to a notched board—over a specified duration of time. The students, as anticipated, reported that the task felt menial and boring. After they had manipulated the pegs for awhile, the students were told that the experiment had concluded and they were free to leave.

Before anyone actually left, however, experimenters requested, on an individual basis, a small favor from each student. Festinger's assistants explained that one of their colleagues had been unable to attend as planned. Now, someone else had to help administer the experiment. Could this student lend a hand? The challenge: Try to persuade another student, who had also participated in the peg activity, that the task had actually felt intriguing and engaging. For their trouble, some subjects were offered the then-significant sum of $20. Others were offered $1, and a control group of students were not requested to perform the favor.

Following this exercise, the volunteers compensated $1 convincingly displayed far more fondness for the peg activity than the students in either of the other two groups. On one hand, this was surprising, because one would expect that the students paid for their efforts would associate the task itself with the experience of receiving compensation; therefore, in that regard, the students receiving $20 would have had the best experience. Cognitive dissonance theory, however, correctly predicted that the volunteers compensated only $1 would actually internalize the more positive recollection that they had been induced to express to their peers. Although all participants initially harbored the same basic impression—that the peg task was not pleasurable—the students asked to help "administer" the second portion of the experiment became subject to cognitive dissonance, since the cognition that they voiced to their fellow students contradicted their genuine opinion. Unable to associate the experience of manipulating the pegs with the more significant compensation offered to the students in the $20 group, the students in the $1 group had to fabricate some other justification that would align their own, privately held views about the experiment with the outlook they were attempting to communicate to their peers. Hence, they became more inclined to regard the peg activity as inherently rewarding, which synchronized their own preexisting cognitions with those that they advocated in the second phase of the experiment and, therefore, relieved the dissonance. Figure 7.2 represents graphically the students' mental predicament and subsequent potential paths to resolving that predicament.

Implications for Investors.   Investors, like everyone else, need to be able to live with their decisions. Many wealth management practitioners note that clients often go to great lengths to rationalize decisions on prior investments, especially failed investments. Moreover, people displaying this tendency might also irrationally delay unloading assets that are not generating adequate returns. In both cases, the effects of cognitive dissonance are preventing investors from acting rationally and, in certain cases, preventing them from realizing losses for tax purposes and reallocating at the earliest opportunity. Furthermore, and perhaps even more important, the need to maintain self-esteem may prevent investors from learning from their mistakes. To ameliorate dissonance arising

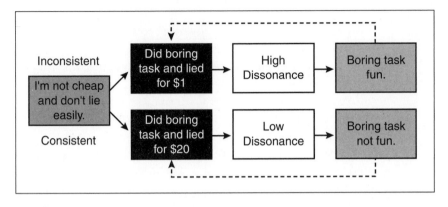

FIGURE 7.2 Modeling Cognitive Dissonance in Festinger's Peg Experiment
Reprinted from R. H. Rolla, "Cognitive Dissonance Theory," with permission by
Psychology World. Department of Psychology, University of Missouri—http:// www.
umr.edu/~psyworld.

from the pursuit of what they perceive to be two incompatible goals—
self-validation and acknowledgment of past mistakes—investors will
often attribute their failures to chance rather than to poor decision
making. Of course, people who miss opportunities to learn from past
miscalculations are likely to miscalculate again, renewing a cycle of
anxiety, discomfort, dissonance, and denial.

Both selective perception (information distortion to meet a need,
which gives rise to subsequent decision-making errors) and selective decision making (an irrational drive to achieve some specified result for the
purpose of vindicating a previous decision) can have significant effects on
investors. Box 7.1 illustrates four behaviors that result from cognitive
dissonance and that cause investment losses.

RESEARCH REVIEW

In their superb work entitled "Cognitive Dissonance and Mutual Fund
Investors," Professor William N. Goetzmann, of the Yale School of
Management, and Nadav Peles, of J. P. Morgan, examined the tendency of investors to "stick," irrationally, with struggling mutual
funds. Their theory was that cognitive dissonance played a significant

1. Cognitive dissonance can cause investors to hold losing securities position that they otherwise would sell because they want to avoid the mental pain associated with admitting that they made a bad decision.
2. Cognitive dissonance can cause investors to continue to invest in a security that they already own after it has gone down (average down) to confirm an earlier decision to invest in that security without judging the new investment with objectivity and rationality. A common phrase for this concept is "throwing good money after bad."
3. Cognitive dissonance can cause investors to get caught up in herds of behavior; that is, people avoid information that counters an earlier decision (cognitive dissonance) until so much counter information is released that investors herd together and cause a deluge of behavior that is counter to that decision.
4. Cognitive dissonance can cause investors to believe "it's different this time." People who purchased high-flying, hugely overvalued growth stocks in the late 1990s ignored evidence that there were no excess returns from purchasing the most expensive stocks available. In fact, many of the most high-flying companies are now far below their peaks in price.

BOX 7.1 Cognitive Dissonance Bias: Behaviors That Can Cause Investment Mistakes

role in compelling investors to hold losing fund positions. The researchers theorized that people do not permit themselves to accept new evidence that suggests that it might be time to evacuate a fund because they feel committed to whatever rationale initially inspired the purchase. In 1998, Goetzmann told CNN that investors "are selective about the information they collect about their mutual funds. People like to think that they made a good choice in the past and don't like to look at evidence that their fund did poorly."[2]

The study by Goetzmann and Peles[3] showed that investors, when deciding whether to sell or to retain an investment, are affected by the disparity in value between the security's purchase price and its current price.

The researchers observed an imbalance between cash inflows and out-flows for most mutual funds and discovered that investors rapidly poured money into funds that performed well but tended to vacate the poorest-performing funds. This behavior suggests susceptibility to availability bias but also indicates that investors in a losing fund may suffer from selective perception, ignoring evidence that discredits the earlier decision to buy into the fund. In some instances, people also feel compelled to "double down," or to continue an investment in a risky situation in an attempt to break even, just to avoid the embarrassment of reporting a losing investment.

Goetzmann and Peles noted:

We present evidence from questionnaire studies of mutual fund investors about recollections of past fund performance. We find that investor memories exhibit a positive bias, consistent with current psychological models. We find that the degree of bias is conditional upon previous investor choice, a phenomenon related to the well-known theory of cognitive dissonance.

The magnitude of psychological and economic frictions in the mutual fund industry is examined via a cross-sectional study of equity mutual funds. We find an unusually high frequency of poorly performing funds, consistent with investor "inertia." Analysis of aggregate dollar investments, however, shows the net effect of this inertia is small. Thus the regulatory implications with respect to additional disclosure requirements are limited. We examine one widely documented empirical implication of mutual fund investor inertia: the differential response of investment dollars to past performance. We perform tests that control for the crucial problem of survivorship. These confirm the presence of differential response, but find the effect is confined to the top quartile. There is little evidence that the response to poor performance is unusual.[4]

The researchers' final comment, here—that the response documented in their study appears widespread—suggests that this chapter might have especially broad implications. Understanding, detecting, and countering the behavioral biases associated with cognitive dissonance are objectives that, when undertaken successfully, could help numerous individual investors.

DIAGNOSTIC TESTING

This test begins with a scenario that illustrates some criteria that can determine susceptibility to cognitive dissonance.

Cognitive Dissonance Bias Test

Scenario: Suppose that you recently bought a new car, Brand A, Model B. You are very pleased with your purchase. One day, your neighbor finds you in your driveway washing your new car and comments on your new purchase: "Wow, love the new car. I know this model. Did you know that Brand Y, Model Z (Model Z is nearly identical to Model B), was giving away a free navigation system when you bought the car?"

You are initially confused. You were unaware, until now, that Model Z was including a navigation system with purchase of the car. You would have liked to have it. Perhaps, you wonder, was getting Model B a bad decision? You begin to second-guess yourself. After your neighbor leaves, you return to your house.

Question: Your next action is, most likely, which of the following?
  a. You immediately head to your home office and page through the various consumer magazines to determine whether you should have purchased Model B.
  b. You proceed with washing the car and think, "If I had it to do all over again, I may have purchased Model Z. Even though mine doesn't have a navigation system, I'm still pleased with Model B."
  c. You contemplate doing some additional research on Model Z. However, you decide not to follow through on the idea. The car was a big, important purchase, and you've been so happy with it—the prospect of discovering an error in your purchase leaves you feeling uneasy. Better to just put this thought to rest and continue to enjoy the car.

Test Results Analysis

Answering "c" may indicate a propensity for cognitive dissonance. The next section gives advice on coping with this bias.

ADVICE

Cognitive dissonance does not in and of itself preordain biased decision making. The driving force behind most of the irrational behavior discussed is the tendency of individuals to adopt certain detrimental *responses* to cognitive dissonance in an effort to alleviate their mental discomfort. Therefore, the first step in overcoming the negative effects of cognitive dissonance is to recognize and to attempt to abandon such counterproductive coping techniques. People who can recognize this behavior become much better investors. Specifically, there are three common responses to cognitive dissonance that have potentially negative implications for personal finance and, consequently, should be avoided: (1) modifying beliefs, (2) modifying actions, and (3) modifying perceptions of relevant action(s). Each will be addressed in detail, following a brief overview. Advisors should take note of how these types of resolutions can affect investors.

Cognitive Dissonance: Common Coping Responses

People can and do recognize inconsistencies between actions and beliefs. When they act in ways that contradict their own beliefs, attitudes, or opinions, some natural "alarm" tends to alert them. For example, you believe that it is wrong to hit your dog; yet, somehow, if you find yourself engaged in the act of hitting your dog, you will register the inconsistency. This moment of recognition will generate cognitive dissonance, and the unease that you experience will motivate you to resolve the contradiction. You will be expected, usually, to try to reconcile your conflicting cognitions in one of three ways:

1. *Modifying beliefs.* Perhaps the easiest way to resolve dissonance between actions and beliefs is simply to alter the relevant beliefs. In the aforementioned incident, for example, you could just recategorize "hitting one's dog" as a perfectly acceptable behavior. This would take care of any dissonance. When the principle in question is important to you, however, such a course of action becomes unlikely. People's most basic beliefs tend to remain stable; they don't just go around modifying their fundamental moral matrices on a day-to-day basis.

Investors, however, do sometimes opt for this path of least resistance when attempting to eliminate dissonance (although the belief-modification mechanism is the least common, in finance, of the three coping tactics discussed here). For example, if the behavior in question was not "hitting your dog" but rather "selling a losing investment," you might concoct some rationale along the lines of "it is okay not to sell a losing investment" in order to resolve cognitive dissonance and permit yourself to hold onto a stock. This behavior, obviously, can pose serious hazards to your wealth.

2. *Modifying actions.* On realizing that you have engaged in behavior contradictory to some preexisting belief, you might attempt to instill fear and anxiety into your decision in order to averse-condition yourself against committing the same act in the future. Appalled at what you have done, you may emphasize to yourself that you will never hit your dog again, and this may aid in resolving cognitive dissonance. However, averse conditioning is often a poor mechanism for learning, especially if you can train yourself, over time, to simply tolerate the distressful consequences associated with a "forbidden" behavior.

Investors may successfully leverage averse conditioning. For example, in the instance wherein a losing investment must be sold, an individual could summon such anxiety at the prospect of ever again retaining an unprofitable stock that actually doing so seems inconceivable. Thus, the dissonance associated with having violated a basic precept of investment strategy dissipates. However, some investors might undergo repeated iterations of this process and eventually become numb to their anxieties, nullifying the effects of averse conditioning on behavior.

3. *Modifying perceptions of relevant action(s).* A more difficult approach to reconciling cognitive dissonance is to rationalize whatever action has brought you into conflict with your beliefs. For example, you may decide that while hitting a dog is generally a bad idea, the dog whom you hit was not behaving well; therefore, you haven't done anything wrong. People relying on this technique try to recontextualize whatever action has generated the current state of mental discomfort so that the action no longer appears to be inconsistent with any particular belief.

An investor might rationalize retaining a losing investment: "I don't really need the money right now, so I won't sell" is a justifica-

tion that might resolve cognitive dissonance. It is also a very dangerous attitude and must be avoided.

CONCLUSION

The bottom line in overcoming the negative behavioral effects of cognitive dissonance is that clients need to immediately admit that a faulty
cognition has occurred. Rather than adapting beliefs or actions in order
to circumnavigate cognitive dissonance, investors must address feelings
of unease at their source and take an appropriate *rational* action. If you
think you may have made a bad investment decision, analyze the decision; if your fears prove correct, confront the problem head-on and rectify the situation. In the long run, you'll become a better investor.

CHAPTER 8

Availability Bias

It is ironic that the greatest stock bubble coincided with the greatest amount of information available. I always thought this would be a good thing, but maybe it was not so good.

—James J. Cramer, financial news analyst for CNBC

BIAS DESCRIPTION

Bias Name: Availability Bias
Bias Type: Cognitive

General Description. The *availability bias* is a rule of thumb, or mental shortcut, that allows people to estimate the probability of an outcome based on how prevalent or familiar that outcome appears in their lives. People exhibiting this bias perceive easily recalled possibilities as being more likely than those prospects that are harder to imagine or difficult to comprehend.

One classic example cites the tendency of most people to guess that shark attacks more frequently cause fatalities than airplane parts falling from the sky do. However, as difficult as it may be to comprehend, the latter is actually 30 times more likely to occur. Shark attacks are probably assumed to be more prevalent because sharks invoke greater fear or because shark attacks receive a disproportionate degree of media attention. Consequently, dying from a shark attack is, for most respondents, easier to imagine than death by falling airplane parts. In sum, the availability rule of thumb underlies judgments about the likelihood or frequency of an occurrence based on readily available information, not necessarily based on complete, objective, or factual information.

Technical Description.   People often inadvertently assume that readily available thoughts, ideas, or images represent unbiased indicators of statistical probabilities. People estimate the likelihoods of certain events according to the degree of ease with which recollections or examples of analogous events can be accessed from memory. Impressions drawn from imagination and past experience combine to construct an array of conceivable outcomes, whose real statistical probabilities are, in essence, arbitrary. There are several categories of availability bias, of which the four that apply most to investors are: (1) *retrievability,* (2) *categorization,* (3) *narrow range of experience,* and (4) *resonance.* Each category will be described and corresponding examples given.

1. *Retrievability.* Ideas that are *retrieved* most easily also seem to be the most credible, though this is not necessarily the case. For example, David Kahneman, Paul Slovic, and Amos Tversky performed an experiment in which subjects were read a list of names and then were asked whether more male or female names had been read.[1] In reality, the majority of names recited were unambiguously female; however, the subset of male names contained a much higher frequency of references to celebrities (e.g., "Richard Nixon"). In accordance with availability theory, most subjects produced biased estimates indicating, mistakenly, that more male than female names populated the list (this particular concept will be reviewed further in Chapter 20).

2. *Categorization.* In Chapter 5, "Representativeness Bias," we discussed how people's minds comprehend and archive perceptions according to certain classification schemes. Here, we will discuss how people attempt to categorize or summon information that matches a certain reference. The first thing that their brains do is generate a set of search terms, specific to the task at hand, that will allow them to efficiently navigate their brain's classification structure and locate the data they need. Different tasks require different search sets, however; and when it is difficult to put together a framework for a search, people often mistakenly conclude that the search simply references a more meager array of results. For example, if a French person simultaneously tries to come up with a list of high-quality U.S. vineyards

and a corresponding list of French vineyards, the list of U.S. vine-yards is likely to prove more difficult to create. The French person, as a result, might predict that high-quality U.S. vineyards exist with a lower probability than famous French vineyards, even if this is not necessarily the case.

3. *Narrow range of experience.* When a person possesses a too-restrictive frame of reference from which to formulate an objec-tive estimate, then *narrow range of experience bias* often results. For example, assume that a very successful college basketball player is drafted by a National Basketball Association (NBA) team, where he proceeds to enjoy several successful seasons. Because this person encounters numerous other successful former college basketball players on a daily basis in the NBA, he is likely to overestimate the relative proportion of successful college bas-ketball players that go on to play professionally. He will, likewise, probably underestimate the relative frequency of failed college basketball players, because most of the players he knows are those who have gone on to reap great rewards from their undergradu-ate basketball careers. In reality, only an extremely small percent-age of college basketball players will ever graduate to the NBA.

4. *Resonance.* The extent to which certain, given situations *resonate* vis-à-vis individuals' own, personal situations can also influence judgment. For example, fans of classical music might be likely to overestimate the portion of the total population that also listens to classical music. Those who dislike classical music would probably underestimate the number of people who listen to classical music.

PRACTICAL APPLICATION

Each variation of the availability bias just outlined has unique implica-tions in personal finance, both for advisory practitioners and for clients. Let's explore these now.

1. *Retrievability.* Most investors, if asked to identify the "best" mutual fund company, are likely to select a firm that engages in heavy adver-tising, such as Fidelity or Schwab. In addition to maintaining a high public relations profile, these firms also "cherry pick" the funds with the best results in their fund lineups, which makes this belief more "available" to be recalled. In reality, the companies that manage

some of today's highest-performing mutual funds undertake little to no advertising. Consumers who overlook these funds in favor of more widely publicized alternatives may exemplify retrievability/availability bias.

2. *Categorization.* Most Americans, if asked to pinpoint one country, worldwide, that offers the best investment prospects, would designate their own: the United States. Why? When conducting an inventory of memories and stored knowledge regarding "good investment opportunities" in general, the country category that most Americans most easily recall is the United States. However, to dismiss the wealth of investment prospects abroad as a result of this phenomenon is irrational. In reality, over 50 percent of equity market capitalization exists outside the United States. People who are unduly "patriotic" when looking for somewhere to invest often suffer from availability bias.

3. *Narrow range of experience.* Assume that an employee of a fast-growing, high-tech company is asked: "Which industry generates the most successful investments?" Such an individual, who probably comes into contact with other triumphant tech profiteers each and every day, will likely overestimate the relative proportion of corporate successes stemming from technologically intensive industries. Like the NBA star who got his start in college and, therefore, too optimistically estimates the professional athletic prospects of college basketball players, this hypothetical high-tech employee demonstrates narrow range of experience availability bias.

4. *Resonance.* People often favor investments that they feel match their personalities. A thrifty individual who discount shops, clips coupons, and otherwise seeks out bargains may demonstrate a natural inclination toward value investing. At the same time, such an investor might not heed the wisdom of balancing value assets with more growth-oriented ventures, owing to a reluctance to front the money and acquire a quality growth stock. The concept of value is easily available in such an investor's mind, but the notion of growth is less so. This person's portfolio could perform suboptimally as a result of resonance availability bias.

A Classic Example of Availability Bias. In the period 1927 to 1999, which political party's leadership has correlated with higher stock market returns? Many Wall Street professionals are known to lean Republican; so a lot of people, given this readily available information, might speculate that the markets benefit from Republican political hegemony. After all, why would so many well-informed individuals, whose livelihoods depend on the success of the stock market, vote for Republicans if Democrats produced higher returns? According to a study done by University of California at Los Angeles professors Pedro Santa-Clara and Rossen Valkanov,[2] the 72-year period between 1927 and 1999 showed that a broad stock index, similar to the Standard & Poor's (S&P) 500, returned approximately 11 percent more a year on average under a Democratic president than safer, three-month Treasury bonds (T-bonds). By comparison, the index returned 2 percent a year more than the T-bonds when Republicans were in office. If your natural reaction was to answer "Republican" to this question, you may suffer from availability bias.

Implications for Investors.   Box 8.1 summarizes the primary implications for investors of susceptibility to availability bias in each of the four forms we've reviewed. In all such instances, investors ignore potentially beneficial investments because information on those investments is not readily available, or they make investment decisions based on readily available information, avoiding diligent research.

RESEARCH REVIEW

A 2002 working paper by Terrance Odean and Brad Barber, entitled "All That Glitters: The Effect of Attention and News on the Buying Behavior of Individual and Institutional Investors,"[3] asks a simple question: How do investors choose the stocks that they buy? Odean and Barber tested the proposition that individual investors buy stocks that happen to catch their attention. In this work, Odean and Barber pointed out that when buying stocks, investors are faced with a formidable decision task because there are over 7,000 U.S. common stocks from which to choose. They proposed that investors manage the search problem by limiting their search to stocks that have recently caught their attention. They tested the hypothesis that individual investors are more likely to be net buyers of attention-grabbing stocks than are institutional investors by looking at three indications of how likely stocks are to catch investors' attention: (1) daily abnormal trading volume, (2) daily returns, and (3)

1. *Retrievability*. Investors will choose investments based on information that is available to them (advertising, suggestions from advisors, friends, etc.) and will not engage in disciplined research or due diligence to verify that the investment selected is a good one.
2. *Categorization*. Investors will choose investments based on categorical lists that they have available in their memory. In their minds, other categories will not be easily recalled and, thus, will be ignored. For example, U.S. investors may ignore countries where potentially rewarding investment opportunities may exist because these countries may not be an easily recalled category in their memory.
3. *Narrow range of experience*. Investors will choose investments that fit their narrow range of life experiences, such as the industry they work in, the region they live in, and the people they associate with. For example, investors who work in the technology industry may believe that only technology investments will be profitable.
4. *Resonance*. Investors will choose investments that resonate with their own personality or that have characteristics that investors can relate to their own behavior. Taking the opposite view, investors ignore potentially good investments because they can't relate to or do not come in contact with characteristics of those investments. For example, thrifty people may not relate to expensive stocks (high price/earnings multiples) and potentially miss out on the benefits of owning these stocks.

BOX 8.1 Availability Bias: Behaviors That Can Cause Investment Mistakes

daily news. They examined the buying and selling behavior associated with abnormal trading volume for four samples of investors:

1. Investors with accounts at a large discount brokerage.
2. Investors at a smaller discount brokerage firm that advertises its trade execution quality.

3. Investors with accounts at a large retail brokerage.
4. Professional money managers.

As news agencies routinely report the prior day's big winners and big losers, stocks that soar or dive catch people's attention. As predicted, Odean and Barber found that individual investors tend to be net buyers on high attention days: Investors at the large discount brokerage made nearly twice as many purchases as sales of stocks experiencing unusually high trading volume (e.g, the highest 5 percent). They also found that attention-driven investors tend to be net buyers of companies on days that those companies are in the news. (See Figure 8.1.)

Odean and Barber also found that professional investors are less likely to indulge in attention-based purchases. With more time and resources, professionals are able to continuously monitor a wider range of stocks and they are unlikely to consider only attention-grabbing stocks. Furthermore, many professionals may solve the problem of searching through too many stocks by concentrating on a particular sector or on stocks that have passed an initial screen. Perhaps the most important and relevant finding is that investors who engage in attention-based buying do not benefit from doing so. Abnormal volume and extreme return

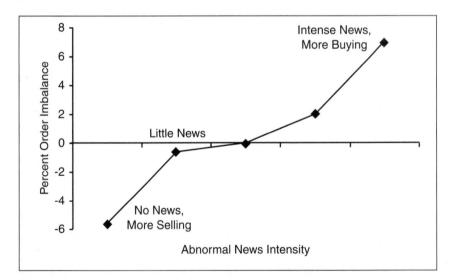

FIGURE 8.1   Order Imbalance as a Function of News Intensity
Reprinted with permission by Brad M. Barber and Terrance Odean (working paper, Cornell University 2002).

analysis that Odean and Barber performed showed that attention-grabbing stocks do not outperform the market.

In this paper, Odean and Barber illustrated a direct practical application of availability bias in individual finance: People tend to deviate from rationally prescribed economic behavior because, in this instance, they lack the capacity to process the utterly massive quantities of data that ought to contextualize a truly "rational" stock purchase. Information that is literally available to investors—information that is published on a daily basis—simply isn't always *cognitively* available. When pertinent information isn't available in this latter, practical sense, decisions are ultimately flawed.

DIAGNOSTIC TEST

This brief test helps detect investor availability bias.

Availability Bias Test

Question 1: Suppose you have some money to invest and you hear about a great stock tip from your neighbor who is known to have a good stock market sense. He recommends you purchase shares in Mycrolite, a company that makes a new kind of lighter fluid for charcoal grills. What is your response to this situation?
   a. I will likely buy some shares because my neighbor is usually right about these things.
   b. I will likely take it under advisement and go back to my house and do further research before making a decision.

Question 2: Suppose that you are planning to buy stock in a generic drug maker called "Generics Plus." Your friend Marian sent you a report on the company and you like the story, so you plan to purchase 100 shares. Right before you do, you hear on a popular financial news show that "GN Pharmaceuticals," another generic drug maker, just reported great earnings and the stock is up 10 percent on the news. What is your response to this situation?
   a. I will likely take this information as confirmation that generics are a good area to be in and proceed with my purchase of Generics Plus.
   b. I will pause before buying Generics Plus and request research on GN prior to proceeding with the purchase of Generics Plus.

    c. I will purchase GN rather than Generics Plus because GN appears to be a hot stock and I want to get in on a good thing.

Question 3: Which claims more lives in the United States?

    a. Lightning.

    b. Tornadoes.

Test Results Analysis

Question 1: Respondents choosing "a" are likely to be susceptible to availability bias.

Question 2: Respondents choosing "c" are likely to be susceptible to availability bias.

Question 3: Respondents choosing "b" are likely to be susceptible to availability bias. More Americans are killed annually by lightning than by tornadoes. Media attention, drills, and other publicity, however, make tornado fatalities memorable and therefore more "available" for people.[4]

ADVICE

Generally speaking, in order to overcome availability bias, investors need to carefully research and contemplate investment decisions before executing them. Focusing on long-term results, while resisting chasing trends, are the best objectives on which to focus if availability bias appears to be an issue. Be aware that everyone possesses a human tendency to mentally overemphasize recent, newsworthy events; refuse to let this tendency compromise you. The old axiom that "nothing is as good or as bad as it seems" offers a safe, reasonable recourse against the impulses associated with availability bias.

    When selecting investments, it is crucial to consider the effects of the availability rule of thumb. For example, stop and consider how you decide which investments to research before making an investment. Do you frequently focus on companies you've read about in *Businessweek* or the *Wall Street Journal* or on investments that have been mentioned on popular financial news programs? A Cornell University researcher named Christopher Gadarowski in 2001 investigated the relationship between stock returns and press coverage. He found that the stocks receiving the most press coverage actually went on to underperform the market in the two years following their exposure in the news.[5]

It is also important to keep in mind that people tend to view things that occur more than a few years ago as past history. For example, if you got a speeding ticket last week, you will probably reduce your speed over the course of the next month or so. However, as time passes, you are likely to revert to your old driving habits. Likewise, availability bias causes investors to overreact to present-day market conditions, whether they are positive or negative. The tech bubble of the late 1990s provided a superb illustration of this phenomenon. Investors, swept up in the euphoria of the "new economy," disregarded elementary risks. When the market corrected itself, these same investors lost confidence and over-focused on the short-term, negative results that they were experiencing.

Another significant problem is that much of the information investors receive is inaccurate and is based on insufficient information and multiple opinions. Furthermore, the information can be outdated or confusingly presented. Availability bias causes people to attribute disproportionate degrees of credibility to such information when it arrives amid a flurry of media attention. Many investors, suffering from information overload, overlook the fact that they often lack the training, experience, and objectivity to filter or interpret this deluge of data. As a result, investors often believe themselves to be more accurately informed than is, ultimately, the case. Because availability bias is a cognitive bias, often it can be corrected with updated information.

CHAPTER 9

Self-Attribution Bias

Heads I win, tails it's chance.

—Ellen Langer and Jane Roth, 1975

BIAS DESCRIPTION

Bias Name: Self-Attribution Bias
Bias Type: Cognitive

General Description.   *Self-attribution bias* (or self-serving attributional bias) refers to the tendency of individuals to ascribe their successes to innate aspects, such as talent or foresight, while more often blaming failures on outside influences, such as bad luck. Students faring well on an exam, for example, might credit their own intelligence or work ethic, while those failing might cite unfair grading. Similarly, athletes often reason that they have simply performed to reflect their own superior athletic skills if they win a game, but they might allege unfair calls by a referee when they lose a game.

Technical Description.   Self-attribution is a cognitive phenomenon by which people attribute failures to situational factors and successes to dispositional factors. Self-serving bias can actually be broken down into two constituent tendencies or subsidiary biases.

1. *Self-enhancing bias* represents people's propensity to claim an irrational degree of credit for their successes.

2. *Self-protecting bias* represents the corollary effect—the irrational denial of responsibility for failure.

Self-enhancing bias can be explained from a cognitive perspective. Research has shown that if people intend to succeed, then outcomes in accordance with that intention—successes—will be perceived as the result of people acting to achieve what they've originally intended. Individuals, then, will naturally accept more credit for successes than failures, since they intend to succeed rather than to fail. *Self-protecting bias* can be explained from an emotional perspective. Some argue that the need to maintain self-esteem directly affects the attribution of task outcomes because people will protect themselves psychologically as they attempt to comprehend their failures. Because these cognitive and emotional explanations are linked, it can be difficult to ascertain which form of the bias is at work in a given situation.

PRACTICAL APPLICATION

Dr. Dana Dunn, a professor of psychology at Moravian College in Bethlehem, Pennsylvania, has done some excellent work regarding self-serving bias. She observed that her students often have trouble recognizing self-serving attributional bias in their own behaviors. To illustrate this phenomenon, she performs an experiment in which she asks students to take out a sheet of paper and draw a line down the middle of the page. She then tells them to label one column "strengths" and the other "weaknesses" and to list their personal strengths and weaknesses in the two columns. She finds that students consistently list more strengths than weaknesses.[1]

Dunn's result suggests that her students tend to suffer from self-serving attributional bias. Investors are not immune from this behavior. The old Wall Street adage "Don't confuse brains with a bull market" is relevant here. When an investor who is susceptible to self-attribution bias purchases an investment and it goes up, then it was due, naturally, to their business and investment savvy. In contrast, when an investor who is susceptible to self-attribution bias purchases an investment and it goes down, then it was due, naturally, to bad luck or some other factor that was not the fault of the investor. People's strengths, generally, consist of personal qualities that they believe empower them to succeed, whereas weaknesses are traits they possess that predispose them to fail. Investors subject to self-attributional bias perceive that investment successes are more often attributable to innate characteristics and that investment failures are due to exogenous factors.

Implications for Investors

Irrationally attributing successes and failures can impair investors in two primary ways. First, people who aren't able to perceive mistakes they've made are, consequently, unable to learn from those mistakes. Second, investors who disproportionately credit themselves when desirable outcomes do arise can become detrimentally overconfident in their own market savvy. Box 9.1 describes the pitfalls of self-serving behavior that often lead to financial mistakes.

RESEARCH REVIEW

A very pertinent discussion of self-serving bias is "Learning to Be Overconfident," written by Terrance Odean and Simon Gervais.[2] They developed a model that describes how novice traders who exhibit susceptibility to self-serving bias end up unjustifiably confident in their investment skills because they tend to take inadequate degrees of responsibility for losses they've incurred. Self-attribution teaches investors to unwittingly take on inappropriate degrees of financial risk and to trade too aggressively, amplifying personal market volatility. This study revealed that while the novice investors are consistently overconfident that they can outperform the market, most fail to do so.

Gervais and Odean developed three hypotheses that are all backed by statistical data.

1. Periods of general prosperity are usually followed by periods of higher-than-expected trading volume, a trend signifying the impact of overconfidence on investor decision making.
2. During periods in which overconfidence increases trading volume, lower-than-average profits are the result.
3. Traders who are both young and successful tend to trade the most and demonstrate the most overconfidence.

1. Self-attribution investors can, after a period of successful investing (such as one quarter or one year) believe that their success is due to their acumen as investors rather than to factors out of their control. This behavior can lead to taking on too much risk, as the investors become too confident in their behavior.

2. Self-attribution bias often leads investors to trade too much than is prudent. As investors believe that successful investing (trading) is attributed to skill versus luck, they begin to trade too much, which has been shown to be "hazardous to your wealth."

3. Self-attribution bias leads investors to "hear what they want to hear." That is, when investors are presented with information that confirms a decision that they made to make an investment, they will ascribe "brilliance" to themselves. This may lead to investors that make a purchase or hold an investment that they should not.

4. Self-attribution bias can cause investors to hold underdiversified portfolios, especially among investors that attribute the success of an company's performance to their own contribution, such as corporate executives, board members, and so on. Often the performance of a stock is not attributed to the skill of an individual person, but rather many factors, including chance; thus, holding a concentrated stock position can be associated with self-attribution and should be avoided.

BOX 9.1   Self-Attribution Bias: Behaviors That Can Cause Investment Mistakes

Gervais and Odean, in an excerpt from "Learning to Be Overconfident," summarized their approach and their findings:

> In assessing his ability, the trader takes too much credit for his successes. This leads him to become overconfident. A trader's expected level of overconfidence increases in the early stages of his career. Then, with more experience, he comes to better recognize his own ability. An overconfident trader trades too aggressively, thereby increasing trading volume and market volatility

while lowering his own expected profits. Though a greater number of successes indicate greater probable ability, a more successful trader may actually have lower expected profits in the next period than a less successful trader due to his greater overconfidence. Since overconfidence is generated by success, overconfident traders are not the poorest traders. Their survival in the market is not threatened. Overconfidence does not make traders wealthier, but the process of becoming wealthy can make traders overconfident.[3]

DIAGNOSTIC TESTING

This diagnostic quiz can help to detect susceptibility to self-attribution bias.

Self-Attribution Test

Question 1: After making an investment, assume that you overhear a news report that has negative implications regarding the potential outcome of the investment you've just executed. How likely are you to then seek information that could confirm that you've made a bad decision?
a. Very unlikely.
b. Unlikely.
c. Likely.
d. Very likely.

Question 2: When returns to your portfolio increase, to what do you believe the change in performance is mainly due?
a. Your investment skill.
b. A combination of investment skill and luck.
c. Luck.

Question 3: After you make a successful trade, how likely are you to put your profits to work in a quick, subsequent trade, rather than letting the money idle until you're sure you've located another good investment?
a. When I sell a profitable investment, I usually invest the money again right away.

b. I will usually wait until I find something I really like before making a new investment.

c. Some combination of choices A and B.

Question 4: Relative to other investors, how good an investor are you?
   a. Below average.
   b. Average.
   c. Above average.
   d. Well above average.

Test Results Analysis

Question 1: People whose response indicates that they would be unlikely to seek information that could implicate them in a previous poor decision are likely to suffer from self-attribution bias. This is so because an investment failure is due not to poor decision making, but to bad luck.

Question 2: Attributing financial success to skill tends to indicate susceptibility to self-attribution bias.

Question 3: Investors who roll over their money immediately without carefully plotting their next move are, often, disproportionately attributing their successes to their own market savvy. Therefore, they are likely to suffer from self-attribution bias.

Question 4: Investors who rate themselves as "above average" or "well above average" in skill are likely to suffer from self-attribution bias.

ADVICE

Recall again the old Wall Street adage that perhaps provides the best warning against the pitfalls of self-attribution bias: "Don't confuse brains with a bull market."

Oftentimes, when financial decisions pan out well, investors like to congratulate themselves on their shrewdness. When things don't turn out so profitably, however, they can console themselves by concluding that someone or something else is at fault. In many cases, neither explanation is entirely correct. Winning investment outcomes are typically due to any number of factors, a bull market being the most prominent;

stocks' decline in value, meanwhile, can be equally random and complex. Sometimes, the fault does lie in arenas well beyond an investor's control, such as fraud or mismanagement.

One of the best things investors can do is view both winning and losing investments as objectively as possible. However, most people don't take the time to analyze the complex confluence of factors that helped them realize profit or to confront the potential mistakes that aggravated a loss. Postanalysis is one of the best learning tools at any investor's disposal. It's understandable but, ultimately, irrational to fear an examination of one's past mistakes. The only real, grievous error is to continue to succumb to overconfidence and, as a result, to repeat the same mistakes!

Advisors and individual investors should perform a postanalysis of each investment: Where did you make money? Where did you lose money? Mentally separate your good, money-making decisions from your bad ones. Then, review the beneficial decisions and try to discern what, exactly, you did correctly: Did you purchase the stock at a particularly advantageous time? Was the market, in general, on an upswing? Similarly, you should review the decisions that you've categorized as poor: What went wrong? Did you buy stocks with poor earnings? Were those stocks trading at or near their recent price highs when you purchased them, or did you pick up the stocks as they were beginning to decline? Did you purchase a stock aptly and simply make an error when it came time to sell? Was the market, in general, undergoing a correction phase?

When reviewing unprofitable decisions, look for patterns or common mistakes that perhaps you were unaware of making. Note any such tendencies that you discover, and try to remain mindful of them by, for example, brainstorming a rule or a reminder such as: "I will not do X in the future" or "I will do Y in the future." Being conscious of these rules will help you overcome any bad habits that you may have acquired and can also reinforce your reliance on the strategies that have served you well.

Remember: Admitting and learning from your past mistakes is the best way to become a smarter, better, and more successful investor!

CHAPTER 10

Illusion of Control Bias

I claim not to have controlled events, but confess plainly that events have controlled me.

—Abraham Lincoln

BIAS DESCRIPTION

Bias Name: Illusion of Control
Bias Type: Cognitive

General Description. The *illusion of control* bias describes the tendency of human beings to believe that they can control or at least influence outcomes when, in fact, they cannot. This bias can be observed in Las Vegas, where casinos play host to many forms of this psychological fallacy. Some casino patrons swear that they are able to impact random outcomes such as the product of a pair of tossed dice. In the casino game "craps," for example, various research has demonstrated that people actually cast the dice more vigorously when they are trying to attain a higher number. Some people, when successful at trying to predict the outcome of a series of coin tosses, actually believe that they are "better guessers," and some claim that distractions might diminish their performance at this statistically arbitrary task.

Technical Description. Ellen Langer, Ph.D., of Harvard University's psychology department, defines the illusion of control bias as the "expectancy of a personal success probability inappropriately higher than the objective probability would warrant."[1] Langer found that choice, task familiarity, competition, and active involvement can all inflate confidence and generate such illusions. For example, Langer observed that people who were permitted to select their own numbers in a hypothetical lottery game were also willing to pay a higher price per ticket than subjects gambling on randomly assigned numbers. Since this initial study, many other researchers uncovered similar situations where people perceived themselves to possess more control than they did, inferred causal connections where none existed, or displayed surprisingly great certainty in their predictions for the outcomes of chance events.

A relevant analogy can be found in a humorous, hypothetical anecdote: In a small town called Smallville, a man marches to the town square every day at 6 P.M. carrying a checkered flag and a trumpet. When the man reaches an appointed spot, he brandishes the flag and blows a few notes on the trumpet. Then, he returns home to the delight of his family.

A police officer notices the man's daily display and eventually asks him, "What *are* you doing?"

The man replies, "Keeping the elephants away."

"But there aren't any elephants in Smallville," the officer replies.

"Well, then, I'm doing a fine job, aren't I?" At this, the officer rolls his eyes and laughs.

This rather absurd tale illustrates the fallacy inherent in the illusion of control bias.

PRACTICAL APPLICATION

When subject to illusion of control bias, people feel as if they can exert more control over their environment than they actually can. An excellent application of this concept was devised by Andrea Breinholt and Lynnette Dalrymple, two researchers at Westminster College in Salt Lake City, Utah. Their study entitled "The Illusion of Control: What's Luck Got to Do with It?"[2] illustrates that people often harbor unfounded illusions of control.

Breinholt and Dalrymple sought to examine subjects' susceptibility to illusions of control as determined by the intersection of two common impulses: the desire for control, and the belief in good luck as a controllable attribute. Two hundred eighty-one undergraduate students participated in the study, and all rated themselves based on a "Desirability of Control Scale" and a "Belief in Luck Scale" immediately prior to the experiment. The subjects then participated in an online, simulated gambling task. Participants were randomly assigned either a high-involvement or a low-involvement condition and, also randomly, were rewarded with either a descending or a random sequence of outcomes.

All participants played 14 hands of "Red & Black," using four cards from a standard poker deck. Each card was presented facedown on the screen, and subjects were asked to wager as to whether a chosen card matched a selected, target color. Each player began with 50 chips. In each hand, participants could wager between zero and five chips; winning increased the participant's total stock of chips by the wagered amount. Likewise, following a lost hand, a player's supply of chips automatically decreased by the wagered amount. The odds of winning each hand were calibrated at 50:50.

Participants randomly assigned to the high-involvement condition were allowed to "shuffle" and "deal" the cards themselves. They could also choose, in each hand, the target color and the amount wagered. After the high-involvement participants chose their cards, the computer revealed each result accordingly. This sequence repeated over the course of 14 trials. The high-involvement condition was designed to maximize the participants' perception that they were controlling the game.

In the low-involvement condition, the computer shuffled and dealt the cards. The participants chose the amounts wagered, but the computer randomly selected the card on which the outcome of each hand would rest.

The descending outcome sequence was designed to maximize the illusion of control, letting the majority of successful outcomes occur during the first seven trials.[3] The descending sequence, for example, consisted of the outcomes depicted in Figure 10.1.

FIGURE 10.1   A Sample Distribution of the Descending Outcome Sequence in "The Illusion of Control: What's Luck Got to Do with It?"
Source: Breinhold and Dalrymple, 2004.

The random outcome sequence was designed to minimize the illusion of control by spacing the successful outcomes more evenly over the course of the fourteen trials. Figure 10.2 demonstrates a sample distribution.

Ultimately, participants in the high-involvement condition tended to wager more chips on each hand than participants in the low-involvement condition did. Moreover, in the low-involvement condition, wagers did not differ reliably as a function of Distributed Feature Composition (DFC)—in other words, participants receiving the descending sequence of outcomes did not wager more or less, on average, than did participants allotted the random outcome sequence. In contrast, in the high-involvement condition, high DFC participants wagered more than low DFC participants did. These findings support the presence of an *illusion of control phenomenon* in the traditional sense.

This study clearly demonstrates the illusion-of-control bias in practice. Investors are very much susceptible to this bias.

Implications for Investors.   In Box 10.1 are listed four primary behaviors that can lead to investment mistakes by investors who are susceptible to illusion of control bias.

RESEARCH REVIEW

This section examines the results of a relatively new paper published in May 2004 by Gerlinde Fellner of the Max Planck Institute for Research into Economic Systems in Jena, Germany. In her work, "Illusion of Control as a Source of Poor Diversification: An Experimental Approach,"[4] Fellner explored the mechanics of this bias as they apply, specifically, to investing behavior. She hypothesized that the illusion of control bias accounts for systematic capital shifts toward investments (stocks) that offer investors the illusion of control. The paper investigated factors influencing individual

FIGURE 10.2   A Sample Distribution of the Random Outcome Sequence in "The Illusion of Control: What's Luck Got to Do with It?"
Source: Breinhold and Dalrymple, 2004.

1. Illusion of control bias can lead investors to trade more than is prudent. Researchers have found that traders, especially online traders, believe themselves to possess more control over the outcomes of their investments than they actually do. An excess of trading results, in the end, in decreased returns.[5]
2. Illusions of control can lead investors to maintain underdiversified portfolios. Researchers have found that investors hold concentrated positions because they gravitate toward companies over whose fate they feel some amount of control. That control proves illusory, however, and the lack of diversification hurts the investors' portfolios.
3. Illusion of control bias can cause investors to use limit orders and other such techniques in order to experience a false sense of control over their investments. In fact, the use of these mechanisms most often leads to an overlooked opportunity or, worse, a detrimental, unnecessary purchase based on the occurrence of an arbitrary price.
4. Illusion of control bias contributes, in general, to investor overconfidence. (Please see Chapter 4 for a detailed discussion of related pitfalls and compensation techniques.)

BOX 10.1 Illusion of Control Bias: Behaviors That Can Cause Investment Mistakes

portfolio allocations. The fundamental question asked was, "Do individuals invest more in a "lottery" (stocks) for which they can control the chance move?" Her hypothesis proved correct. In her words: "Results indicate that subjects invest more in an alternative when they can exercise control on its return and less in the alternative where they do not. This is especially pronounced when subjects can choose the investment alternative on which to exercise control."[6]

In summary, Fellner's research showed that investors prefer to make investments over which they *believe* they can control the outcome. Many practitioners know that investors have no control over the outcome of investments they make, only the decision to invest or not to invest (in rare cases, one individual may have influence over the outcome, but this is the exception, not the rule). Thus, practitioners need to be fully cognizant of this tendency to want to make "controlled" investments and dissuade investors of the notion that they have control over investment outcomes.

DIAGNOSTIC TESTING

This diagnostic test helps to determine whether people taking the test harbor illusions of control.

Illusion of Control Bias Test

Question 1: When you participate in games of chance that involve dice—such as Backgammon, Monopoly, or Craps—do you feel most in control when you roll the dice yourself?
a. I feel more in control when I roll the dice.
b. I am indifferent as to who rolls the dice.

Question 2: When returns to your portfolio increase, to what do you mainly attribute this turn of events?
a. The control that I've exercised over the outcome of my investments.
b. Some combination of investment control and random chance.
c.. Completely random chance.

Question 3: When you are playing cards, are you usually most optimistic with respect to the outcome of a hand that you've dealt yourself?
a. A better outcome will occur when I am controlling the dealing of the cards.
b. It makes no difference to me who deals the cards.

Question 4: When and if you purchase a lottery ticket, do you feel more encouraged, regarding your odds of winning, if you choose the number yourself rather than using a computer-generated number?
a. I'm more likely to win if I control the numbers picked.
b. It makes no difference to me how the numbers are chosen.

Test Results Analysis

Question 1: People who feel more confident rolling the dice themselves, rather than allowing someone else to roll, are more likely to be susceptible to illusion of control bias.

Question 2: People who feel that they are able to exert control over their investments are likely to be susceptible to illusion of control bias.

Question 3: Question 3 parallels Question 1. People who perceive that they have more control over the outcome of a hand of cards when dealing the cards themselves are likely to be susceptible to illusion of control bias.

Question 4: Respondents selecting "a," indicating that they feel more optimistic when choosing their own lottery numbers instead of accepting randomized numbers, are likely to be susceptible to illusion of control bias.

ADVICE

What follows are four advisories that investors can implement to stem the detrimental financial effects of illusions of control.

1. *Recognize that successful investing is a probabilistic activity.* The first step on the road to recovery from illusion of control bias is to take a step back and realize how complex U.S. and global capitalism actually is. Even the wisest investors have absolutely no control over the outcomes of the investments that they make.

2. *Recognize and avoid circumstances that trigger susceptibility illusions of control.* A villager blows his trumpet every day at 6 P.M., and no stampede of elephants ensues. Does the trumpet really keep the elephants away? Applying the same concept to investing, just because you have deliberately determined to purchase a stock, do you really control the fate of that stock or the outcome of that purchase? Rationally, it becomes clear that some correlations are arbitrary rather than causal. Don't permit yourself to make financial decisions on what you can logically discern is an arbitrary basis.

3. *Seek contrary viewpoints.* As you contemplate a new investment, take a moment to ponder whatever considerations might weigh against the trade. Ask yourself: Why am I making this investment? What are the downside risks? When will I sell? What might go wrong? These important questions can help you to screen the logic behind a decision before implementing that decision.

4. Once you have decided to move forward with an investment, one of the best ways to keep illusions of control at bay is to maintain

records of your transactions, including reminders spelling out the rationale that underlie each trade. Write down some of the important features of each investment that you make, and emphasize those attributes that you have determined to be in favor of the investment's success.

If you want proof that this fourth habit, in particular, pays off, look no further than renowned former Fidelity Magellan Fund manager Peter Lynch. Lynch was a meticulous record keeper, documenting his opinions on different companies at every opportunity. When I was a young analyst in Boston right out of college, I had the occasion to visit some colleagues at Fidelity and met Mr. Lynch in his office. What I saw was astounding. Lynch maintained an archive of notebooks filled with information. His office was literally wall-to-wall research papers. He expected his subordinates to be equally thorough. When analysts made a recommendation, Lynch would require a written presentation outlining the details and the basis of each recommendation. Average investors should strive to reach this standard.

FINAL THOUGHT

Rationally, we know that returns on long-term investments aren't impacted by the immediate-term beliefs, emotions, and impulses that often surround financial transactions. Instead, success or lack thereof is usually a result of uncontrollable factors like corporate performance and general economic conditions. During periods of market turmoil, though, it can be difficult to keep this in mind. One of the best ways to prevent your biases from affecting your decisions is to keep the rational side of your brain engaged as often as possible. Success in investing ultimately is found by investors who can conquer these daily psychological challenges and keep a long-term perspective in view at all times. Also, if you habitually use limit orders, keep track of your successes and failures. Don't worry so much about overpaying by a quarter or an eighth to buy a stock. If you maintain your position for the long term, paying an extra quarter or eighth of a point will not impact your return.

CHAPTER 11

Conservatism Bias

To invest successfully over a lifetime does not require a stratospheric IQ, unusual business insight, or inside information. What's needed is a sound intellectual framework for decisions and the ability to keep emotions from corroding that framework.

—Warren Buffett

BIAS DESCRIPTION

Bias Name: Conservatism
Bias Type: Cognitive

General Description. *Conservatism bias* is a mental process in which people cling to their prior views or forecasts at the expense of acknowledging new information. For example, suppose that an investor receives some bad news regarding a company's earnings and that this news negatively contradicts another earnings estimate issued the previous month. Conservatism bias may cause the investor to *underreact* to the new information, maintaining impressions derived from the previous estimate rather than acting on the updated information. It is important to note that the conservatism bias may appear to conflict with representativeness bias, described in Chapter 5; in representativeness, people *overreact* to new information. People can actually exhibit both biases: If new data appears to fit, or appears representative of, an underlying model, then people may overweight that data in accordance with representativeness bias. However, if no representative relationship is evident, conservatism can dominate, which subsequently underemphasizes new data.

Technical Description. Conservatism causes individuals to overweight base rates and to underreact to sample evidence. As a result, they fail to react as a rational person would in the face of new evidence. A classic experiment by Ward Edwards[1] in 1968 eloquently illustrated the technical side of conservatism bias. Edwards presented subjects with two urns—one containing 3 blue balls and 7 red balls, the other containing 7 blue balls and 3 red ones. Subjects were given this information and then told that someone had drawn randomly 12 times from one of the urns, with the ball after each draw restored to the urn in order to maintain the same probability ratio. Subjects were told that this draw yielded 8 reds and 4 blues. They were then asked, "What is the probability that the draw was made from the first urn?" While the correct answer is 0.97, most people estimate a number around 0.7. They apparently overweight the base rate of 0.5—the random likelihood of drawing from one of two urns as opposed to the other—relative to the "new" information regarding the produced ratio of reds to blues.

Professor David Hirshleifer of Ohio State University[2] noted that one explanation for conservatism is that processing new information and updating beliefs is cognitively costly. He noted that information that is presented in a cognitively costly form, such as information that is abstract and statistical, is weighted less. Furthermore, people may overreact to information that is easily processed, such as scenarios and concrete examples. The costly-processing argument can be extended to explain base rate underweighting. If an individual underweights new information received about population frequencies (base rates), then base rate underweighting is really a form of conservatism. Indeed, base rates are underweighted less when they are presented in more salient form or in a fashion that emphasizes their causal relation to the decision problem. This costly-processing-of-new-information argument does not suggest that an individual will underweight his or her preexisting internalized prior belief. If base rate underweighting is a consequence of the use of the representativeness heuristic, there should be underweighting of priors.

Portions of this analysis resonate interestingly with Edwards's experiment. For example, perhaps people overweight the base rate probability of drawing randomly from one of two urns, relative to the sample data probability of drawing a specific combination of items, because the former quantity is simply easier to compute.

PRACTICAL APPLICATION

James Montier is author of the 2002 book B*ehavioural Finance: Insights into Irrational Minds and Markets*[3] and analyst for DKW in London. Montier has done some exceptional work in the behavioral finance field. Although Montier primarily studied the stock market in general, concentrating on the behavior of securities analysts in particular, the concepts presented here can and will be applied to individual investors later on.

Commenting on conservatism as it relates to the securities markets in general, Montier noted: "The stock market has tendency to underreact to fundamental information—be it dividend omissions, initiations, or an earnings report. For instance in the US, in the 60 days following an earnings announcement, stocks with the biggest positive earnings surprise tend to outperform the market by 2 percent, even after a 4–5 percent outperformance in the 60 days prior to the announcement."

In relating conservatism to securities analysts, Montier wrote:

People tend to cling tenaciously to a view or a forecast. Once a position has been stated, most people find it very hard to move away from that view. When movement does occur, it does so only very slowly. Psychologists call this conservatism bias. The chart below [Figure 11.1] shows conservatism in analysts' forecasts. We have taken a linear time trend out of both the operating earnings numbers and the analysts' forecasts. A cursory glance at the chart reveals that analysts are exceptionally good at telling you what has just happened. They have invested too heavily in their view and hence will only change it when presented with indisputable evidence of its falsehood.[4]

This is clear evidence of conservatism bias in action. Montier's research documents the behavior of securities analysts, but the trends observed can easily be applied to individual investors, who also forecast securities prices, and will cling to these forecasts even when presented with new information.

FIGURE 11.1 Montier Observes That Analysts Cling to Their Forecasts
Source: Dresdner Kleinwort Wasserstein, 2002

Implications for Investors. Investors too often give more attention to forecast outcomes than to new data that actually describes emerging outcomes. Many wealth management practitioners have observed clients who are unable to rationally act on updated information regarding their investments because the clients are "stuck" on prior beliefs. Box 11.1 lists three behaviors stemming from conservatism bias that can cause investment mistakes.

---

1. Conservatism bias can cause investors to cling to a view or a forecast, behaving too inflexibly when presented with new information. For example, assume an investor purchases a security based on the knowledge that the company is planning a forthcoming announcing regarding a new product. The company then announces that it has experienced problems bringing the product to market. The investor may cling to the initial, optimistic impression of some imminent, positive development by the company and may fail to take action on the negative announcement.

2. When conservatism-biased investors do react to new information, they often do so too slowly. For example, if an earnings announcement depresses a stock that an investor holds, the conservative investor may be too slow to sell. The preexisting view that, for example, the company has good prospects, may linger too long and exert too much influence, causing an investor exhibiting conservatism to unload the stock only after losing more money than necessary.

3. Conservatism can relate to an underlying difficulty in processing new information. Because people experience mental stress when presented with complex data, an easy option is to simply stick to a prior belief. For example, if an investor purchases a security on the belief that the company is poised to grow and then the company announces that a series of difficult-to-interpret accounting changes may affect its growth, the investor might discount the announcement rather than attempt to decipher it. More clear-cut and, therefore, easier to maintain is the prior belief that the company is poised to grow.

BOX 11.1 Conservatism Bias: Behaviors That Can Cause Investment Mistakes

RESEARCH REVIEW

What happens when important news hits the financial markets? Suppose a company reports earnings much higher than expected or announces a big acquisition. Traders and investors rush to digest the information and push stock prices to a level they think is consistent with what they have heard. But do they get it right? Do they react properly to the news they receive? Recent evidence suggests investors make systematic errors in processing new information that may be profitably exploited by others. In a 1997 paper, "A Model of Investor Sentiment," University of Chicago Graduate School of Business assistant professor of finance Nicholas Barberis and finance professor Robert Vishny, along with former Chicago faculty member Andrei Shleifer of Harvard University, argued that there is evidence that in some cases investors react too little to news and that in other cases they react too much.[5]

Investor Overreaction

In an important paper published in 1985, Werner De Bondt of the University of Wisconsin and Richard Thaler of the University of Chicago Graduate School of Business discovered what they claimed was evidence that investors overreact to news. Analyzing data dating back to 1933, De Bondt and Thaler found that stocks with extremely poor returns over the previous five years subsequently dramatically outperformed stocks with extremely high previous returns, even after making the standard risk adjustments.[6] Barberis, Vishy, and Shleiter's work corroborated these findings. "In other words," observed Barberis, "if an investor ranks thousands of stocks based on how well they did over the past three to five years, he or she can then make a category for the biggest losers, the stocks that performed badly, and another for the biggest winners. What you will find is that the group of the biggest losers will actually do very well on average over the next few years. So it is a good strategy to buy these previous losers or undervalued stocks."[7]

How might investor overreaction explain these findings? Suppose that a company announces good news over a period of three to five years, such as earnings reports that are consistently above expectations. It is possible that investors overreact to such news and become excessively optimistic about the company's prospects, pushing its stock price to unnaturally high levels. In the subsequent years, however, investors realize that they were unduly optimistic about the business and that the stock price will correct itself downward. In a similar way, loser stocks may simply be stocks that investors have become excessively pessimistic about. As the misperception is corrected, these stocks earn high returns.

Investor Underreaction

Barberis, Vishny, and Shleifer believe that investors sometimes also make the mistake of underreacting to certain types of financial news. Suppose a company announces quarterly earnings that are substantially higher than expected. The evidence suggests that investors see this as good news and send the stock price higher but, for some reason, not high enough. Over the next six months, this mistake is gradually corrected as the stock price slowly drifts upward toward the level it should have attained at the time of the announcement. Investors who buy the stock immediately after the announcement will benefit from this upward drift and enjoy higher returns.

The same underreaction principle applies to bad news. If bad news is announced—like if a company announces it is cutting its dividend—then the stock price will fall. However, it does not fall enough at the time of the announcement and instead continues to drift downward for several months. In both cases, when investors are faced with either good or bad announcements, they initially underreact to this news and only gradually incorporate its full import into the stock price. This signals an inefficient market. So what strategy should smart investors adopt? In the long run, it is better to invest in value stocks, stocks with low valuations (overreaction theory); but in the short run, the best predictor of returns in the next six months is returns over the preceding six months (underreaction theory). "In the short run, you want to buy relative strength," explained Vishny. "This might seem contradictory, but we can explain how both of those facts might be true using some basic psychology and building that into a model for how people form their expectations for future earnings."[8]

Psychological Evidence

In the new field of behavioral finance, researchers seek to understand whether aspects of human behavior and psychology might influence the way prices are set in financial markets. "Our idea is that these market anomalies—underreaction and overreaction—are the results of investors' mistakes," said Vishny. "In this paper, we present a model of investor sentiment—that is, of how investors form beliefs—that is consistent with the empirical findings."[9] In explaining investor behavior, Barberis, Vishny, and Shleifer's model is consistent with two important psychological theories: "convervatism" and the "representative heuristic," the latter referring to the fact that people tend to see patterns in random sequences. Certainly it would be to an investor's advantage to see patterns in financial data, if they were really there.

Unfortunately, investors are often too quick to see patterns that aren't genuine features of the data. In reality, long-run changes in company earnings follow a fairly random pattern. However, when people see a company's earnings go up several years in a row, they believe they have spotted a trend and think that it is going to continue. Such excessive optimism pushes prices too high and produces effects that support Barberis and Vishny's theory of overreaction. There are also well-known biases in human information processing that would predict underreaction to new pieces of information. One such bias, conservatism, states that once individuals have formed an impression, they are slow to change that impression in the face of new evidence. This corresponds directly to underreaction to news. Investors remain skeptical about new information and only gradually update their views.

DIAGNOSTIC TESTING

The following diagnostic quiz can help to detect elements of conservatism bias.

Conservatism Bias Test

Question 1: Suppose that you live in Baltimore, MD, and you make a forecast such as, "I think it will be a snowy winter this year." Furthermore suppose that, by mid-February, you realize that no snow has fallen. What is your natural reaction to this information?
a. There's still time to get a lot of snow, so my forecast is probably correct.
b. There still may be time for some snow, but I may have erred in my forecast.

    c. My experience tells me that my forecast was probably incorrect. Most of the winter has elapsed; not much snow, if any, is likely to arrive now.

Question 2: When you recently hear news that has potentially negative implications for the price of an investment you own, what is your natural reaction to this information?

    a. I tend to ignore the information. Because I have already made the investment, I've already determined that the company will be successful.

    b. I will reevaluate my reasons for buying the stock, but I will probably stick with it because I usually stick with my original determination that a company will be successful.

    c. I will reevaluate my reasoning for buying the stock and will decide, based on an objective consideration of all the facts, what to do next.

Question 3: When news comes out that has potentially negative implications for the price of a stock that you own, how quickly do you react to this information?

    a. I usually wait for the market to communicate the significance of the information and then I decide what to do.

    b. Sometimes, I wait for the market to communicate the significance of the information, but other times, I respond without delay.

    c. I always respond without delay.

Test Results Analysis

People answering "a" or "b" to any of the above may indicate susceptibility to conservatism bias.

ADVICE

Because conservatism is a cognitive bias, advice and information can often correct or lessen its effect. Specifically, investors must first avoid clinging to forecasts; they must also be sure to react, decisively, to new information. This does not mean that investors should respond to events without careful analysis. However, when the wisest course of action becomes clear, it should be implemented resolutely and without hesitation.

Additionally, investors should seek professional advice when trying to interpret information that they have difficulty understanding. Otherwise, investors may not take action when they should.

When new information is presented, ask yourself: How does this impact my forecast? Does it actually jeopardize my forecast? If investors can answer these questions honestly, then they have achieved a very good handle on conservatism bias. Conservatism can prevent good decisions from being made, and investors need to remain mindful of any propensities they might exhibit that make them cling to old views and react slowly toward promising, emerging developments. Offering high-quality, professional advice is probably the best way to help a client avoid the pitfalls of this common bias.

CHAPTER 12

Ambiguity Aversion Bias

*The practical justification for the study of general economics is
a belief in the possibility of improving the quality of human life
through changes in the form of organization of want-satisfying
activity.*

—Frank K. Knight, economist, University of Chicago (1921)

BIAS DESCRIPTION

Bias Name: Ambiguity Aversion
Bias Type: Cognitive

General Description.   People do not like to gamble when probability distributions seem uncertain. In general, people hesitate in situations of ambiguity, a tendency referred to as *ambiguity aversion*. Frank H. Knight, of the University of Chicago, was one of the twentieth century's most eclectic, thoughtful economists and one of the first to write on ambiguity aversion. Knight's 1921 dissertation, entitled "Risk, Uncertainty, and Profit," defined a *risk* as a gamble with a precise probability distribution. "Uncertainty," according to Knight, materializes when the distribution of possible outcomes resulting from a gamble cannot be known. Knight's groundbreaking treatise concluded that people dislike uncertainty (ambiguity) more than they dislike risk.

Ambiguity aversion appears in a wide variety of contexts. For instance, a researcher might ask a subject to estimate the probability that a certain team will win its upcoming college soccer game; the subject might estimate a 50 percent likelihood of success. The researcher might then ask the subject to consider an electronic slot machine, which is guaranteed to display either a "1" or a "0," each with a probability of 50 percent. Would the subject prefer to bet on the football game (an ambiguous bet) or on the slot machine (a bet that offers no ambiguity of the risks involved)? In general, most subjects in such a study would probably choose the slot machine, demonstrating the ambiguity aversion bias.

Technical Description.   Leonard J. Savage, author of the classic 1954 book *The Foundations of Statistics*,[1] developed "Subjective Expected Utility Theory" (SEUT) as a counterpart to the expected utility concept in economics. This theory states that, under certain conditions, an individual's expectation of utility is weighted by that individual's subjective probability assessment.

Using SEUT, Daniel Ellsberg[2] performed a classic ambiguity aversion experiment that examined, technically, ambiguity aversion. His experiment went as follows:

Suppose that subjects are presented with two boxes, referred to here as Box 1 and Box 2. The subjects are advised that Box 2 contains a total of 100 balls, exactly half of which are white, and half of which are black. Box 1 likewise contains 100 balls, again a mix of white and black, but the proportion of white to black balls in Box 1 is kept secret. Subjects are asked to choose one of the following two options, each of which offers a possible payoff of $100, depending on the color of the ball drawn at random from the relevant box.

1A. A ball is drawn from Box 1. The subject receives $100 if the ball is white, $0 if the ball is black.
1B. A ball is drawn from Box 2. The subject receives $100 if the ball is white, $0 if the ball is black.

A similar follow-up scenario is then posed, and subjects choose again between two options.

2A. A ball is drawn from Box 1. The subject receives $0 if the ball is white, $100 if the ball is black.
2B. A ball is drawn from Box 2. The subject receives $0 if the ball is white, $100 if the ball is black.

Ellsberg found that 1B was typically preferred to 1A, and that 2B was likewise preferred to 2A. These choices are inconsistent with SEUT: the choice of 1B implies a subjective probability that fewer than 50 percent of the balls in Box 1 are white, while the choice of 2B implies the opposite. The experiment suggests that people do not like situations where they are uncertain about the probability distribution of a gamble. SEUT does not account for an agent's degree of confidence in a probability distribution, and it fails to accurately predict the outcome of Ellsberg's experiment because it cannot capture ambiguity aversion.

PRACTICAL APPLICATION

When it comes to financial markets, people often make decisions based on subjective probabilities. For example, on learning that the Federal Reserve System (the Fed) is going to increase interest rates by 50 basis points, an investor must determine the probability that, say, Citigroup's stock will fall as a result. Does ambiguity aversion factor into the ensuing subjective probability evaluation? A study by Chip Heath and Amos Tversky[3] concluded that this depends on the investor's subjective competence level. When people feel skillful or knowledgeable, they prefer to stake claims on ambiguous events, whose outcomes they believe they can predict based on their own judgment, rather than on equiprobable chance events (known probability events). By contrast, when people do not feel skillful or knowledgeable, they prefer to wager on chance events. This is known as the *competence effect*, and it is a facet of ambiguity aversion extremely relevant to investors that is explored in more depth later.

John R. Graham, Campbell R. Harvey, and Hai Huang of Duke University illustrated the competence effect with an experiment.[4]

> Participants first report their subjective knowledge level about the game of football. Next, they are asked to predict the winner of a football game and also report their subjective probabilities of the predictions being correct. Then they are asked to choose between two bets, either to bet on their own judgment, or a lottery that provides an equal chance of winning. In this example, subjective competence is captured in two dimensions: the self-rated knowledge level, and the subjective probability of the football prediction

being correct. The results of this experiment are shown in [Figure 12.1] (adapted from Heath and Tversky 1991, Figure 4). The percentage of participants choosing to bet on their own judgments increases with both measures of subjective competence. When subjects feel that they are highly competent in predicting the results of football games, they prefer to bet on their own judgment. In fact, even when presented with a lottery with a greater chance of winning, they would still prefer to bet on their football predictions. In other words, they are willing to pay a premium to bet on their own judgments. When people do not feel competent, however, the matching chance lottery is preferred.

Implications for Investors.   Private-client behavior often demonstrates ambiguity aversion. The most obvious and directly applicable situation

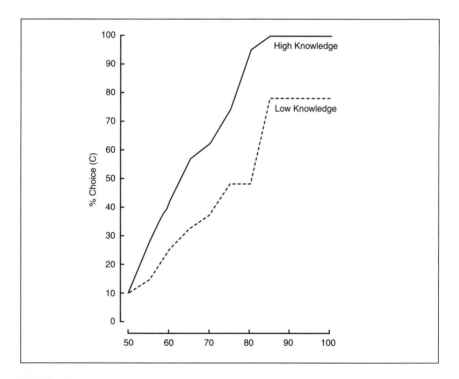

FIGURE 12.1   Percentage of Participants Who Chose Their Own Judgments over Matched Chance Lotteries
Source: Graham, Harvey, and Huang, 2003.

is investor uncertainty regarding the distribution of a security's return. As a prerequisite for investing, uncertain people are likely to demand a higher expected rate of return than they would demand if they felt certain about the risk/return trade-off of the security in question. Pascal Maenhout[5] showed that if investors are concerned about the uncertainty of a model of a stock's returns, they will demand a higher "equity premium" as compensation for the ambiguity in the probability distribution that they intuit. (Barring unreasonably high anxieties about uncertainty, Maenhout did point out that ambiguity aversion only partially solves the equity premium puzzle.)

Ambiguity aversion also sheds light on the problem of insufficient diversification. For example, investors may feel that local stock indexes are more familiar—less ambiguous—than foreign stock indexes. They may also consider firms that are situated close to them geographically to be less ambiguous than those located far away. Other investors may give increased preference to their own employers' stocks, which seem less ambiguous than the stocks of unfamiliar firms. Since less ambiguous assets are attractive, people invest heavily in those and invest little or nothing at all in ambiguous assets. Their portfolios therefore become underdiversified, relative to what modern portfolio theory would recommend.

Another important aspect of ambiguity aversion that is important for investors is the competence effect. Here, investors who believe that they are more skillful or knowledgeable in making financial decisions (i.e., those who do not perceive as much ambiguity in investment situations) are more willing to act on their judgments. For example, investors who feel more competent may trade more frequently than investors who feel less competent. Along these lines, investors are more willing to shift assets overseas when they feel that they understand foreign markets. The Research Review in this chapter further investigates the competence effect as it relates to investor behavior.

Box 12.1 contains a review of investment mistakes that stem from ambiguity aversion.

RESEARCH REVIEW

In their insightful paper "Investor Competence, Trading Frequency, and Home Bias," Graham, Harvey, and Huang[6] argued that investors who perceive themselves as financially savvy are, in accordance with the

1. Ambiguity aversion may cause investors to demand higher compensation for the perceived risks of investing in certain assets. Thus, the investors may hold only conservative investments, which can cause the potential to outlive an asset base, purchasing power erosion, and other consequences.

2. Ambiguity aversion may restrict investors to their own national indexes (e.g., Standard & Poor's 500) because these indexes are more familiar than foreign ones. This is particularly important in light of the boom in exchange traded funds (ETFs), which offer Americans the ability to invest in often unfamiliar locales, such as China and South America. Similarly, ambiguity aversion may cause investors to favor *companies* that are geographically close to them and to ignore investments that seem to be located distantly. Remaining confined to specific national indexes or companies limits options for diversification and prevents investors from exploiting profit opportunities abroad.

3. Ambiguity aversion can cause investors to believe that their employers' stocks are safer investments than other companies' stocks because investments in other companies are ambiguous. Enron, WorldCom, and other crises demonstrate the obvious perils of investing too heavily in a single company's stock.

4. A unique aspect of ambiguity aversion is the competence effect. Here, investors presented with an uncertain probability distribution might be expected to display caution due to ambiguity aversion. However, judging themselves competent in some pertinent realm (e.g., foreign stocks, small company stocks, etc.), these investors actually accept *more* risks than they should.

BOX 12.1   Ambiguity Aversion Bias: Behaviors That Can Cause Investment Mistakes

competence effect, more willing to act on their judgments. Furthermore, they show that investors who feel more competent tend to trade more frequently than investors who feel less competent. The competence effect also contributes to home bias, or the tendency to keep assets geographically nearby. In contrast, when investors feel less competent, they are more likely to avoid investing in foreign assets.

The following is excerpted from the "Introduction" of Graham, Harvey, and Huang's paper.

When people feel skillful or knowledgeable in an area, they would rather bet on their own judgment (even though it is ambiguous) than on an equiprobable chance event (e.g., drawing balls from an urn with known contents), even though the outcome of the chance event has an unambiguous probability distribution. However, when participants do not feel competent, they prefer to bet on the unambiguous chance event. Therefore, the effects of ambiguity aversion are conditional on the subjective competence level of participants.

When people feel less knowledgeable, however, they tend to choose the matched-chance lottery. The competence effect is particularly relevant to understand investor behavior. In financial markets, investors are constantly required to make decisions based on ambiguous, subjective probabilities. It is likely that their educational background and other demographic characteristics make some investors feel more competent than others in understanding the array of financial information and opportunities available to them.

We study two types of investor behavior, namely trading frequency and home bias. Although there exists extensive literatures on both trading frequency and home bias, these two have always been treated separately. In this paper, we argue that these two aspects of behavior are driven (at least in part) by the same underlying psychological bias, namely, the competence effect. With regard to trading frequency, we hypothesize that investors who feel more competent tend to trade more frequently than investors who feel less competent. This occurs because investors who feel more knowledgeable in making financial decisions should be more willing to act on their judgments. . . . Our empirical results are consistent with this hypothesis. We argue that the competence effect also contributes to home bias. Home bias refers to the tendency to overweight domestic equities and underweight international equities in investment portfolios. . . . When an investor feels that he fully understands the benefits and risks involved in investing in foreign assets, he is more willing to invest in foreign securities. In contrast, when an investor feels less competent, he is more likely to avoid foreign assets. Consistent with these predictions, our results suggest that investors with more competence are more likely to invest in international assets.[7]

So, the research that Graham, Harvey, and Huang conducted suggests two important practical applications for ambiguity aversion bias with respect to individual investors: (1) The competence effect holds, and people who feel less competent regarding some key aspect of some financial decision are less likely to heed their judgments than people who feel more competent; (2) ambiguity aversion bias helps to explain home bias. Practitioners need to be keenly aware of these investor tendencies.

DIAGNOSTIC TESTING

This section contains two questions. People who may be subject to ambiguity aversion bias answer both questions.

Ambiguity Aversion Bias Test

Question 1: Suppose you are a big fan of your local AAA baseball team, the Smallville Cougars. You are sitting in the stands just prior to the start of a game, and someone you don't know approaches you and offers you a gamble. First, he asks you what the odds are that the Cougars will win tonight's game. You estimate that the odds are 1 to 1 (50 percent), because the Cougars are playing the Bigville Titans, who linger midpack in the standings but overall have a decent team. The man then asks you if you would be willing to bet money on the game, based on those odds. You feel confident in your assessment, and you agree. You're surprised, however, when the man then produces a handheld, electronic slot machine and suggests that perhaps you would rather wager on the slot machine than on the baseball game. The machine pays off every time three cherries appear, an outcome that occurs 50 percent of the time. Assuming that the amount of money at stake is equal in each case, which bet do you accept?

Question 2: The scenario is the same as in Question 1, but there are some differences: Suppose that you are not only a big fan of your local AAA baseball team, the Smallville Cougars, but that you helped to put the team together and know all of the competitors in the league very well. This time, when the stranger approaches you, assume that you estimate 1 to 2 (67 percent) odds in favor of the Cougars. Since you know a significant amount about the team, you are again confident enough to answer in the affirmative when the man asks, given these odds, if you are willing to bet on the game. Assume that, as before, the man produces a slot machine and says you'll win just as much money if the slot machine produces three cherries as if the Cougars beat the Titans. This time the slot machine pays off—that is, produces three cherries—70 percent of the time. Which gamble do you choose?

Test Results Analysis

Question 1: People who elect the slot machine are more likely to be subject to ambiguity aversion than people who would stick with the baseball bet. The slot machine is a much less ambiguous bet, although to the subject the odds are the same.

Question 2: People who choose to bet on the game may be subject to the competence effect; feelings of expertise or skillfulness may lead these people to accept less optimal odds than they otherwise would. In this case, the outcome of the game has a lower probability than that of the slot machine, and the game was picked anyway as a result of competence effect.

ADVICE

There are two primary topics on which people exhibiting ambiguity aversion might benefit from some advice: We'll look at managing ambiguity aversion, and then we'll look at tactics for addressing the competence effect.

Ambiguity Aversion

As noted earlier, there are several key areas of which investors need to be aware with regard to ambiguity aversion. People who are ambiguity averse may not be investing in certain equity asset classes because they demand too high an equity premium; they may invest only in local or national stock indexes or only in companies located in geographically familiar places. Furthermore, they may unduly favor their own corporations' stocks over stocks of other firms.

When people demand too high a premium for investing in certain equity asset classes (such as small cap, international, etc.) and don't understand the distribution of potential outcomes, education is critical in reforming such potentially unprofitable behavior. Investors need to be educated on how the relevant asset classes perform and how adding these asset classes to a diversified portfolio can be a beneficial action. Clients who only invest in certain familiar indexes because they do not feel they can predict the probable payoffs of investing elsewhere may likewise benefit from more information about the benefits of other options. In short, education is the key to overcoming ambiguity aversion.

Competence Effect

When investors demonstrate the competence effect, it is very important that they be counseled on potential investor mistakes such as trading too frequently, which can be "hazardous to one's wealth." The competence effect also contributes to home bias, or the tendency to keep assets geographically nearby. Graham, Harvey, and Huang demonstrated that the investors most willing to shift a portion of their assets into foreign securities are those who feel most competent about investing in foreign assets. The key advice that can be offered is to not let competence in a certain area prevent investments in other areas as well. For example, if you have an investor who is an expert in real estate, does that mean that he or she should be 100 percent invested in real estate? The obvious answer is no. Stick to the fundamentals of a balanced, well-diversified portfolio.

CHAPTER 13

Endowment Bias

A wise man should have money in his head, but not in his heart.

—Jonathan Swift

BIAS DESCRIPTION

Bias Name: Endowment Bias
Bias Type: Emotional

General Description.   People who exhibit *endowment bias* value an asset more when they hold property rights to it than when they don't. Endowment bias is inconsistent with standard economic theory, which asserts that a person's *willingness to pay* for a good or an object should always equal the person's *willingness to accept dispossession* of the good or the object, when the dispossession is quantified in the form of compensation. Psychologists have found, however, that the minimum selling prices that people state tend to exceed the maximum purchase prices that they are willing to pay for the same good. Effectively, then, ownership of an asset instantaneously "endows" the asset with some added value. Endowment bias can affect attitudes toward items owned over long periods of time or can crop up immediately as the item is acquired.

Technical Description.   *Endowment bias* is described as a mental process in which a differential weight is placed on the value of an object. That value depends on whether one possesses the object and is faced with its loss or whether one does not possess the object and has the potential to gain it. If one loses an object that is part of one's endowment, then the magnitude of this loss is perceived to be greater than the magnitude of the corresponding gain if the object is newly added to one's endowment. Professor Richard Thaler, of the University of Chicago, defines the endowment bias:

> If out-of-pocket costs are viewed as losses and opportunity costs are viewed as foregone gains, the former will be more heavily weighted. Furthermore, a certain degree of inertia is introduced into the consumer choice process since goods that are included in the individual's endowment will be more highly valued than those not held in the endowment, *ceteris paribus*. This follows because removing a good from the endowment creates a loss while adding the same good (to an endowment without it) generates a gain. Henceforth, I will refer to the underweighting of opportunity costs as the *endowment effect*.[1]

In 1989, a researcher named J. L. Knetsch reported results from experiments designed to examine the *endowment bias*.[2] Knetsch's results provided an excellent practical application of endowment bias and concerned an experiment involving two groups of subjects. The 76 subjects in the first group were each given a coffee mug. They were then asked to complete a questionnaire, after which they were shown some candy bars. It had been determined earlier that the 76 subjects were about evenly divided over whether they generally preferred candy bars or coffee mugs if given a choice. But when told that they could substitute a candy bar for the coffee mug they had been given, 89 percent chose to keep the coffee mug. The second group consisted of 87 subjects. Again, about 50 percent preferred candy bars, and 50 percent preferred coffee mugs. The second group participated in the same exercise as the first group, except this time, the candy bars were the endowment good and the coffee mugs were offered subsequently as substitutes. In the second group, 90 percent declined to trade their endowed candy bars. Knetsch concluded that this dramatic asymmetry resulted because "subjects weigh the loss of giving up their initial reference entitlement far more heavily than the foregone gains of not obtaining the alternative entitlement."[3] Neither coffee mugs nor candy bars seemed, in this experiment, innately more desirable by any significant margin; rather, subjects' preferences depended on their respective endowments.

PRACTICAL APPLICATION

Investors prove resistant to change once they become endowed with (take ownership of) securities. We will examine endowment bias as it relates both to inherited securities and purchased securities. Then, we'll look at two common causes of endowment bias.

Inherited Securities

William Samuelson and Richard Zeckhauser[4] performed an enlightening study on endowment bias that aptly illustrates investor susceptibility to this bias. Samuelson and Zeckhauser conducted an experiment in which investors were told to imagine that they had to newly acquire one of four investment options:

1. A moderately risky stock.
2. A riskier stock.
3. A Treasury security.
4. A municipal security.

Another group of investors was given the same list of options. However, they were instructed to imagine that they had already inherited one specified item on the list. If desired, the investors were told, they could cede their hypothetical inheritance in favor of a different option and could do so without penalty. In every case, however, the investors in the second group showed a tendency to retain whatever was "inherited." This is a classic case of endowment bias. Most wealth management practitioners have encountered clients who are reluctant to sell securities bequeathed by previous generations. Often, in these situations, investors cite feelings of disloyalty associated with the prospect of selling inherited securities, general uncertainty in determining "the right thing to do," and tax issues.

Purchased Securities

Endowment bias also often influences the value that an investor assigns to a recently purchased security. Here is an example to illustrate this point: Assume that you have a great need for income. How much would you pay for a municipal bond that pays you triple your pretax income? Further assume that you have purchased this bond and that it is performing as expected. Interest rates have not changed, the market for securities is highly liquid, and you have the type of account that offers unlimited transactions for one fee. How much would you demand in exchange for the bond if someone wanted to buy it from you?

Rational economic theories predict that your willingness to pay (WTP) for the bond would equal your willingness to accept (WTA) compensation for it. However, this is unlikely to be the case. Once you are endowed with the bond, you are probably inclined to demand a selling price that exceeds your original purchase price. Many wealth managers have observed that investor decision making regarding both inherited and purchased securities can exhibit endowment bias and that "decision paralysis" often results: Many clients have trouble making decisions regarding the sale of securities that they either inherited or purchased themselves, and their predicament is attributable to endowment bias.

Implications for Investors.   There are some practical explanations as to why investors are susceptible to endowment bias. Understanding the origins of endowment bias can help to provide intuition that guards against the mistakes that the bias can cause. First, investors may hold onto securities that they already own in order to *avoid the transaction costs* associated with unloading those securities. This is particularly true regarding bonds. Such a rationale can be hazardous to one's wealth, because failure to take action and sell off certain assets can sometimes invite otherwise avoidable losses, while forcing investors to forgo the purchase of potentially more profitable, alternative assets. Second, investors hold onto securities because of familiarity. If investors know from experience the characteristics of the instruments that they already own (the behavior of particular government bonds, for example), then they may feel reluctant to transition into instruments that seem relatively unknown. Familiarity, effectively, has value. This value adds to the actual, market value of a security that an investor possesses, causing WTA to exceed WTP.

Box 13.1 contains a summary of investment mistakes that arise from endowment bias.

1. Endowment bias influences investors to hold onto securities that they have inherited, regardless of whether retaining those securities is financially wise. This behavior is often the result of the heirs' fear that selling will demonstrate disloyalty to prior generations or will trigger tax consequences.
2. Endowment bias causes investors to hold securities they have purchased (already own). This behavior is often the result of decision paralysis, which places an irrational premium on the compensation price demanded in exchange for the disposal of an endowed asset.
3. Endowment bias causes investors to hold securities that they have either inherited or purchased because they do not want to incur the transaction costs associated with selling the securities. These costs, however, can be a very small price to pay when evacuating an unwise investment.
4. Endowment bias causes investors to hold securities that they have either inherited or purchased because they are familiar with the behavioral characteristics of these endowed investments. Familiarity, though, does not rationally justify retaining a poorly performing stock or bond.

BOX 13.1 Endowment Bias: Behaviors That Can Cause Investment Mistakes

RESEARCH REVIEW

Professor John A. List, of the University of Maryland, authored a unique and highly relevant paper entitled "Does Market Experience Eliminate Market Anomalies?"[5] which reviewed some key aspects of endowment bias, the lessons of which can be relevant to investors. In the paper, Professor List tried to ascertain the effect of trading expertise on an individual's susceptibility to endowment bias. List's sample population traded sports cards and other sports memorabilia, and the key result of List's empirical analysis was that traders with more real-world experience were less susceptible to endowment bias. Most professional sports memorabilia dealers, for example, showed little biased behavior. List also demonstrated that people who are net sellers learn how to trade better and more quickly, with less biased behavior, than people who are net buyers. These lessons have direct implications for securities markets, and readers should take note:

> Neoclassical models include several fundamental assumptions. While most of the main tenets appear to be reasonably met, the basic independence assumption, which is used in most theoretical and applied economic models to assess the operation of markets, has been directly refuted in several experimental settings. . . . These experimental findings have been robust across unfamiliar goods, such as irradiated sandwiches, and common goods, such as chocolate bars, with most authors noting behavior consistent with an endowment effect. Such findings have induced even the most ardent supporters of neoclassical theory to doubt the validity of certain neoclassical modeling assumptions. Given the notable significance of the anomaly, it is important to understand whether the value disparity represents a stable preference structure or if consumers' behavior approaches neoclassical predictions as market experience intensifies.
>
> In this study, I gather primary field data from two distinct markets to test whether individual behavior converges to the neoclassical prediction as market experience intensifies. My data gathering approach is unique in that I examine i) trading patterns of sports memorabilia at a sports card show in Orlando, FL, and ii) trading patterns of collector pins in a market constructed by Walt Disney World at the Epcot Center in Orlando, FL. In addition, as an institutional robustness check, I examine explicit statements of value in actual auctions on the floor of a sports card show in Tucson, AZ. All of these markets are natural settings for an experiment on the relationship between market experience and the endowment effect, as they provide natural variation across individual levels of expertise. In the sports card show field experiments, I conduct some of the treatments with professional dealers and others with ordinary consumers. The design was used to capture the distinction between consumers who have intense trading experience (dealers) and those who have less trading experience (non-dealers). A major advantage of this particular field experimental design is that my laboratory is the marketplace: subjects would be engaging in similar activities whether I attended the event or went to the opera. In this sense, I

am gathering data in the least obtrusive way possible, while still maintaining the necessary control to execute a clean comparison between treatments. This highlights the naturalness of this particular setting and the added realism associated with my field experiments.

The main results of the study fall into three categories. First, consistent with previous studies, I observe a significant endowment effect in the pooled data. Second, I find sharp evidence that suggests market experience matters: across all consumer types, market-like experience and the magnitude of the endowment effect are inversely related. In addition, within the group of subjects who have intense trading experience (dealers and experienced non-dealers), I find that the endowment effect becomes negligible. Both of these observations extend quite well to statements of value in auctions, where offers and bids are significantly different for naive consumers, but statistically indistinguishable for experienced consumers.

While these empirical results certainly suggest that individual behavior converges to the neoclassical prediction as market experience intensifies, it remains an open question as to whether the endowment effect is absent for practiced consumers because of experience (treatment effect), or because a prior disposition toward having no such gap leads them to trade more often (selection effect). To provide evidence into this query, I returned to the sports card market approximately one year after the initial sports card trading experiment and examined trading rates for the same group of subjects who participated in the first experiment. Via both unconditional and conditional statistical analyses, which use panel data regression techniques to control for individual static preferences, I find that market experience significantly attenuates the endowment effect.

Whether preferences are defined over consumption levels or changes in consumption merits serious consideration. If preferences are defined over changes in consumption, then a reevaluation of a good deal of economic analysis is necessary since the basic independence assumption is directly refuted. Several experimental studies have recently provided strong evidence that the basic independence assumption is rarely appropriate. These results, which clearly contradict closely held economic doctrines, have led some influential commentators to call for an entirely new economic paradigm to displace conventional neoclassical theory.

In this study, I depart from a traditional experimental investigation by observing actual market behavior. Examining behavior in four field experiments across disparate markets yields several unique insights. First, the field data suggest that there is an overall endowment effect. Second, within both institutions—observed trading rates and explicit value revelation—I find strong evidence that individual behavior converges to the neoclassical prediction as trading experience intensifies.[6]

Overall, List's data and analysis support the idea that trading expertise negatively correlates with endowment bias. Moreover, by examining trading patterns within two separate market institutions, List provided controls for any unobserved effects that may be specific to one trading forum and thereby bias his result. List's findings do not simply pertain to the sports card show or to Epcot, but to both—and can be applied to the investing behavior of private clients.

DIAGNOSTIC TESTING

The following is a brief diagnostic test that can help to detect endowment bias.

Endowment Bias Test

Question 1: Assume that your dearly departed Aunt Sally has bequeathed to you 100 shares of IBM. Your financial advisor tells you that you are too "tech heavy" and recommends that you sell Aunt Sally's shares. What is your most likely course of action?
   a. I will likely hold the IBM shares because Aunt Sally bequeathed them to me.
   b. I will likely listen to my financial advisor and sell the shares.

Question 2: Assume that you have purchased a high-quality municipal bond for your portfolio. It has been providing income for you, and you are happy with it. Your financial advisor analyzes your bond holdings and recommends switching to a corporate bond, of comparable quality, with which you are unfamiliar. Your advisor explains that, after taxes and fees, the corporate bond can be expected to provide a slightly better return than your current municipal bond. What is your most likely response?

a. I will stick with the municipal bond because I am familiar with it.

b. I will sell the municipal bond and purchase the corporate bond, even though I am unfamiliar with the corporate bond.

Question 3: Assume that you purchased 100 shares of GE in a self-directed account and paid a commission on the transaction. Shortly following the purchase, you realize that you momentarily overlooked another 100 shares of GE that you already owned in another account. Now, the redundant holdings are causing an imbalance in your overall portfolio. What is your reaction to this situation?

a. Since I paid a commission and I like GE's stock, I will keep the GE even though it may cause an imbalance in my overall portfolio.

b. I am not comfortable with imbalance in my portfolio. I will sell the GE, even though this means that I will have paid two unnecessary commissions.

Test Results Analysis

Question 1: A reluctance to unload Aunt Sally's IBM shares can signal susceptibility to endowment bias.

Question 2: People who decide that they might likely hold onto the municipal bond, due to familiarity with it, are likelier to exhibit endowment bias than people who would be willing to re-allocate, even into unfamiliar territory, at a financial advisor's request.

Question 3: Respondents who estimate that they'd be willing to tolerate the imbalance caused by the redundant GE holdings are probably susceptible to endowment bias.

ADVICE

Generally, endowment bias tends to impact investors in four main contexts: (1) inherited securities, (2) purchased securities, (3) commission aversion, and (4) desire for familiarity. Advice can be tailored, specifically, to address each case.

Inherited Securities.   If you are a professional wealth advisor and you realize that a client's decisions regarding inherited securities, or any other pertinent asset, are being compromised by endowment bias, then asking the client carefully targeted questions is often a useful first step. This way, you can lead clients to discover the "correct" conclusion themselves. In the case of an inherited security, for example, you might ask: "If you had received, as cash, the current value of this security, what portion of that inheritance would you allocate into this specific security?" Often, the answer is none or very little. It can also be useful to explore the deceased's intent in owning the security. "Do you think that Uncle John's primary intent was to leave you this specific number of shares of this specific security? Is it possible that he was concerned about your general financial security?" Again, clients usually affirm the latter conclusion, paving the way to a more sensible allocation. If the client does believe that his or her deceased relative valued, specifically, the opportunity to bequeath holdings in this exact security, then you might need to try a different line of questioning: "Okay, Uncle John wanted you to have these shares. But, if he really didn't want you to sell them, then . . . what did he want you to do with them?" Stressing the achievement of financial goals usually persuades the client to listen to facts about how selling enhances the chances of achieving a favorable outcome.

Purchased Securities.   A similar line of questioning can also help determine if clients are biased in the area of purchased securities, for example, "If you had to convert your current holdings in Security XYZ into cash and then allocate that cash as you see fit, would you end using it to purchase more of Security XYZ? Do you think you'd purchase the same amount of Security XYZ that you currently own?" Often clients will realize that they might hypothetically behave differently if handling a liquid sum. It is also useful to question the client about his or her intent in owning the security: "What do you hope to accomplish by holding this security, and how is this security helping you to achieve your financial goals?" Often, as in the case of inherited securities, the client will see the light. Stressing a long-term view in financial goals can often persuade clients to be more receptive to facts.

Transaction Cost Aversion.   Commission aversion is a very common phenomenon and can be very detrimental to a portfolio. The "penny wise, pound foolish" proverb is often one of the most salient arguments that you can present to a client in this case, and the best way to do this is to lay out, numerically, potential gains that can be achieved or losses that can be averted by selling versus retaining the security. Then, contrast these sums with the relatively trivial expected sum of any commission fees. More often than not, if you present this logic persuasively, a client will understand the lesson and agree to re-allocate.

Desire for Familiarity. Familiarity can be a difficult craving to overcome. Comfort is crucial to an investor, and it may not be wise to take a portfolio in any direction with which the client seems significantly uncomfortable. This ends up being especially important in cases where your recommendation ultimately goes sour. The best way to address a client's desire for familiarity, when that desire contradicts your financial advice, is to review the historical performance of the unfamiliar securities that you are suggesting the client acquire. Demonstrate the logic underlying your recommendation. Rather than entirely replacing familiar holdings with new, scary ones, perhaps recommend that the client try out a small purchase of the unfamiliar investment you're recommending. This way, your client can develop familiarity with the new investment instrument and achieve a corresponding comfort level.

CHAPTER 14

Self-Control Bias

*Self-reverence, self-knowledge, self-control—these three alone
lead to power.*

—Alfred, Lord Tennyson (1880)

BIAS DESCRIPTION

Bias Name: Self-Control Bias
Bias Type: Emotional

General Description.   Simply put, *self-control bias* is a human behavioral
tendency that causes people to consume today at the expense of saving
for tomorrow. Money is an area in which people are notorious for displaying a lack of self-control. Attitudes toward paying taxes provide a
common example. Imagine that you, a taxpayer, estimate that your income this year will cause your income tax to increase by $3,600, which
will be due one year from now. In the interest of conservatism, you decide to set money aside. You contemplate two choices: Would you rather
contribute $300 per month over the course of the next 12 months to
some savings account earmarked for tax season? Or would you rather increase your federal income tax withholding by $300 each month, sparing
you the responsibility of writing out one large check at the end of the
year? Rational economic thinking suggests that you would prefer the savings account approach because your money would accrue interest and
you would actually net more than $3,600. However, many taxpayers

choose the withholding option because they realize that the savings account plan would be complicated in practice by a lack of self-control.

Self-control bias can also be described as a conflict between people's overarching desires and their inability, stemming from a lack of self-discipline, to act concretely in pursuit of those desires. For example, a student desiring an "A" in history class might theoretically forgo a lively party to study at the library. An overweight person desperate to shed unwanted pounds might decline a tempting triple fudge sundae. Reality demonstrates, however, that plenty of people do sabotage their own long-term objectives for temporary satisfaction in situations like the ones described.

Investing is no different. The primary challenge in investing is saving enough money for retirement. Most of this chapter will focus on the savings behaviors of investors and how best to promote self-control in this often-problematic realm. Perhaps the best framework for understanding how to advise clients on self-control bias is done in the context of *life-cycle hypothesis*, a rational theory of savings behavior. This is a standard finance concept that we will examine and then entertain from a behavioral perspective.

Technical Description. The technical description of self-control bias is best understood in the context of the *life-cycle hypothesis,* which describes a well-defined link between the savings and consumption tendencies of individuals and those individuals' stages of progress from childhood, through years of work participation, and finally into retirement. The foundation of the model is the *saving decision*, which directs the division of income between consumption and saving. The saving decision reflects an individual's relative preferences over present versus future consumption. Because the life-cycle hypothesis is firmly grounded in expected utility theory and assumes rational behavior, an entire lifetime's succession of optimal saving decisions can be computed given only an individual's projected household income stream vis-à-vis the utility function.

The income profile over the life cycle starts with low income during the early working years, followed by increasing income that reaches a peak prior to retirement. Income during retirement, based on assumptions regarding pensions, is then substantially lower. To make up for the lower income during retirement and to avoid a sharp drop in utility at the point of retirement, individuals will save some fraction of their income when they're still working, spending it later during retirement. The main prediction, then, of the life-cycle hypothesis is a lifetime savings profile characterized by a "hump"-shaped curve, with savings building gradually, maxing out, and finally declining again as a function of time.

Two common tendencies of individuals underlie spending patterns, according to the life-cycle hypothesis:

1. Most people prefer a higher standard of living to a lower standard of living; that is, people want to maximize consumption spending in the present.
2. Most people prefer to maintain a relatively constant standard of living throughout their lives. They dislike volatility and don't desire abrupt intervals of feast interspersed with famine.

Basically, the life-cycle hypothesis envisions that people will try to maintain the highest, smoothest consumption paths possible.

Now that we have an understanding of the life cycle hypothesis, we can integrate behavioral concepts that account for real-world savings behavior. In 1998, Hersh Shefrin and Richard Thaler introduced a behaviorally explained life-cycle hypothesis,[1] which is a descriptive model of household savings in which self-control plays a key role. The key assumption of the behavioral life-cycle theory is that households treat components of their wealth as "nonfungible" or noninterchangeable even in the absence of credit rationing. Specifically, wealth is assumed to be divided into three "mental" accounts: (1) current income, (2) current assets, and (3) future income. The temptation to spend is assumed to be greatest for current income and least for future income.

Considerable empirical evidence supporting the behavioral life-cycle theory exists. In a survey of students´ expectations of future consumption, Shefrin and Thaler obtained direct support for the tenets of behavioral life-cycle theory. Specifically, they found that subjects envisioning themselves to be the beneficiaries of some financial windfall predicted that they would consume, immediately, a greater portion of that windfall during the same year if the money was coded as current income rather than current assets. Subjects said that they would consume the smallest portions of income coded as future income. For most people, consumption and income (i.e., saving) are mediated by institutions, not individual decisions. Examples include home mortgage repayment schedules, 401(k) plans, and individual retirement accounts (IRAs); often, these instruments represent an individual's only real savings, with no additional funds being set aside.

Self-control has a cost, and people are willing to pay a price to avoid reigning in their natural impulses. Consumers act as if they are maintaining separate funds within their individual accounting systems, separating income into current income and wealth. The marginal propensity to consume varies according to the source of income (e.g., salary versus bonus), even if the measure taken to activate or to sustain the source of income (e.g., work) is the same. People are more likely to build assets or savings with money they view, or "frame," as wealth, whereas they are less likely to build savings using what they consider to be current income. Many researchers have continued to elaborate on the behavioral life-cycle model, particularly as it relates to retirement savings.

PRACTICAL APPLICATION

Encouraging people to save more is a task that constantly challenges financial advisors. The "Save More Tomorrow Program,"[2] developed by Professors Richard H. Thaler, of the University of Chicago, and Shlomo Benartzi, of the Anderson School of Business at UCLA, aims to help corporate employees who would like to save more but lack the willpower to act on this desire. The program offers many useful insights into saving behavior, and examining it will serve as our practical application discussion in this chapter.

The "Save More Tomorrow Program" has four primary aspects:

1. Employees are approached about increasing their contribution rates a considerable time before their scheduled pay increases occur.
2. The contributions of employees who join the plan are automatically increased beginning with the first paycheck following a raise.
3. Participating employees' contribution rates continue to increase automatically with each scheduled raise, until rates reach a preset maximum.
4. Employees can opt out of the plan at any time.

Let's examine the results of a trial of the Save More Tomorrow Program (SMTP) by a midsize manufacturing company in 1988. Prior to the adoption of the SMTP, the company suffered from a low participation rate as well as low saving rates. In an effort to increase the saving rates of the employees, the company hired an investment consultant and offered this service to every employee eligible for its retirement savings plan. Of the 315 eligible participants, all but 29 agreed to meet with the consultant and get his advice. Based on information that the employee provided, the consultant used commercial software to compute a desired saving rate. The consultant also discussed with each employee how much of an increase in saving would be considered economically feasible. If the employee seemed very reluctant to increase his or her saving rate substantially, the consultant would constrain the program to increase the saving contribution by no more than 5 percent.

Of the 286 employees who talked to the investment consultant, only 79 (28 percent) were willing to accept the consultant's advice, even with the adjustment to constrain some of the saving rate increases to 5 percent. For the rest of the participants, the planner offered a version of the SMTP, proposing that they increase their saving rates by 3 percentage points a year, starting with the next pay increase. Even with the aggressive strategy of increasing saving rates, the SMTP proved to be extremely popular with the participants. Of the 207 participants who were unwilling to accept the saving rate proposed by the investment consultant, 162 (78 percent) agreed to join the SMTP.

The majority of these participants did not change their minds once the saving increases took place. Only 4 participants (2 percent) dropped out of the plan prior to the second pay raise, with 29 more (18 percent) dropping out between the second and third pay raises. Hence, the vast majority of the participants (80 percent) remained in the plan through three pay raises. Furthermore, even those who withdrew from the plan did not reduce their contribution rates to the original levels; they merely stopped the future increases from taking place. So, even these workers are saving significantly more than they were before joining the plan.

The key lesson here is that people are generally poor at planning and saving for retirement. They need to have self-discipline imposed on them consistently in order to achieve savings.

Implications for Investors.   As previously noted, the primary issue with regard to self-control is the lack of ability to save for retirement. In addition, there are several other self-control behaviors that can cause investment mistakes. Box 14.1 summarizes some of these.

1. Self-control bias can cause investors to spend more today at the expense of saving for tomorrow. This behavior can be hazardous to one's wealth, because retirement can arrive too quickly for investors to have saved enough. Frequently, then, people incur inappropriate degrees of risk in their portfolios in effort to make up for lost time. This can, of course, aggravate the problem.

2. Self-control bias may cause investors to fail to plan for retirement. Studies have shown that people who do not plan for retirement are far less likely to retire securely than those who do plan. Studies have shown that people who do not plan for retirement are also less likely to invest in equity securities.

3. Self-control bias can cause asset-allocation imbalance problems. For example, some investors prefer income-producing assets, due to a "spend today" mentality. This behavior can be hazardous to long-term wealth because too many income-producing assets can inhibit a portfolio to keep up with inflation. Other investors might favor different asset classes, such as equities over bonds, simply because they like to take risks and can't control their behavior.

4. Self-control bias can cause investors to lose sight of basic financial principles, such as compounding of interest, dollar cost averaging, and similar discipline behaviors that, if adhered to, can help create significant long-term wealth.

BOX 14.1   Self-Control Bias: Behaviors That Can Cause Investment Mistakes

RESEARCH REVIEW

This research review examines two academic studies done by Professor Annamaria Lusardi, of Dartmouth College. In 2000, Lusardi wrote "Explaining Why So Many Households Do Not Save."[3] In 1999, she wrote "Information, Expectations, and Savings for Retirement."[4] Lusardi's work examined household savings and asset-ownership behavior in an attempt to assess how differences in planning and saving across households are explained by various factors. In essence, the studies address whether *lack of planning* (which may be interpreted as lack of self-control) plays a key role in explaining differences in savings behavior. The analysis relies on data obtained from the Health and Retirement Study (HRS), a survey based on a sample of U.S. householders born between 1931 and 1941; and the triennial, Federal Reserve–sponsored Survey of Consumer Finances (SCF). Lusardi took two measures to gauge the extent of retirement planning.

1. Planning is measured by responses to the question "How much have you thought about retirement?" Responses, grouped at various income levels, are summarized in Table 14.1. Lusardi classified respondents as "planners" or "nonplanners" on the basis of their responses; those who have "hardly" thought about retirement are nonplanners, whereas those who have thought at least "a little" about retirement are planners.
2. Planning is measured via a "planning index." The index is constructed by assigning "points" to respondents based on survey results. Points are awarded to reflect the extent to which a respondent claims to have thought about retirement ("hardly at all" merits one point, while "a lot" earns four), and points are added if respon-

TABLE 14.1 Thinking about Retirement and Savings

	How much have you thought about retirement?			
Percentile	A lot	Some	A little	Hardly at all
5	0	2,010	–120	–500
25	41,300	50,500	28,500	8,800
50	116,200	128,000	92,000	60,000
75	241,000	266,800	208,000	147,000
90	437,000	474,500	485,700	346,500
95	636,500	752,000	1,009,000	613,350
Mean	224,252	239,298	245,304	165,367
(Std. Dev.)	(504,987)	(422,639)	(638,957)	(448,924)
Number of observations	1,331	1,039	681	1,438

Note: This table reports the distribution of total net worth across different responses to the question "How much have you thought about retirement?" All figures are weighted using survey weights.
Source: Lusardi, 2000. Reprinted with permission.

dents report engaging in additional planning activities. For example, respondents who have asked the Social Security Administration to calculate their expected retirement benefits receive one extra point. Respondents also receive points for having attended retirement seminars.

Lusardi's empirical analysis showed that householders not planning for retirement tend to have much lower savings than householders who have given thought to retirement. The study controlled for numerous additional variables that might arguably impact savings and also tried substituting various measures of asset accumulation (e.g., financial or total net worth) as proxy variables to provide alternative planning measures. Still, the result remains conclusive: Savings levels depend significantly on whether a householder has planned for retirement.

Additionally, planning may have an effect not only on wealth but also on portfolio choice. If obtaining information about complex investment assets, such as stocks, required too much effort, families facing retirement will be less likely to invest in those assets. Thus, the question of whether planning affects stock ownership is also important and can be examined using regression analysis. Again, Lusardi incorporated a wide array of proxy variables to control for resource and preference attributes of households that, though not explicitly measurable, could be expected to bias results. Rather than considering total pension wealth, for example, the analysis distinguished between households whose heads maintain defined contribution, defined benefit, or other types of pensions. The underlying logic here is that plan structure might impact the degree of discretion employees exercise over the allocation of pension assets and that this, in turn, might impact allocation of nonpension assets. The results of this analysis showed that lack of planning is also a strong determinant of portfolio choice. Households that do not plan are less likely to invest in stocks; this result is consistent even after a variety of factors have been accounted for.

In the HRS, respondents were asked to rate their retirement experiences, and to state how they felt retirement compared to their working years. (See Table 14.2.) More than 54 percent of those respondents who had not thought about retirement rated their retirement experiences poor with respect to their preretirement years. A large proportion of respondents (79 percent) who thought "a lot" about retirement described their quality of life during retirement as equaling or exceeding that of

TABLE 14.2   How Has Your Retirement Turned Out?

| | Retirement and Planning | | | |
| | How much have you thought about retirement? | | | |
How has your retirement turned out to be?	A lot	Some	A little	Hardly at all
Very satisfying	0.68	0.50	0.35	0.22
Moderately satisfying	0.28	0.41	0.46	0.35
Not at all satisfying	0.04	0.09	0.19	0.43
Number of observations	343	217	92	520

| | Retirement and Planning | | | |
| | How much have you thought about retirement? | | | |
How is your retirement compared to the years just before you retired?	A lot	Some	A little	Hardly at all
Better	0.57	0.44	0.35	0.18
About the same	0.22	0.31	0.36	0.24
Not as good	0.11	0.15	0.22	0.54
Retired less than one year ago	0.10	0.10	0.07	0.04
Number of observations	343	217	92	520

Note: This table reports the fraction of respondents according to how they have rated retirement and how much they have thought about retirement.
Source: Lusardi, 2000. Reprinted with permission.

their preretirement years. This evidence suggestively coincides with the low amount of asset accumulation estimated for nonplanners in Lusardi's previous regressions. Rationally, households that accumulate less savings are probably more likely to experience an unpleasant "surprise" after retirement.

It can be concluded that a large percentage of U.S. households nearing retirement age inadequately plan for retirement. Although many explanations can be generated for these statistics, the reality is that people often simply do not think about retirement or do not want to sacrifice today to have future benefits. Lack of self-control (planning), Lusardi demonstrated, correlates with low aggregate wealth and results in portfolios that are less likely to contain high-return assets, such as stocks. Much research is needed to determine why households fail to plan for retirement and whether the provision of information (e.g., Social Security and pension benefits) might perhaps improve the financial security of many U.S. households.

DIAGNOSTIC TESTING

This section contains a brief diagnostic quiz that deals with issues of self-control.

Question 1: Suppose that you are in need of a new automobile. You have been driving your current car for seven years, and it's time for a change. Assume that you do face some constraints in your purchase as "money does not grow on trees." Which of the following approaches are you most likely to take?

   a. I would typically underspend on a car because I view a car as transportation, and I don't need anything fancy. Besides, I can save the extra money I might have spent on a fancy car and put it away in my savings accounts.

   b. I would typically purchase a medium-priced model, with some fancy options, simply because I enjoy a nice car. I may forgo other purchases in order to afford a nice car. I don't imagine that I'd go crazy and purchase anything extravagant, but a nice car is something that I value to an extent and am willing to spend money to obtain this.

   c. When it comes to cars, I like to indulge myself. I'd probably splurge on a top-of-the-line model and select most or all available luxury options. Even if I must purchase this car at the expense of saving money for the long term, I believe that it's vital to live in the moment. This car is simply my way of living in the moment.

Question 2: How would you characterize your retirement savings patterns?

   a. I consult my advisors and make sure that every tax-favored investment vehicle is maxed out (401(k), IRA, etc.), and I will often save additional funds in taxable accounts.

   b. I will usually take advantage of most tax-favored investment vehicles, though in some cases I'm sure that details may have escaped

my attention. I may or may not save something in taxable investment accounts.

c. I hardly ever save for retirement. I spend most of my disposable income, so very little remains available for savings.

Question 3: How well would you rate your own self-discipline?

a. I always achieve a goal if it is important to me. If I want to lose 10
pounds, for example, I will diet and exercise relentlessly until I am
satisfied.

b. I can often attain my goals, but sometimes I have trouble sticking
to certain difficult things that I have resolved to accomplish.

c. I have a tremendous amount of difficulty keeping promises to myself. I have little or no self-discipline, and I often find myself reaching out to others for help in attaining key goals.

Test Results Analysis

Questions 1, 2, and 3: People answering "b" or "c" to any of these questions may be susceptible to self-control bias. Please note that self-
control is a very common bias!

ADVICE

When a practitioner encounters self-control bias, there are four primary topics on which advice can generally be given: (1) spending control, (2) lack of planning, (3) portfolio allocation, and (4) the benefits
of discipline.

Spending Control.   Self-control bias can cause investors to spend more
today rather than saving for tomorrow. People have a strong desire to
consume freely in the present. This behavior can be counterproductive to
attaining long-term financial goals because retirement often arrives before investors have managed to save enough money. This may spur people into accepting, at the last minute, inordinate amounts of risk in their
portfolios to make up for lost time—a tendency that actually places one's
retirement security at increased risk. Advisors should counsel their clients
to pay themselves first, setting aside consistent quantities of money to ensure their comfort later in life, especially if retirement is still a long way
off. If an advisor encounters investors who are past age 60 and have not

saved enough for retirement, then a more difficult situation emerges. A careful balance must be struck between saving, investing, and risk taking in order to increase the pot of money for retirement. Often, these clients might benefit from examining additional options, such as part-time work (cycling in and out of retirement) or cutting back on consumption. In either case, emphasizing paying oneself first—assigning a sufficient level of priority to future rather than present-day consumption—is critical.

Lack of Planning.   Self-control bias may cause investors to not plan adequately for retirement. Studies have shown that people who do not plan for retirement are much less likely not to retire securely than those who do plan. People who do not plan for retirement are also less likely to invest in equity securities. Advisors must emphasize that investing without planning is like building without a blueprint. Planning is the absolute key to attaining long-term financial goals. Furthermore plans need to be written down so that they can be reviewed on a regular basis. Without planning, investors may not be apt to invest in equities, potentially causing a problem with keeping up with inflation. In sum, people don't plan to fail—they simply fail to plan.

Portfolio Allocation.   Self-control bias can cause asset allocation imbalance problems. Investors subject to this bias may prefer income-producing assets, due to a "spend today" mentality. This behavior can be counterproductive to attaining long-term financial goals because an excess of income-producing assets can prevent a portfolio from keeping up with inflation. Self-control bias can also cause people to unduly favor certain asset classes, such as equities over bonds, due to an inability to reign in impulses toward risk. Advisors must emphasize the importance of adhering to a planned asset allocation. There is a litany of information on the benefits of asset allocation, which can be persuasively cited for a client's benefit. Whether they prefer bonds or equities, clients exhibiting a lack of self-control need to be counseled on maintaining properly balanced portfolios so that they can attain their long-term financial goals.

Benefits of Discipline.   Self-control bias can cause investors to lose sight of very basic financial principles, such as compounding of interest or dollar cost averaging. By failing to reap these discipline profits over time, clients can miss opportunities for accruing significant long-term wealth. Perhaps the most critical issue is to counsel your clients on the benefits of compounding. There are a number of very effective software programs that can demonstrate that even a minimal, 1 to 2 percent disparity in returns, if compounded over decades, can mean the difference between a comfortable and a subpar retirement. To return to an example that arises frequently in discussions of willpower—the matter of exercising—the benefits of self-discipline in investing, as in physical fitness, are difficult to obtain. The results, however, are well worth it.

CHAPTER 15

Optimism Bias

Even apart from the instability due to speculation, there is the instability due to the characteristic of human nature that a large proportion of our positive activities depend on spontaneous optimism rather than on a mathematical expectation, whether moral or hedonistic or economic.

—John Maynard Keynes, *The General Theory of Employment, Interest, and Money* (1936)

BIAS DESCRIPTION

Bias Name: Optimism
Bias Type: Emotional

General Description. Most people have heard of "rose-colored glasses" and know that those who wear them tend to view the world with undue optimism. Empirical studies referred to in previous chapters demonstrate that, with respect to almost any personal trait perceived as positive— driving ability, good looks, sense of humor, physique, expected longevity, and so on—most people tend to rate themselves as surpassing the popu- lation mean. Investors, too, tend to be overly optimistic about the mar- kets, the economy, and the potential for positive performance of the investments they make. Many overly optimistic investors believe that bad investments will not happen to them—they will only afflict "others." Such oversights can damage portfolios because people fail to mindfully acknowledge the potential for adverse consequences in the investment decisions they make.

Technical Description. Nobel Prize winner Daniel Kahneman, of Princeton University, and Daniel Lovallo, of the University of New South Wales, Australia, describe *optimism bias* in more technical terms. They note a tendency of investors to adopt an inside view, in lieu of the outside view that is often more appropriate when making financial decisions.[1] An inside view is one that focuses on a current situation and reflects personal involvement. An outside view, however, dispassionately assesses a current situation in the context of results obtained in past, related situations. The inside-versus-outside thought process distinguishes investors exhibiting optimism bias from investors exhibiting rational economic decision making, because most unreasonably rosy forecasts tend to derive from biased feelings about specific, current situations while largely ignoring the outcomes of previous, related situations. Consideration of such outcomes might help investors make more realistic judgments.

Investors are encouraged to take an outside view, also known as *reference-class forecasting.* This technique focuses less on the characteristics of an individual investment at hand and, instead, encourages investors to examine the experiences of a class of similar investments. Investors should lay out a rough distribution of outcomes for a similar investment class and then try to forecast returns on a new prospective investment by positioning it within that asset class distribution. This outside view is more likely than an inside view is to produce accurate forecasts—and less likely to deliver unexpected outcomes. The contrast between inside and outside views has been confirmed in systematic research. Studies have shown that when people are asked simple questions designed to instill an outside view, their forecasts become significantly more objective and reliable.

Most individuals, however, are inclined toward an inside view of their investments. This approach is traditional, ingrained, and intuitive. The natural way to think about a complex investment is to focus on the investment itself—to bring forth all available data, paying special attention to unique or unusual details. The thought of going out and gathering statistics about related cases seldom enters an investor's mind. Optimism in and of itself is not a bad thing. However, investors must examine downside risks, particularly when large sums of money are at stake. There needs to be a balance between optimism and realism, between goals and forecasts. Inside views can generate potentially successful investment ideas, but outside-view forecasts should ultimately determine whether an individual makes a specific investment in the first place.

PRACTICAL APPLICATION

One of the most striking observed instances of optimism bias involves the purchase of company stock by employees in their retirement plans. At the end of 2000, 62 percent of Enron's 401(k) plan assets were invested in Enron common stock. Do you think that Enron employees were optimistic regarding the prospects of their company? Given what is now known, the answer to that question is definitely "yes." Perhaps it is not surprising that Enron's 401(k) wasn't that different from many other companies in terms of the percentage of company stock held by employees.

Most 401(k) plans maintained by large, public companies offer employer stock funds. What is not commonly known is that employees who participate in 401(k) plans that offer employer stock funds tend to invest, on average, a third of their plan assets in company stock.[2] One in five companies' 401(k) plan assets invested *at least* 50 percent in the company's own stock; at some firms, this threshold is actually much higher. In 2002, Procter & Gamble's 401(k) funds were 94.7 percent invested in employer securities; for Sherwin-Williams, the figure was 91.6 percent; at Abbott Laboratories, 90.2 percent; and at Pfizer, 85.5 percent.

Undue optimism by employees is a key driver of this phenomenon because optimism leads people to perceive their own firms as being exceptionally unlikely to suffer from economic misfortunes. Therefore, people feel that their employer's stock is a less risky investment than other companies' stock, and they feel an upbeat sense of assurance when they allocate their assets accordingly. This is particularly understandable when employees do not benefit from any investment advice; given a vast array of unexplained investment options, an employer's stock seems especially familiar and comfortable. When people do seek advice, it is helpful for practitioners to understand their optimism and to respond by counseling the pitfalls of overinvesting in company stock.

Implications for Investors.   Undue optimism can be financially harmful because it creates, for investors, the illusion of some unique insight or upper hand. Often, people on some level believe that they can "see" inaccurately priced securities, when in fact they cannot. This section is devoted to exploring some of the behaviors related to optimism that can cause investment mistakes. First, many investors falsely believe themselves to be above-average investors. Numerous studies demonstrate that, as with driving ability and good looks, market savvy is an arena in which the majority of individuals estimate themselves to outshine the majority of individuals, which is statistically problematic. One study found that "over half of the overly optimistic investors actually believed they were beating the market, and yet were underperforming by 5 to 15 percent. Their denial just made things worse, and made improvement darn near impossible."[3]

DALBAR, Inc., conducted the well-known *Quantitative Analysis of Investor Behavior*. DALBAR's 2003 study,[4] previously referenced in Chapter 5, demonstrated that investors do not outperform the market as decisively as they think that they do. The average equity investor earned a 2.57 percent average annual return over the period 1984 through 2002; given a 3.14 percent inflation rate and a 12.22 percent return on the Standard & Poor's 500 over the exact same period, it is safe to say that outperforming did not occur. Naturally, this is not to say that *all* investors underperformed, but the *average* investor did.

Other studies show that optimism bias can correlate with *home bias*—the desire to invest close to home—because people may be unduly optimistic about prospects in their own geographic vicinities. The research review later in this chapter elaborates on this subject. As we've discussed already, optimism bias can also cause investors to load up on company stock, potentially to the detriment of their long-term financial goals.

Finally, some thought leaders in the investment industry continuously warn investors about the lack of "real returns" that investors actually attain. People, of course, do not perceive their own situations this way—they often *think* that they are obtaining good real returns. However, optimism bias is arguably the mechanism that shields most investors from this epiphany. Box 15.1 reviews behaviors related to optimism bias that can cause investment mistakes.

RESEARCH REVIEW

Advisors often need to understand their own potential biases. When advisors are responsible for managing assets for clients, they should en-

1. Optimism bias can cause investors to potentially overload themselves with company stock because optimism biases can make them think that other companies are more likely to experience downturns than their own. Also, employees feel a greater comfort and optimism with the stock of their employer, feeling that an investment there is less risky than an investment elsewhere.

2. Optimism bias can cause investors to believe they are getting marketlike returns, when in fact they need to be wary of things like inflation, fees, and taxes that eat away at these returns and eliminate the long-term benefits of compounding returns.

3. Optimism bias can cause investors to read too much into "rosy" forecasts such as earnings estimates of analysts or their own research done by reading company reports that show rosy outlooks. Additionally, investors prefer to get good news about the markets or their investments and so may be predisposed to optimism versus pessimism.

4. Optimism bias can cause investors to think they are above-average investors, simply because they are optimistic people in general, or to believe that they are above average in other areas of their life, such as driving ability or social skills.

5. Optimism bias can cause investors to invest near their geographic region (home bias) because they may be unduly optimistic about the prospect of their local geographic area.

BOX 15.1 Optimism Bias: Behaviors That Can Cause Investment Mistakes

deavor to be as unbiased as possible. The research paper chosen for this chapter presents information that may be critically useful to advisors, especially as it relates to investing (or not investing) internationally. In an excellent work entitled "What Drives Home Bias? Evidence from Fund Managers' Views," Torben Lütje and Lukas Menkhoff of the University of Hannover, Germany, examined the propensity toward "home bias" among institutional and individual asset managers. Their multivariate analyses indicated that home bias, as exhibited by these so-phisticated investors, mainly relates to *relative optimism*. It is interesting that the study finds that observed patterns of bias do not apply to bond managers. Basically, it is equity managers who invest disproportionately close to home; they do so because they are unduly optimistic about market prospects in their own geographic areas. This excerpt highlights Lütje and Menkhoff's findings as they relate to relative return optimism.

> Regarding "relative optimism," the ten-year stock return expectations for the major markets in the world were inquired about. [Our findings] show that the preference for home assets is positively related to a relatively better expectation for the German market. This relative optimism is statistically highly significant in comparison with the rest of Europe and the USA. Regarding subgroups within the market, the finding is particularly strong for equity managers, but does not hold for bond managers. The response of bond managers does not change either if we relate their degree of home bias to the expected bond market return.[5]

The hypothesis of relative optimism was originally advanced in the work "Why Did the Nikkei Crash?" by Robert Shiller, Fumiko Kon-Ya, and Yoshiro Tsutsui.[6] The idea put forth in this work is that local investors view the fundamental economic prospect in their home country more optimistically than would other investors viewing the same country from a *foreign* perspective. This does not imply that local investors give their home country an absolute advantage—even relative advantage justifies a portfolio allocation that overweights the home market. What Shiller, Kon-Ya, and Tsutsui measured in the United States and Japan for the first time has been extended by other researchers and is now well-known among fund managers. Thus, "relative optimism" can now be regarded as a stylized fact helping to understand home bias.

A lesson to take away from these studies is that relative optimism—the expectation that nearby investments will perform better than foreign investments—emerges in this analysis as a huge driver of home bias and therefore explains why some investors are averse to investing abroad. Given the diversification benefits of investing in foreign countries, wherever that might be globally, practitioners should endeavor to educate their clients as to these benefits and discount undue optimism about their home geographic area vis-à-vis investing opportunities abroad.

DIAGNOSTIC TESTING

These questions are designed to detect signs of cognitive bias stemming from excess optimism.

Optimism Bias Test

Question 1: Relative to other drivers on the road, how good a driver are you?
   a. Below average.
   b. Average.
   c. Above average.

Question 2: How optimistic are you about the investing opportunities close to home versus those overseas?
   a. I am much more optimistic about investment opportunities close to home.
   b. I am optimistic about investment opportunities in foreign locations.

Question 3: Relative to other investors, how good an investor are you?
   a. Below average.
   b. Average.
   c. Above average.

Question 4: Look at the five rates of return, and choose the one that you believe you have earned in the past five years.

Rates of Return

   1. Below 0 percent.
   2. Between 0 percent and 3.9 percent.
   3. Between 4 percent and 7.9 percent.
   4. Between 8 percent and 10 percent.
   5. Over 10 percent.

   If you picked numbers 2, 3, or 4, answer this question: How confident are you that you earned this as a "real" return (after taxes, fees, etc.)?

a. I am optimistic that I earned a good "real return."

b. I am not optimistic that I earned a good "real return."

Test Results Analysis

Questions 1 and 3: An answer of "b" or "c" tends to indicate susceptibility to optimism bias.

Questions 2 and 4: An answer of "a" tends to indicate susceptibility to
optimism bias.

ADVICE

Fundamentally, there are four main pieces of advice from which investors
exhibiting optimism bias might generally benefit.

1. *"Live below your means, and save regularly."* This piece of advice is
   essential. Saving and investing are the keys to attaining long-term financial goals. Succumbing too frequently to optimism bias usually
   deteriorates savings, so people attempting to combat this bias should
   try to save responsibly and to invest wisely at every opportunity.
2. *"Asset allocation is the key to a successful portfolio."* Optimism bias
   can cause investors to excessively favor certain asset classes, while
   neglecting others. Advisors should encourage clients to build balanced asset allocations and to stick with them!
3. *"Compounding contributes significantly to long-term financial success."* Optimism bias can obscure the benefits of disciplined investing. Encourage clients to let their money accumulate, compounding
   year after year. Consider the dieting and exercise analogies discussed
   earlier: Sure, adhering to such a regime can be difficult, but the results are well worth it.
4. *"Encourage the use of a financial advisor."* It goes without saying
   that nothing can replace the benefit of objective advice. Using the
   services of a quality financial advisor can partially compensate for
   the discipline that individual investors sometimes lack. By utilizing
   an advisory service, clients can reap the benefits of regular, rational
   investing behavior.

CHAPTER 16

Mental Accounting Bias

It has been my experience that competency in mathematics, both in numerical manipulations and in understanding its conceptual foundations, enhances a person's ability to handle the more ambiguous and qualitative relationships that dominate our day-to-day financial decision making.

—Alan Greenspan

BIAS DESCRIPTION

Bias Name: Mental Accounting
Bias Type: Cognitive

General Description. First coined by University of Chicago professor Richard Thaler, *mental accounting* describes people's tendency to code, categorize, and evaluate economic outcomes by grouping their assets into any number of nonfungible (noninterchangeable) mental accounts.[1] A completely rational person would never succumb to this sort of psychological process because mental accounting causes subjects to take the irrational step of treating various sums of money differently based on where these sums are mentally categorized, for example, the way that a certain sum has been obtained (work, inheritance, gambling, bonus, etc.) or the nature of the money's intended use (leisure, necessities, etc.).

The concept of *framing* is important in mental accounting analysis. In framing, people alter their perspectives on money and investments

171

according to the surrounding circumstances that they face. Thaler[2] performed an experiment in which he offered one group of people $30 and an accompanying choice: either pocket the money, no strings attached, or gamble on a coin toss, wherein a win would add $9 and a loss would subtract $9 from the initial $30 endowment. Seventy percent of the people offered this choice elected to gamble, because they considered the $30 to be "found" money—a little fortuitous windfall, not the sum of pennies meticulously saved and not the wages of hours spent slaving at some arduous task. So, why not have a little fun with this money? After all, what did these subjects really stand to lose?

A second group of people confronted a slightly different choice. Outright, they were asked: Would you rather gamble on a coin toss, in which you will receive $39 for a win and $21 for a loss? Or, would you rather simply pocket $30 and forgo the coin toss? The key distinction is that these people were not awarded $30, seemingly out of the blue, in the initial phase, as was the first group. Rather, at the outset of the exercise, the options were presented in terms of their ultimate payoffs. As you might expect, the second group reacted differently from the first. Only 34 percent of them chose to gamble, even though the economic prospects they faced were identical to those offered to group one. Sometimes people create mental accounts in order to justify actions that seem enticing but that are, in fact, unwise. Other times, people derive benefits from mental accounting; for example, earmarking money for retirement may prevent some households from spending that money prematurely. Such concepts will be explored at greater length later in this chapter.

Technical Description.   Mental accounting refers to the coding, categorization, and evaluation of financial decisions. There are numerous interpretations of mental accounting, two of which will be reviewed here.

The first interpretation stems from Shefrin and Thaler's behavioral life-cycle theory, reviewed in the previous chapter, and submits that people mentally allocate wealth over three classifications: (1) current income, (2) current assets, and (3) future income. The propensity to consume is greatest from the current income account, while sums designated as future income are treated more conservatively.

Another interpretation of mental accounting describes how distinct financial decisions may be evaluated *jointly* (i.e., as though they pertain to the same mental account) or *separately*. For example, Kahneman and Tversky[3] conducted a study in which a majority of subjects declined to pay for a new theater ticket, which they were told would replace an identically priced ticket previously bought and lost. However, when the premise was altered and the subjects were told to imagine that they had not mislaid a previous ticket but, rather, an equivalent sum of cash—and so were contemplating the ticket purchase itself for the first time—a majority *did* decide to pay. Kahneman and Tversky concluded that subjects tended to evaluate the loss of a ticket and the purchase price of a new ticket in the same mental account; losing a ticket and shelling out for a new one would represent two losses incurred successively, debited from the same cluster of assets. The loss of actual cash, however, and the purchase of a ticket were debits evaluated separately. Therefore, the same aggregate loss felt less drastic when disbursed over two different accounts.

PRACTICAL APPLICATION

Marketing professors Drazen Prelec and Duncan Simester of Massachusetts Institute of Technology (MIT) brought mental accounting to life through an ingenious experiment.[4] Prelec and Simester organized a sealed-bid auction for tickets to a Boston Celtics game during the team's victorious Larry Bird era. Half the participants in the auction were told that whoever won the bidding would need to pay for the tickets in cash within 24 hours. The other half were informed that the winning bidder would pay by credit card. Prelec and Simester then compared the average bids put forth within each group. As predicted, bidders who thought that they were relying on their credit cards wagered, on average, nearly twice the average cash bid.

This experiment illustrated that people put money in separate "accounts" when presented with a financial decision. In this case, auction participants value cash more highly than credit card remittances, even though both forms of payment draw, ultimately, from the participant's own money. People may allocate money to a "cash" (expenditures only paid in cash) account, while simultaneously placing additional funds in a "credit card" (expenditures only paid by credit card) account. Viewed in light of the life-cycle theory mentioned in the previous section, the cash might be more likely to represent a "current asset," and the credit card might represent "future income," which are two separate accounts. It probably goes without saying that this behavior touches on another bias previously reviewed: self-control.

Implications for Investors. Mental accounting is a deep-seated bias with many manifestations, and it can cause a variety of problems for investors. The most basic of these problems is the placement of investment assets into discrete "buckets" according to asset type, without regard for potential correlations connecting investments across categories. Tversky and Kahneman[5] contended that the difficulty individuals have in addressing interactions between investments leads investors to construct portfolios in a layered, pyramid format. Each tier addresses a particular investment goal independently of any additional investment goals. For example, when the objective is to preserve wealth, investors tend to target low-risk investments, like cash and money market funds. For income, they rely mostly on bonds and dividend-paying stocks. For a chance at a more drastic reward, investors turn to riskier instruments, like emerging market stocks and initial public offerings (IPOs). Combining different assets whose performances do *not* correlate with one another is an important consideration for risk reduction, but it is often neglected in this "pyramid" approach. As a result, investment positions held without regard to correlations might offset one another in a portfolio context, creating suboptimal inefficiencies. People quite often fail to evaluate a potential investment based on its contribution to overall portfolio return and aggregate portfolio risk; rather, they look only at the recent performance of the relevant asset layer. This common, detrimental oversight stems from mental accounting.

Box 16.1 reviews five investment mistakes that mental accounting can cause. Please note that this list is not exhaustive, as mental accounting bias

---

1. Mental accounting bias can cause people to imagine that their investments occupy separate "buckets," or accounts. These categories might include, for example, college fund or money for retirement. Envisioning distinct accounts to correspond with financial goals, however, can cause investors to neglect positions that offset or correlate across accounts. This can lead to suboptimal aggregate portfolio performance.
2. Mental accounting bias can cause investors to irrationally distinguish between returns derived from income and those derived from capital appreciation. Many people feel the need to preserve capital (i.e., principal) sums and prefer to spend interest. As a result, some investors chase income streams and can unwittingly

erode principal in the process. Consider, for example, a high-income bond fund or a preferred stock that pays a high dividend yet, at times, can suffer a loss of principal due to interest rate fluctuations. Mental accounting can make instruments like these appealing, but they may not benefit the investor in the long run.

3. Mental accounting bias can cause investors to allocate assets differently when employer stock is involved. Studies have shown that participants in company retirement plans that offer no company stock as an option tend to invest in a balanced way between equities and fixed-income instruments. However, when employer stock is an option, employees usually allocate a portion of contributions to company stock, with the remainder disbursed evenly over equity and fixed-income investments. Total equity allocation, then, could be too high when company stock was offered, causing these investors' portfolios to potentially be underdiversified. This can be a suboptimal condition because these investors do not fully comprehend the risk that exists in their portfolio.

4. In the same vein as anchoring bias, mental accounting bias can cause investors to succumb to the "house money" effect, wherein risk-taking behavior escalates as wealth grows. Investors exhibiting this rationale behave irrationally because they fail to treat all money as fungible. Biased financial decision making can, of course, endanger a portfolio. (In the Research Review of this chapter, we will review some excellent research on the house money effect.)

5. Mental accounting bias can cause investors to hesitate to sell investments that once generated significant gains but, over time, have fallen in price. During the bull market of the 1990s, investors became accustomed to healthy, unrealized gains. When most investors had their net worth deflated by the market correction, they hesitated to sell their positions at the then-smaller profit margin. Many today still regret not reaping gains when they could; a number of investments to which people clung following the 1990s boom have become nearly worthless.

BOX 16.1 Mental Accounting Bias: Behaviors That Can Cause Investment Mistakes is a vast, varied topic in application to private clients. Advice on each of the five potential pitfalls will follow in subsequent portions of this chapter.

RESEARCH REVIEW

In their working paper entitled "An Experimental Examination of the House Money Effect in a Multi-Period Setting," Lucy F. Ackert, Narat Charupat, Bryan K. Church, and Richard Deaves cited evidence attesting to the influence exerted by prior monetary gains and losses over present-day risk-taking behavior. Their analysis confirmed that when endowed with "house money," people become more inclined to take risks. It is, incidentally, the first study to successfully employ an experimental methodology in corroborating the existence of "house money effect" in a dynamic, financial setting. The paper compared market outcomes across sessions that begin with participants benefiting from cash endowments at different levels (i.e., "low" versus "high" endowments). The study demonstrated that the traders' bids, their price predictions, and the market prices ultimately negotiated are all influenced by the level of the endowment that traders receive prior to trading. The paper carried significant implications for practitioners and investors: Namely, it implied that investors take more risks as wealth increases. This phenomenon, in turn, can endanger investors' portfolios. A rational investor should treat every dollar as "fungible"—of interchangeable value. However, if the value of each dollar decreases as the abundance of endowed dollars grows, then this assumption is clearly upset, and neoclassical theory no longer applies. Given the length and complexity of the paper, only one of the two main hypotheses will be reviewed. This hypothesis is that *market prices become higher when traders' endowments are larger.*

> The purpose of the experiment is to test for a house money effect in a dynamic market setting. According to the house money effect, people are more willing to take risk after prior gains. To examine the impact of prior gains, we compare behavior across our low endowment (1–5) and high endowment (6–9) sessions. [Table 16.1] summarizes the experimental design. Across the sessions, we vary the initial endowment: low ($60) and high ($75).

TABLE 16.1 Experimental Design

Treatment	Session	Number of Traders	Number of Markets	Number of Periods	Endowment of Cash
Low endowment	1	8	6	3	$60
	2	8	6	3	$60
	3	8	6	3	$60
	4	8	6	3	$60
	5	8	6	3	$60
High endowment	6	8	8	3	$75
	7	8	8	3	$75
	8	8	8	3	$75
	9	8	8	3	$75

Source: Ackert, Charupat, Church, and Deaves (2003)

Each session includes eight participants who bid to acquire a stock whose life is limited to a single period. Sessions include six or eight markets with three trading periods.

With larger monetary endowments, or more house money, market valuations will reflect greater risk taking. Traders with larger endowments will be more willing to gamble to acquire the stock, which translates into a higher market price for the stock. On this basis market prices are expected to differ across the two treatments. Hypothesis 1: The market price is higher when traders' endowments are larger. In testing hypothesis 1 we compare market prices across the low and high endowment treatments. Subsequent behavior is examined by looking at price changes in response to changes in market wealth. As a subset of the traders acquires the stock and the stock pays a positive dividend with a probability of 50 percent, incorporating the prior evolution of the market is important. Barberis, Huang, and Santos (2001)[6] assert that people are less risk averse as their wealth rises because prior gains cushion subsequent losses.

At the beginning of each session, participants receive a set of instructions and follow along as an experimenter reads aloud. Sessions 1–5 (6–9) consist of six (eight) three-period markets. Participants are given tickets on which to record their bids for the stock. Prior to the beginning of each market period, participants are also asked to predict the purchase price of the stock for the upcoming period. Participants record their predictions on the confidential bid tickets. Participants are instructed that the roll of a die determines the dividend paid to asset holders at period end. If the roll of the die results in 1, 2, or 3, the dividend is $0, otherwise the dividend is $40, so that each dividend is equally likely. Participants are invited to examine the die at any time. The bidding procedure works as follows. All eight participants submit sealed bids for the stock by recording the amount of money they are willing to pay for one share of stock. The four shares are allocated to the four highest bidders at the fifth highest bid. After the shares are allocated, one of the traders is specifically asked to observe the experimenter toss the die to ensure confidence that the dividend payment is randomly determined.

At the conclusion of the first period, the second period commences and four shares of an identical single-period stock are auctioned off in the exact same fashion. A trader's cash balance is carried forward across periods within a market. As before, subsequent to allocation with a Vickrey auction, a die roll determines payout. A third period follows with identical procedures. The advantage of this approach is that it is possible to generate a reasonable number of identical dividend evolutions. Six or eight markets are conducted in a similar manner bringing the session to a close. The traders' endowments are reinitialized at the beginning of each market. Subjects are told at the outset that they will be paid based on the results of only one of the markets, and this market is chosen by a die roll (or, in the case of sessions 6–9, by a card draw). Since ex ante the students have no way of knowing the identity of the payout market it is in their interest to treat all markets equally seriously. Participants' experimental earnings include their cash endowment, less payments to acquire stock, plus dividends earned on stock held in the one randomly selected market. In addition, the participant with the lowest absolute prediction error in the randomly selected market receives a bonus of $20. At the beginning of each period, participants are informed that the participant with the lowest sum of the three absolute prediction errors in the selected market will receive the bonus. At the conclusion of each session, participants compute the amount of cash they will receive and complete a post-experimental questionnaire. The purpose of the questionnaire is to collect general information about the participants and how they view the experiment. The average compensation across sessions 1–5 (6–9) is $66.75 ($79.66). Participants' responses on a post-experiment questionnaire indicate that they found the experiment interesting and the monetary incentives motivating.

[Table 16.2] reports information concerning the prices, bids, and price predictions for each period in the low and high endowment treatments. Along with the number of observations (N), the table reports the mean, minimum, and maximum observed value. The final columns report the difference in means across the treatments and the p-value for a test of difference in means. The table reports the test results for hypothesis 1. The average initial price in the low endowment sessions is $17.10, while the average in the high endowment sessions is $20.37. Our results are consistent with a house money effect in a financial setting. Market prices are higher when traders have more found money. Further, the statistics reported in [Table 16.2] indicate that, compared to the low endowment sessions, average prices in the high endowment sessions are also significantly higher in periods 2 and 3 at $p < 0.05$. Thus, the house money effect persists over time.[7]

This excerpt is revealing because it describes, as experimentally observed, one of the irrational financial behaviors that can occur as a result of mental accounting. When people fail to consistently value their wealth—when, for example, their demonstrated risk aversion varies according to a criterion as arbitrary as endowment size—they distinguish themselves sharply from Homo economicus. Moreover, they sometimes place their own financial security at risk.

DIAGNOSTIC TESTING

These questions are designed to detect signs of cognitive bias stemming from mental accounting. To complete the test, select the answer choice that best characterizes your response to each item.

TABLE 16.2 Prices, Bids, and Predictions across Treatments

Period	Variable	Low Endowment Sessions				High Endowment Sessions				Difference in Mean	p-value
		N	Mean	Min	Max	N	Mean	Min	Max		
1	Price	30	17.10	5.01	26.00	32	20.37	9.00	30.00	3.27	0.0336
	Bid	240	19.70	0	60.00	256	24.95	0	75.00	5.25	0.0001
	Prediction	240	17.69	1.00	60.00	256	20.17	2.00	70.00	2.48	<0.0001
2	Price	30	17.33	6.50	26.00	32	20.49	9.00	30.00	3.17	0.0334
	Bid	240	19.97	0	87.25	256	22.10	0.01	92.00	2.13	0.0795
	Prediction	240	17.53	4.75	50.00	256	20.61	8.00	35.00	3.07	<0.0001
3	Price	30	15.94	7.00	25.00	32	19.13	8.00	34.50	3.20	0.0296
	Bid	240	19.13	0	99.01	256	22.13	0	100.00	3.00	0.0213
	Prediction	240	16.97	5.50	28.00	256	20.56	8.50	34.50	3.59	<0.0001

Source: Ackert, Charupat, Church, and Deaves (2003)

Mental Accounting Bias Test

Question 1—Part A: Suppose that you are at a warehouse store, where you intend to purchase a flat screen television. The model you've selected is priced at $750, and you are about to pay. However, at the last minute, you notice a discarded advertising flier featuring the same television—at a price of $720. You retrieve the ad, examine it more closely, and discover that the offer is still valid. To receive the discount, you'll need to drive to a competing electronics outlet about 10 minutes away. Will you get into your car and travel to the other store to take advantage of the lower price?
a. Yes.
b. No.

Question 1—Part B: Now suppose that you are in the same warehouse store, this time to buy a mahogany table. The table that you want costs $4,000, and you are willing to pay. While you are waiting, you strike up a conversation with another store patron, who reveals that she's seen the same table available for $3,970 at a competing local furniture store about 10 minutes away. Will you get into your car and drive to the other store to obtain the lower price?
a. Yes.
b. No.

Question 2—Part A: Suppose that you have purchased a ticket to a concert by your favorite music artist. You arrive at the venue excited, but quickly panic as you realize that you have misplaced your ticket! You paid $100 for the ticket initially and discover that some similar seats are still available at the same price. What is the probability that you will purchase another $100 ticket in order to see the show?
a. 100 percent.
b. 50 percent.
c. 0 percent.

Question 2—Part B: Suppose that you have not purchased any concert tickets in advance but planned to buy one for $100 at the door. When you arrive at the box office to buy your ticket, you panic because you realize you've lost $100 on the subway en route to the show. There is an ATM close by, so you can still get cash and purchase a ticket. What is the probability that you will make a cash withdrawal and then purchase a ticket for $100 to see the show?

a. 100 percent.

b. 50 percent.

c. 0 percent.

Question 3—Part A: Suppose that you've taken half a day off work to shop for a new, ride-on lawn mower. You have a big yard, and trimming it with your current, push-propelled mower simply takes too long. You have been eyeing the Model A300, which offers all the features you require at a cost of $2,000. As luck would have it, you won $500 the previous evening playing bingo at your local Rotary Club. When you arrive at the lawn mower shop, you notice that they also stock Model A305, which has some fancy, desirable new options. This premium model costs $2,250. Considering the previous night's winnings, what is the probability that you will indulge yourself by purchasing the A305?

a. 100 percent.

b. 50 percent.

c. 0 percent.

Question 3—Part B: Suppose that your budget and your needs regarding the lawn mower are exactly as described in Question 3A and that again you've taken half a day off work to go buy the simpler-but-sufficient A300. However, imagine that while you've not been especially lucky at bingo, you do discover a $500 check in your jacket pocket. You recall that the money was a gift from your mother last year, something to be "put away for a rainy day." You apparently forgot that you put it in your jacket and have just come up on it. When you arrive at the lawn mower shop, you again notice the pricier A305 for $2,250, with its coveted, innovative mowing features. Considering the check you just found, what is the probability that you will go ahead purchase the A305?

a. 100 percent.

b. 50 percent.

c. 0 percent.

Test Results Analysis

Question 1—Parts A and B: Most people would probably drive an extra 10 minutes to save $30 on the television but wouldn't go to the same trouble to save the same amount of money on the table. While both scenarios net a savings of $30, a typical mental accounting scheme doesn't envision things this way. So people who are more likely to go out of their way to receive a discount in Part A than in Part B are likely susceptible to mental accounting bias.

Question 2—Parts A and B: If the respondent is like most people, he or she answered "no" to the first question and "yes" to the second, even though both scenarios present the same prospect: an initial loss of $100, an additional $100 outlay for the ticket. Mental accounting causes people to perceive in the first scenario an aggregate cost of $200 for the show—two tickets, each costing $100. Conversely, for most people the loss of $100 cash and the additional $100 ticket price are somehow separate in the second scenario. Mentally, these sums are debited from two independent categories or accounts, meaning that no single, larger loss of $200 ever registers. In both cases, of course, the concert costs $200. If the respondent indicated a greater willingness to pay for a ticket in Part B than in Part A, then mental accounting bias is likely present.

Question 3—Parts A and B: Most people would answer "yes" in Part A and "no" in Part B. They would be willing to allocate the bingo winnings but not the check from Mom toward the purchase of the premium lawn mower. This is because most people engage in mental accounting. In this instance, mental accounting values dollars obtained from different sources differently. However, money is indeed fungible. Responses demonstrate that this all-too-typical inconsistency between Parts A and B probably indicates mental accounting bias.

ADVICE

The following advice has been incremented to correspond to each of the five investment errors discussed in Box 16.1. It is important to note that mental accounting is very common and that nearly everyone is susceptible to this bias in some way or another. Remember, moreover, that mental accounting can sometimes serve as a beneficial rather than as a harmful cognitive mechanism for investors. This section concludes with a special "bonus" discussion of the helpful aspects of mental accounting.

Correlations between Investment "Buckets."   The most effective method to prevent investors from viewing their money in terms of discrete investment buckets is demonstrating how investments identified with separate mental accounts can actually correlate with one another, impacting portfolio performance. A straightforward discussion of the harms of excessive correlation and the benefits of sufficient diversification ought to effectively refute the bucket rationale. Since mental accounting is a cognitive bias, education can often defeat it.

Total Returns as Priority.   The best way to prevent mental accounting from weakening total returns is to remind your client that total returns are, after all, the number-one priority of any allocation. A renewed focus on global portfolio performance—not simply piecemeal aspects, such as principal or income—is often achievable. As clients become more conscious of total returns, they will likely recognize the pitfalls of excessive mental accounting, and the problem will remedy itself.

Company Stock and Diversification.   Persuading clients to diversify away from company stock is indeed a theme that emerges again and again in contending with various behavioral biases. This problem arises once more with mental accounting. As in previous instances involving portfolios overly dominated by company stock, the client must be educated as to the benefits of a balanced, diversified portfolio. Excessive concentration in any stock is not good, but a variety of behavioral biases can crop up and cause investors to feel irrationally comfortable with their own companies' stocks.

House Money Effect.   As the research review demonstrates, the house money effect is a manifestation of mental accounting that can cause people to take on more risk as their wealth increases. This specific bias is perhaps the most pernicious of any reviewed in this chapter; however, education can help clients overcome it. Gentle but straightforward reminders regarding the risk of a chosen investment or the fungibility of money in general can diminish the house money effect. The house money effect causes investors to devalue a dollar as aggregate dollars accumulate. Recall that this rationale causes investors to devalue individual dollars. They sense that they are now playing with the "house's" money, not their own. Remember, dollars won or found seem, for many people, irrationally expendable. When clients appear subject to the house money effect, it is crucial to stress the underlying truth that *a dollar equals a dollar*—no matter which mental account each dollar occupies.

Clinging to Formerly Gainful Investments.   Mental accounting bias prevailed during the collapse of the tech boom in 2000 and 2001. Any investor who recalls those years should be somewhat inoculated against this behavior. Unfortunately, however, many people have short memories. If a company's prospects today do not look good and if it is still possible to divest from that company and capture a gain, then the client should evacuate the position immediately. The investment may have generated great profits in the past, but most clients should rationally grasp that the present-day outlook matters most. A convenient reminder is: "No one ever got hurt taking a profit."

Bonus Section: The Potential Benefits of Mental Accounting

It is important for practitioners to recognize that mental accounting can sometimes generate benefits. If clients regard college funds or retirement funds, for example, as sacrosanct, then they may be less inclined to disturb sound long-term investment plans by interfering with money stashed away. Of course, an instinct to preserve certain assets does not guarantee that those assets will be managed wisely. In the instance of a college fund, practitioners should recommend multiple shifts toward more conservative investments as the child's teen years approach. This will likely result in less resistance to change when reallocating funds.

Some financial advisors adhere to "goals-based planning," which leverages mental accounting for the benefit of the client. These practitioners argue that clients should set multiple, distinct investment goals, a practice that contrasts with many interpretations of traditional investment theory. Conventional approaches suggest that an allocation should be oriented toward total portfolio gains. Risk, in this view, is likewise managed at the global portfolio level, using an estimate of an investor's overall risk tolerance. Daniel Nevins argued that it is difficult to reconcile this single portfolio framework with the existence of separate mental accounts linked to specific investment goals.[8] An alternative to this traditional approach is to allow more than one strategy, as discussed also by

Jean Brunel: "Each strategy is linked to a goal and managed according to the risk measures and risk tolerance that are most appropriate for that goal. This approach, which we call goals-based investing, is compatible with mental accounting. Another advantage is that it manages the risk of not achieving goals rather than relying on traditional risk measures."[9]

So, there are observable benefits of mental accounting. Practitioners, moreover, can often leverage this bias to the benefit of their clients.

CHAPTER 17

Confirmation Bias

It is the peculiar and perpetual error of the human understanding to be more moved and excited by affirmatives than by negatives.

—Francis Bacon

BIAS DESCRIPTION

Bias Name: Confirmation Bias
Bias Type: Cognitive

General Description.   *Confirmation bias* refers to a type of selective perception that emphasizes ideas that confirm our beliefs, while devaluing whatever contradicts our beliefs. For example, you may believe that more red automobiles drive by your house during the summer than during any other time of the year; however, this belief may be due to confirmation bias, which causes you to simply *notice* more red cars during the summer, while overlooking them during other months. This tendency, over time, unjustifiably strengthens your belief regarding the summertime concentration of red cars. To describe this phenomenon another way, we might say that confirmation bias refers to our all-too-natural ability to convince ourselves of whatever it is that we want to believe. We attach undue emphasis to events that corroborate the outcomes we desire and downplay whatever contrary evidence arises.

Technical Description. Confirmation bias can be thought of as a form of selection bias in collecting evidence for supporting certain beliefs, whereby decision makers observe, overvalue, or actively seek out information that confirms their claims, while simultaneously ignoring or devaluing evidence that might discount their claims. A classic demonstration of confirmation bias, of which there are many versions, is one in which subjects are shown four cards, each with a number on one side and a letter on the other. They are then told the following rule: "If the card has a vowel on one side, then it *must* have an even number on the other side." The cards are then laid out as depicted in Figure 17.1. Subjects are then asked, "Which two cards would you turn over to test the rule?"

When this experiment is run, most participants do not choose the correct cards (the card reading "A" and the card reading "9"). Instead, the most frequent responses are "A" and "2." This pairing demonstrates a common logical fallacy: People choose "2" because the discovery of an accompanying vowel could indeed uphold the hypothesis. However, exposing the opposite side of the "2" card can't possibly invalidate the hypothesized condition, so this can't be the correct response. People more readily identify "2" rather than "9" because confirmation bias makes them *want* to validate the hypothesis—not refute it as directed.

Another lesson here is that beliefs don't need to be logically entrenched in order to kindle confirmation bias. The hypothesis as stated becomes an immediate if subtle aspect of the participant's choice of cards. Even though subjects have no reason to accept the hypothesis, they become loyal enough to its validity that they are unable to recognize the correct answer choice. In fact, when beliefs *are* firmly established in evidence, the effects of confirmation bias become less overt. This is due to a tendency to give more attention and weight to data that fit with beliefs with stronger foundations.

FIGURE 17.1 Classic Confirmation Bias Experiment

Numerous studies have demonstrated that people excessively value confirmatory information, that is, positive or supportive data. The "most likely reason for the excessive influence of confirmatory information is that it is easier to deal with cognitively"[1] than contradictory information is; that is, most people find it easier to discern how a piece of data might support rather than challenge a given position. Researchers are sometimes guilty of confirmation bias, as they occasionally design experiments or frame data in ways likely to confirm their hypotheses. To compound the problem, some scholars also avoid dealing with data that would contradict their hypotheses.

PRACTICAL APPLICATION

To demonstrate confirmation bias, we discuss employees' penchant for overconcentrating in company stock. Most practitioners have encountered clients who rationalize their disproportionate holdings by citing the promising "big things" that are developing at their companies. (Of course, numerous shareholders in Enron and WorldCom probably speculated that great growth was under way—if only these investors had had some clue as to the nature of the "big things" that would soon befall their employers!) When employees load up on company stock en masse and bullish commentary on employer stock prices dominates water cooler conversation, inauspicious details can be easily overlooked. We don't have to focus exclusively on the tech bubble of the late 1990s to find evidence of confirmation bias. A strong cautionary tale emerged earlier that decade at a well-established tech firm: IBM.

In the early 1990s, many IBM employees were convinced that their company's OS/2 operating system would achieve industry standard status. They frequently ignored unfavorable signs, including evidence of competition from Microsoft Windows. These employees loaded up on IBM stock, anticipating that OS/2's performance would drive the company forward. In 1991, IBM stock reached a split-adjusted peak of $35 per share. Over the course of the next two years, however, IBM slid to a low of $10. It would not reach $35 again until the end of 1996. During this five-year slump, IBM employees rallied around seemingly positive developments that "confirmed" that IBM was making a comeback. Some even delayed retirement. Unfortunately, in an effort to engineer a turnaround, IBM laid off a number of its employees. In the end, OS/2 caused many people to become less wealthy. For some, the failed operating system even led to unemployment. This is a classic case of confirmation bias in action.

Experienced practitioners have seen similar scenarios play out repeatedly. Clients ignore downside risks of, for example, employer stock and focus only on the upside potential. Why? In this case, confirmation bias played a significant role in the behavior of the IBM employees. It led them to accept information that supported their rosy predictions regarding IBM while discounting evidence of increased competition from Microsoft. Consequently, these employees lost money as IBM's stock price fell. Only those few who were able to hang on, over the course of five years of uncertainty—history, remember, shows us that most investors "panic" in such a situation—had the opportunity to profit in the end.

Implications for Investors.   Anyone who has played a hand or two of poker knows well the downside of confirmation bias. Suppose you are entrenched in a game, and you have three kings. Your opponent raises the pot, and you are only happy to raise him back. Your cards are telling you "You can't lose." You are oblivious to the fact that someone else at the table might have a better hand than you do. Oops, someone had a full house, and you lose.

In the context of the poker analogy, what's important to note is that, by "listening" only to information that confirms your beliefs, you ignore the other players' cards. Focusing on the payoff of the present hand might eventually earn a profit; however, you don't analyze the implications of a loss—even if some indication has cropped up during the game that another player might be harboring aces. While the poker metaphor isn't flawless, it gets the point across: People believe what they want to believe and ignore evidence to the contrary. This is the essence of confirmation bias.

In finance, the effects of confirmation bias can be observed almost daily. Investors often fail to acknowledge anything negative about investments they've just made, even when substantial evidence begins to argue against these investments. A classic example took place on the Internet message boards during the technology stock boom of the late 1990s. Many of these chat roomers would harass anyone who voiced a negative opinion of the company they invested in. Rather than try to glean some useful insight into their company through other investors, they only sought confirmations of their own beliefs.

Box 17.1 summarizes investment mistakes that can be caused by confirmation bias.

RESEARCH REVIEW

Professor Meir Statman and investment professional Ken Fisher provided an excellent example of confirmation bias in action in their paper

---

1. Confirmation bias can cause investors to seek out only information that confirms their beliefs about an investment that they have made and to not seek out information that may contradict their beliefs. This behavior can leave investors in the dark regarding, for example, the imminent decline of a stock.
2. When investors believe strongly in predetermined "screens," such as stocks breaking through a 52-week price high, confirmation bias is usually at work. These investors only use information that confirms their beliefs. They may blind themselves to information that demonstrates that a stock breaking through its 52-week high may not make a good investment.
3. Confirmation bias can cause employees to overconcentrate in company stock. As IBM and other examples demonstrate, intraoffice buzz about a company's prospects does not justify indiscriminate reliance by employees on company stock. People naturally tend to unduly emphasize evidence suggesting that the companies they work for will do well.
4. Confirmation bias can cause investors to continue to hold underdiversified portfolios. Many practitioners have seen clients become infatuated with certain stocks—not always the stocks of employer corporations. Over the course of years, such a client might accrue a large position that ultimately produces a lopsided portfolio. These clients do not want to hear anything negative about favored investments but rather seek, single-mindedly, confirmation that the position will pay off.

BOX 17.1   Confirmation Bias: Behaviors That Can Cause Investment Mistakes

"Cognitive Biases in Market Forecasts."[2] Here, Statman and Fisher test the commonly held belief that price/earnings (P/E) ratios can forecast stock returns. It seems logical to most investors that when P/Es surpass historical averages, shareholders should sell. Likewise, conventional wisdom dictates that stocks whose P/Es fall below historical averages make good buys. Statman and Fisher examined the validity of these principles.

> We can overcome the confirmation bias by examining all data, confirming as well as disconfirming. Consider, in particular, an examination of the hypothesis that low dividend yields forecast low returns while high dividend yields forecast high returns. Define dividend yields as high if they exceed their median over the 128 years from 1872 through 1999 and as low if they fall below it. The median dividend yield for the period was 4.43 percent. Define one-year returns as high and low in a similar fashion. The median return was 10.50 percent. [Table 17.1] presents a schematic view of the frequency of observations in the four cells of a matrix. The first cell includes observations where dividend yields were low and subsequent returns were low. These are positive hits. The fourth cell has observations where dividend yields were high and subsequent returns were also high. These are negative hits. Positive hits and negative hits are confirming evidence, observations consistent with the hypothesis that low dividend yields forecast low returns and high dividend yields forecast high returns. The other two cells have disconfirming evidence. That is, the second cell includes false positive observations where dividend yields were low but subsequent returns were high, and the third cell is the false negatives, observations

TABLE 17.1   Relationship between Dividend Yields and Future Returns

	Below-Median Return	Above-Median Return
Below-median dividend yield	Positive hit	False positive
Above-median dividend yield	False negative	Negative hit

where dividend yields were high but subsequent returns were low. False positives and false negatives are discomfirming evidence. Correct analysis of the hypothesis requires examination of all four cells. Those who examine only the positive and negative hits fall prey to the confirmation bias. The confirmation bias is common. Consider, for example, Prechter's discussion of low dividend yield as a forecaster of low returns, "August 1987 saw a historically high valuation of dividends, beating out even that of 1929. The result was a 1,000 point crash."[3] Prechter's observation is a positive hit, an observation consistent with the hypothesis that low dividend yields (i.e., "high valuation of dividends") forecast low returns. But we need an account of false positives and false negatives as well. Consider dividend yields as forecasters of one-year returns. It turns out, as presented in [Table 17.2], that there are 33 positive hits in the first cell and 33 negative hits in the fourth.

These are consistent with the hypothesis that low dividend yields forecast low returns, while high dividend yields forecast high returns. But the evidence against the hypothesis is almost as strong as the evidence for it; there are 31 false positives in the second cell and 31 false negatives in the third. The deviations of actual observations from those expected by chance alone are too small to be statistically significant. We can conclude only that dividend yields enable no statistically significant forecasts of returns

TABLE 17.2 Relationship between Dividend Yields at Beginning of a Year and Stock Returns over Following Year, 1872–1999

	Below-Median Return	Above-Median Return	Total
Below-median dividend yield	33	31	64
Above-median dividend yield	31	33	64
Total	64	64	128

Chi-square = 0.03.

in the following year. We also find no statistically significant relationship between dividend yields and returns in the following (nonoverlapping) two-year returns, as depicted in [Table 17.3].

The same is true for the relationship between P/E ratios and returns during the following year or during the following two (nonoverlapping) years, as depicted in [Tables 17.4, 17.5, and 17.6].

For example, while high P/E ratios were followed by low returns in 32 years, high P/E ratios were followed by high returns in an equal 32 years. Low dividend yields are followed almost equally by low returns and high returns, and high dividend yields are followed almost equally by high returns and low returns. The same is true for high and low P/E ratios. Thus, dividend yields and P/E ratios are unreliable forecasters of future returns because they provide so many bad forecasts along with the good ones.

TABLE 17.3 Relationship between Dividend Yields at Beginning of Year and Stock Returns over Following (Nonoverlapping) Two Years 1872–1999

	Below-Median Return	Above-Median Return	Total
Below-median dividend yield	17	15	32
Above-median dividend yield	15	17	32
Total	32	32	64

Chi-square = 0.06.
Critical chi-square for 5% level of significance is 3.841.
Median dividend yield over 128 years (1872–1999) is 4.43%.
Median return during a year is 10.50%.

TABLE 17.4 Relationship between P/E Ratios and Future Returns

	Below-Median Return	Above-Median Return
Above-median P/E ratios	Positive hit	False positive
Below-median P/E ratios	False negative	Negative hit

TABLE 17.5 Relationship between P/E Ratios at Beginning of a Year and Stock Returns over Following Year 1872–1999

	Below-Median Return	Above-Median Return	Total
Above-median P/E ratios	32	32	64
Below-median P/E ratios	32	32	64
Total	64	64	128

Chi-square = 0.00.

TABLE 17.6 Relationship between P/E Ratios at Beginning of Year and Stock Returns over Following (Nonoverlapping) Two Years 1872–1999

	Below-Median Return	Above-Median Return	Total
Above-median P/E ratios	19	13	32
Below-median P/E ratios	13	19	32
Total	32	32	64

Chi-square = 1.56.
Median P/E ratio over 128 years (1872–1999) is 13.6%. Median return during a year is 10.50%.
Tables 17.5 and 17.6 are reprinted with permission from Institutional Investor, Inc. They originally appeared in the Fall 2000 issue of *Journal of Portfolio Management* It is illegal to make unauthorized copies. For more information please visit www.iijournals.com. All rights reserved.

DIAGNOSTIC TESTING

These questions are designed to detect cognitive errors stemming from confirmation bias. To complete the test, select the answer choice that best characterizes your response to each item.

Confirmation Bias Test

Question 1: Suppose you have invested in a security after some careful research. Now, you come on a press release that states that the company you've invested in may have a problem with its main product line. The second paragraph, however, describes a completely new product that the company might debut later this year. What is your natural course of action?

a. I will typically take notice of the new product announcement and research that item further.

b. I will typically take notice of the problem with the company's product line and research that item further.

Question 2: Suppose you have invested in a security after some careful research. The investment appreciates in value but not for the reason you predicted (e.g., you were enticed by some buzz surrounding a new product, but resurgence by an older product line ultimately buoyed the stock). What is your natural course of action?

a. Since the company did well, I am not concerned. The shares I've selected have generated a profit. This confirms that the stock was a good investment.

b. Although I am pleased, I am concerned about the investment. I will do further research to confirm the logic behind my position.

Question 3: Suppose you decide to invest in gold as a hedge against inflation. You performed careful research to determine the relationship between gold values and inflation levels. Three months after you invest, you realize that gold prices have risen with no commensurate change in inflation. This is not what you expected. How do you react?

a. I will just "go with it." The reason that an investment performs well is not important. What's important it that I made a good investment.

b. I will do research to try and determine why gold prices and inflation aren't correlating in the manner I'd predicted. This will help me determine if I should remain invested in gold.

Test Results Analysis

Question 1: People who select answer choice "a," indicating they would more readily research the new product line than the potential complications in the old product line, are likely to be susceptible to confirmation bias. They are avoiding information that might confirm—

but, crucially, might also overrule—the previous decision to invest in the company.

Question 2. People who select "a" are more likely to exhibit confirmation bias than people who select "b." Rationalizing that only the company's recent performance is relevant, answer choice "a" implies that the respondent will avoid seeking out information that might contradict previously held beliefs regarding the quality of the (hypothetical) investment. "b" is the more economically rational choice.

Questions 3. Again, "a" is the response that signals susceptibility to confirmation bias. To "just go with it," in this instance, means adopting some arbitrary rationale just because it happens to confirm a previous conviction ("I made a good investment decision"). Answer choice "b", which entails further research, is unattractive to people suffering from confirmation bias. This is because further research might unearth information that contradicts a previous conviction ("I made a good investment decision").

ADVICE

The following advice corresponds to each of the four problem areas listed in Box 17.1.

General Confirmation Bias Behavior. The first step toward overcoming confirmation bias is to recognize that the bias exists. Then people can mindfully compensate by making sure to seek out information that could contradict—not just confirm—their investment decisions. It is important to remember that the mere existence of contradictory evidence does not necessarily mean an investment was unwise. Rather, uncovering all available data simply facilitates informed decisions. Even the most precisely calculated judgments can go awry; however, when investors make sure to consider all available contingencies and perspectives, they are less likely to make mistakes.

Selection Bias. When an investment decision is based on some preexisting criterion—such as a trend regarding stocks that break through 52-week highs—it is advisable to cross verify the decision from additional angles. Fundamental research on a company, industry, or sector, for example, can often provide another informative dimension. This will help to ensure that investment selections don't blindly adhere to preconceived principles while ignoring practical considerations.

Company Stock.   Overconcentrating in company stock is inadvisable for numerous reasons. In guarding against confirmation bias, employees should monitor any negative press regarding their own companies and conduct research on any competing firms. While it is easy to become desensitized toward bad news regarding one's own company, remember: "Where there's smoke, there's (too often) fire." Employee investors should heed the warning signs—or risk getting burned.

Overconcentration.   Company stock isn't the only investment with which people can become unduly enamored. People who demonstrate a disproportionate degree of commitment to any stock whatsoever should remember to seek out unfavorable data regarding that stock. This is especially true for investors whose portfolios concentrate discernibly in a favored investment.

CHAPTER 18

Hindsight Bias

You didn't know it all along, You just think you did.

—James Montier

BIAS DESCRIPTION

Bias Name: Hindsight Bias
Bias Type: Cognitive

General Description.   Described in simple terms, *hindsight bias* is the impulse that insists: "I knew it all along!" Once an event has elapsed, people afflicted with hindsight bias tend to perceive that the event was predictable—even if it wasn't. This behavior is precipitated by the fact that *actual* outcomes are more readily grasped by people's minds than the infinite array of outcomes that could have but didn't materialize. Therefore, people tend to overestimate the accuracy of their own predictions. This is not to say, obviously, that people cannot make accurate predictions, merely that people may believe that they made an accurate prediction in hindsight. Hindsight bias has been demonstrated in experiments involving investing—a few of which will be examined shortly—as well as in other diverse settings, ranging from politics to medicine. Unpredictable developments bother people, since it's always embarrassing to be caught off guard. Hindsight bias alleviates embarrassment under these circumstances, blunting the ugliest of surprises and populating our horizon, instead, with inevitabilities.

Technical Description.   Hindsight bias is the tendency of people, with the benefit of hindsight following an event, to falsely believe that they predicted the outcome of that event in the beginning. Hindsight bias affects future forecasting. A person subject to hindsight bias assumes that the outcome he or she ultimately observes is, in fact, the only outcome that was ever possible. Thus, he or she underestimates the uncertainty preceding the event in question and underrates the outcomes that could have materialized but did not.

Baruch Fischoff[1] described an experiment in which he asked subjects to answer general knowledge questions from almanacs and encyclopedias. Later, after revealing the correct answers, Fischoff asked his subjects to recall their original responses from memory. The results are revealing: In general, people overestimated the quality of their initial knowledge and forgot their initial errors. Hindsight bias is a serious problem for market followers. Once an event is part of market history, there is a tendency to see the sequence that led up to it, making the event appear inevitable. As Richard Posner[2] noted, outcomes exert irresistible pressure on their own interpretations. In hindsight, blunders with happy results are described as brilliant tactical moves, and unfortunate results of choices that were well-grounded in available information are described as avoidable blunders.

One detriment of hindsight bias is that it can prevent learning from mistakes. People with hindsight bias connected to another psychological bias, anchoring, find it difficult to reconstruct an unbiased state of mind—it is easier to argue for the inevitability of a reported outcome and convince oneself that it would not have turned out otherwise. In sum, hindsight bias leads people to exaggerate the quality of their foresight.

PRACTICAL APPLICATION

Many people have observed hindsight bias in the investment realm. They watch people fool themselves into thinking that they could have predicted the outcome of some financial gamble, but they achieve such crystal-clear insight only after the fact. Perhaps the most obvious example recalls the prevailing response by investors to the behavior of the U.S. stock market between 1998 and 2003. In 1998 and 1999, virtually nobody viewed the soaring market indexes as symptomatic of a short-lived "bubble" (or if they did harbor such misgivings, investors did not act on them). Above-average returns were the norm, though even a casual glance at historical business-cycle trends should have foretold that, eventually, the 1990s bull market had to recede. Still, sadly, even some of the most sophisticated investors succumbed to the fantasy: "It's different this time!" Now, in 2006, most people concede the reality of the bubble. In fact, chatting with most investors today, you'll get the impression that they were not fooled by the "irrational exuberance" that Greenspan diagnosed. Often, people insist that the collapse of late-1990s prosperity was "clearly in the cards," or they comment: "Wasn't it obvious that we were in a bubble?" Most investors who lived through the 1990s, of course, were statistically more likely to have bought into the bull market rather than to have remained as aloof as their retrospectives imply. Giving in to hindsight bias can be very destructive, because it leads investors to believe that they have better predictive powers than they actually do. Relying on these "powers" can invite poor decision making in the future.

Implications for Investors.   Perhaps the hindsight bias's biggest implication for investors is that it gives investors a false sense of security when making investment decisions. This can manifest itself in excessive risk-taking behavior, and place people's portfolios at risk. Box 18.1 reviews some common behaviors, rooted in hindsight bias that can cause investment mistakes.

RESEARCH REVIEW

This chapter's research review discusses hindsight bias in the context of fund manager selection. In their insightful paper entitled "On the Predictability of Stock Returns in Real Time," Michael Cooper of Purdue University, Roberto Gutierrez of Texas A&M University, and William Marcum of Wake Forest University argued that some money manager's track records are unduly criticized due to hindsight bias.[3]

The basic thrust of the argument is that money managers with long track records might be inordinately blamed for not outperforming a certain strategy that "worked" over a given time period. This happens when the researchers who are examining the track record of the fund manager are comparing the manager's track record to a strategy that has only recently been recognized as an accepted size or style strategy. For example, suppose a fund manager launched a fund in 1980 with the objective of

1. When an investment appreciates, hindsight-biased investors tend to rewrite their own memories to portray the positive developments as if they were predictable. Over time, this rationale can inspire excessive risk taking, because hindsight-biased investors begin to believe that they have superior predictive powers, when, in fact, they do not. The bursting of the technology bubble is an example of this bias in action.

2. Hindsight-biased investors also "rewrite history" when they fare poorly and block out recollections of prior, incorrect forecasts in order to alleviate embarrassment. This form of self-deception, in some ways similar to cognitive dissonance, prevents investors from learning from their mistakes. A clear example of this bias took place in the early 1980s, when energy stocks generated over 20 percent of Standard & Poor's (S&P) 500 returns, and lots of investors were caught up in the boom. By the 1990s, though, the energy bubble subsided, and many stockholders lost money. Most now prefer, in hindsight, to not recognize that the speculative frenzy clouded their judgments.

3. Hindsight-biased investors can unduly fault their money managers when funds perform poorly. Looking back at what has occurred in securities markets, these investors perceive every development as inevitable. How, then, could a worthwhile manager be caught by surprise? In fact, even top-quartile managers who implement their strategies correctly may not succeed in every market cycle. Managers of small-cap value funds in the late 1990s, for example, drew a lot of criticism. However, these people weren't poor managers; their style was simply out of favor at the time.

4. Conversely, hindsight bias can cause investors to unduly praise their money managers when funds perform well. The clarity of hindsight obscures the possibility that a manager's strategy might simply have benefited from good timing or good fortune. Consider the wisdom attributed to managers of aggressive-growth tech funds in the late 1990s.

BOX 18.1 Hindsight Bias: Behaviors That Can Cause Investment Mistakes finding undervalued stocks. Further suppose that from 1980 to 2004, the manager outperformed the S&P 500. Unfortunately, during the same time period, the manager lagged his benchmark, a value index. Is this lagging a valid criticism?

Cooper, Gutierrez, and Marcum argued implicitly that since true value indexes weren't created until after 1992, when Eugene Fama and Ken French came out with their now groundbreaking paper entitled "The Cross-Section of Expected Stock Returns" (*Journal of Finance*, 1992), the managers are being unduly criticized. In this example, the money manager would have no reason in 1980 to think that low price-to-book ratio stocks would outperform the market because that was not a recognized strategy. Thus, this manager's track record should only be compared to a value index from 1992 to 2005 rather than from 1980 to 2005.

An analogy can be found in the sport of baseball. The concept of "relief pitching" did not appear until after the turn of the twentieth century. To make a point, assume that prior to 1900 pitchers only pitched complete games and that after 1900 relief pitching came into being. Also assume that immediately after relief pitching began, the idea of "earned run average" (ERA) began to be used (in actuality, there were some years in between these events, but this scenario approximates reality). For those unfamiliar with baseball, ERA is the number of earned runs a pitcher gives up per nine innings pitched.

Prior to 1900, pitchers were routinely expected to pitch complete games. Thus, the only way to measure their effectiveness was to look at their won-loss (W-L) record. After the ERA was introduced, pitchers were evaluated on both W-L and ERA. Suppose that a statistician went back and calculated the ERA for pitchers who pitched prior to 1900 and found that their ERAs were much higher (bad) than those who were evaluated after relief pitching was introduced. Evaluating the pre-1900 pitchers by ERA is unfair because ERA was not known prior to 1900 as a measure of effectiveness of a pitcher, as pitchers were forced to pitch complete games. This situation is analogous to the previous example of value managers prior to 1992.

From their paper, Cooper, Gutierrez, and Marcum noted:

> In this study, we address the *ex ante* predictability of the cross section of stock returns by investigating whether a real-time investor could have used book-to-market equity, firm size,

and one-year lagged returns to generate portfolio profits during the 1974–97 period. We develop variations on common recursive out-of-sample methods and demonstrate a marked difference between *ex post* and *ex ante* predictability, suggesting that the current notion of predictability in the literature is exaggerated.[4]

(There is much more to this article. At this writing, it can be found at http://lcb1.uoregon.edu/rcg/research/Realtime.pdf.)

A similar example lies with small capitalization stocks. These managers should be judged from the early 1980s forward, when the idea of small capitalization stocks outperforming large capitalization stocks came into popularity. The point to be duly noted here is that before you criticize a fund manager's track record for any given asset class, make sure you know when his or her strategy gained popularity. Judge the track record from there.

DIAGNOSTIC TESTING

These questions are designed to detect cognitive errors caused by hindsight bias. To complete the test, select the answer choice that best characterizes your response to each item.

Hindsight Bias Test

Question 1: Suppose you make an investment, and it increases in value. Further suppose, though, that your reasons for purchasing the stock did not touch on the forces underlying its growth. How might you naturally react?

a. I do not concern myself with the reasons a stock does well. If it performs well, it means I did a good job as an investor, and doing well makes me more confident about the next investment I make.

b. Even though the stock went up, I'm concerned that the factors I thought were important didn't end up impacting its performance. In cases like this, I usually try to revisit the reasons that I bought the stock, and I also try to understand why it succeeded. Overall, I think I'd be more cautious the next time around.

Question 2: Suppose you make an investment, and it goes down. What is your natural reaction to this situation?

a. Generally, I don't fault myself—if an investment doesn't work out, this may simply be due to bad luck. I'll sell the stock and move on, rather than pursuing the details of what went wrong.

b. I would want to investigate and determine why my investment failed. In fact, I'm very interested in finding out what went wrong. I put a lot of emphasis on the reasons behind my investment decisions, so I need to be aware of the reasons behind my investment's performance.

Question 3: Suppose you are investigating a money manager for inclusion in your portfolio. Your advisor suggests a large cap value manager for you. What is your natural approach to examining the manager's performance?

a. I tend to look primarily at a manager's track record, comparing his or her performance to some relevant benchmark. I don't concern myself with the strategy that the manager employs. The results that a manager achieves are most important. If returns impress me, then I will select that manager; if I see a mediocre history, I'll pass.

b. I look at the returns, which are important, but I also look at the manager's strategy and try to determine what the manager was doing during the time frame I'm examining. In the case of the value manager, I will look, for example, at 2002—the manager was probably down, but by how much? Which companies did the manager invest in at the time? Evidence of a sound strategy makes me more likely to select this money manager.

Test Results Analysis

Questions 1, 2, and 3: Hindsight bias is a difficult bias to measure because people are rarely aware that they harbor it. So, few are likely to take a test like this and effectively respond: "Yes, I am susceptible to 'I-knew-it-all-along' behavior." Even people with reason to believe, objectively, that they might suffer from hindsight bias are unlikely to admit it to themselves. So, this diagnostic test looks for clues that might indicate *symptoms* of potential hindsight bias. For each item, respondents identifying with the rationale in "a" should be aware that they exhibit such symptoms and that they may suffer from hindsight bias.

ADVICE

In order to overcome hindsight bias, it is necessary, as with most biases, for the investors to understand and admit their susceptibility. Advisors should get their clients to understand that they are vulnerable and they counsel them on addressing specific problems that might arise. Here are some thoughts to help clients better deal with hindsight bias.

"Rewriting History"—Predicting Gains.   When a client overestimates the degree to which some positive investment outcome was foreseeable, and you suspect this is due to hindsight bias, the best course of action is to gently point to the facts. Storytelling is a strategy that might help communicate your point without offending the client. You might make reference, for example, to the collapse of the tech bubble in the 2000–2002 period, when risks fueled by false hubris cost stockholders billions. In the face of rationales like "I knew that stock was going to go up! I told you so," a cautionary tale can highlight the pitfalls of overestimating one's own predictive powers.

"Rewriting History"—Predicting Losses.   Advisors need to recognize that many people prefer to block recollections of poor investment decisions. Understanding why investments go awry, however, is critical to obtaining insight into markets and, ultimately, to finding investment success. Counsel clients to carefully examine their investment decisions, both good and bad. Encourage self-examination. This will help eliminate repeats of past investment mistakes.

Unduly Criticizing Money Managers for Poor Performance.   Clients need to understand that markets move in cycles and that, at certain times, an investment manager will underperform in his or her class, relative to other asset classes. Investors should understand that a good manager adheres to a consistent, valid style, through good times and bad. A manager is hired to do a job, and that job is to implement a defined investment strategy. Education is critical here. Just because many growth managers underperformed in the early 2000s, when values of many stocks were in a downward cycle, does not mean that growth managers are categorically unskilled.

Unduly Praising a Money Manager for Good Performance.   Using the same line of reasoning, counsel clients against becoming too giddy over the prospects offered by managers who happen to be in the right asset class at the right time. There are plenty of investment managers who benefit circumstantially from market cycles and still do not meet benchmarks. These are the managers to avoid. Again, education is critical; once clients understand the role that a manager plays in determining fund performance, hindsight bias can be curtailed.

CHAPTER 19

Loss Aversion Bias

Win as if you were used to it, lose as if you enjoyed it for a change.

—Ralph Waldo Emerson

BIAS DESCRIPTION

Bias Name: Loss Aversion Bias
Bias Type: Emotional

General Description. *Loss aversion bias* was developed by Daniel Kahneman and Amos Tversky in 1979 as part of the original prospect theory[1] specifically, in response to prospect theory's observation that people generally feel a stronger impulse to avoid losses than to acquire gains. A number of studies on loss aversion have given birth to a common rule of thumb: Psychologically, the possibility of a loss is on average twice as powerful a motivator as the possibility of making a gain of equal magnitude; that is, a loss-averse person might demand, at minimum, a two-dollar gain for every one dollar placed at risk. In this scenario, risks that don't "pay double" are unacceptable.

Loss aversion can prevent people from unloading unprofitable investments, even when they see little to no prospect of a turnaround. Some industry veterans have coined a diagnosis of "get-even-itis" to describe this widespread affliction, whereby a person waits too long for an investment to rebound following a loss. Get-even-itis can be dangerous because, often, the best response to a loss is to sell the offending security and to redeploy those assets. Similarly, loss aversion bias can make investors dwell excessively on risk avoidance when evaluating possible gains, since dodging a loss is a more urgent concern than seeking a profit. When their investments do begin to succeed, loss-averse individuals hasten to lock in profits, fearing that, otherwise, the market might reverse itself and rescind their returns. The problem here is that divesting prematurely to protect gains limits upside potential. In sum, loss aversion causes investors to hold their losing investments and to sell their winning ones, leading to suboptimal portfolio returns.

Technical Description. The technical definition of loss aversion comes from prospect theory, wherein Kahneman and Tversky don't explicitly mention concrete, relative preferences (e.g., "I prefer avoiding a loss to realizing a gain"). Rather, they discuss loss aversion in the context of the S-shaped, utility representative value function that models the entire evaluation stage in prospect theory. According to Kahneman and Tversky, people weigh all potential gains and losses in relation to some benchmark reference point (the point of origin on the graph in Figure 19.1).

The value function that passes through this point is asymmetric; and its profile implies, given the same variation in absolute value, a bigger

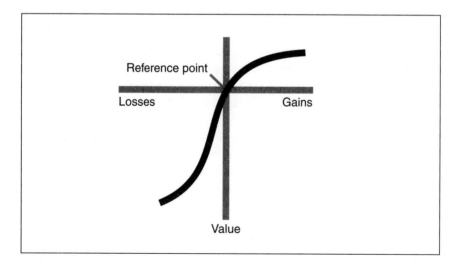

FIGURE 19.1 The Value Function—a Key Tenet of Prospect Theory
Source: The Econometric Society. Reprinted by permission.

impact of losses than of gains. The result is that risk-seeking behavior prevails in the domain of losses (below the x axis), while risk-averse behavior prevails in the domain of gains (above the x axis). An important concept embedded in this utility representation is Hersh Shefrin and Meir Statman's *disposition effect*.[2] The disposition effect is the desire to hold losing investments too long (risk-seeking behavior) and to sell winning investments too quickly (risk-avoidance behavior).

PRACTICAL APPLICATION

Loss aversion bias, observed in practice as the *disposition effect*, is seen often by wealth management practitioners. Investors open up the monthly statements prepared by their advisors, skim columns of numbers, and usually notice both winners and losers. In classic cases of loss aversion, clients dread selling the securities that haven't performed well. Get-even-itis takes hold, and the instinct is to hold onto a losing investment until, at the very least, it rebounds enough for the client to break even. Often, however, research into a losing investment would reveal a company whose prospects don't forecast a rebound. Continuing to hold stock in that company actually adds risk to an investor's portfolio (hence, the client's behavior is risk seeking, which accords with the path of the value function in Figure 19.1).

Conversely, when the monthly statement indicates that profits are being made, the loss-averse client is gripped by a powerful urge to "take the money and run," rather than to assume continued risk. Of course, frequently, holding onto a winning stock isn't a risky proposition, if the company is performing well; that is, profitable investments that the loss-averse investor wants to sell might actually be improving the portfolio's risk/return profile. Therefore, selling deteriorates that risk/return profile and eliminates the potential for further gains. When the increased risks associated with holding onto losing investments are considered in combination with the prospect of losing future gains that occur when selling winners, the degree of overall harm that a loss-averse investor can suffer begins to become clear.

A final thought on taking losses: Some investors, remarking on losing investments that haven't yet been sold, rationalize that "it's only a paper loss." In one sense, yes, this is true. Inasmuch as the investment is still held, a loss has technically not been triggered for tax purposes. In reality, though, this kind of rationale covers up the fact that a loss has taken place. If you went to the market to sell, having just incurred a "paper loss," the price you would obtain for your investment would be lower than the price you paid—effecting a very "real" loss indeed. Thus, if holding onto a losing investment does not objectively enhance the likelihood of recouping a loss, then it is better to simply realize the loss, which won't remain on paper forever.

Implications for Investors. Loss aversion is a bias that simply cannot be tolerated in financial decision making. It instigates the exact opposite of what investors want: increased risk, with lower returns. Investors should take risk to increase gains, not to mitigate losses. Holding losers and selling winners will wreak havoc on a portfolio. Box 19.1 summarizes some common investment mistakes linked to loss aversion bias.

---

1. Loss aversion causes investors to hold losing investments too long. This behavior is sometimes described in the context of a debilitating disease: *get-even-itis*. This is the affliction in which investors hold losing investments in the hope that they get back what they lost. This behavior has seriously negative consequences by depressing portfolio returns.
2. Loss aversion can cause investors to sell winners too early, in the fear that their profit will evaporate unless they sell. This behavior limits upside potential of a portfolio, and can lead to too much trading, which has been shown to lower investment returns.
3. Loss aversion can cause investors to unknowingly take on more risk in their portfolio than they would if they simply eliminated the investment and moved into a better one (or stayed in cash).
4. Loss aversion can cause investors to hold unbalanced portfolios. If, for example, several positions fall in value and the investor is unwilling to sell due to loss aversion, an imbalance can occur. Without proper rebalancing, the allocation is not suited to the long-term goals of the client, leading to suboptimal returns.

BOX 19.1 Loss Aversion Bias: Behaviors That Can Cause Investment Mistakes

RESEARCH REVIEW

Over the course of the twentieth century, one investment enigma lingered: Given the respective risk elements of the two asset classes, why had equity returns so markedly and consistently exceeded fixed income returns over time? In 1985, Rajnish Mehra and Edward C. Prescott wrote a paper entitled "The Equity Premium: A Puzzle," which demonstrated that the *equity premium*—the gap between the average rate of return on stocks and the lower, average rate of return on riskless Treasury bills (T-bills)—had steadily averaged 6.18 percent over the preceding century.[3] A more recent study has since observed that, from 1900 to 2002, U.S. stocks earned a 5.3 percent annual premium over T-bills.[4] So, why don't investors reject low-paying bonds and purchase equities instead? Mehra and Prescott quantified the conundrum using coefficients of relative risk aversion.

Professors Shlomo Benartzi and Richard Thaler[5] suggested a solution to the equity risk premium puzzle based on what they call "myopic loss aversion." Their explanation is grounded in two behavioral concepts: loss aversion and myopia. Loss-averse investors are more sensitive to losses than gains, with losses estimated to be two times more influential than gains of the same size. Myopia denotes shortsightedness. When loss aversion is combined with myopia, investors who evaluate their portfolios most frequently are also the most likely to experience losses and, hence, to suffer from loss aversion. It follows that myopic, loss-averse investors would invest in bonds.

Benartzi and Thaler argued that most investors evaluate their portfolios in a relatively shortsighted way and that, as loss aversion implies, they are highly sensitive to losses that have occurred over the examined time period. Using a number of simulation approaches, the evaluation time period implied in their model (consistent with the realized equity risk premium) is about one year. Benartzi and Thaler demonstrated that nonmyopic investors (investors with long time horizons who don't give in to the temptation to evaluate their portfolios frequently) are more willing to invest in risky assets than short-term investors are (people who evaluate their portfolios more often). In this case, then, an asset's value depends on an investor's time horizon.

Practitioners need to be sensitive to the fact that many clients will evaluate their portfolios myopically and, as a result, may become loss averse. Stress the long-term benefits of asset allocation, and counsel clients not to pay too much attention to short-term market fluctuations.

DIAGNOSTIC TESTING

These questions are designed to detect signs of emotional bias stemming from loss aversion. To complete the test, select the answer choice that best characterizes your response to each item.

Loss Aversion Bias Test

Question 1: Suppose you make a plan to invest $50,000. You are presented with two alternatives. Which scenario would you rather have?
  a. Be assured that I'll get back my $50,000, at the very least—even if I don't make any more money.
  b. Have a 50 percent chance of getting $70,000 and a 50 percent chance of getting $35,000.

Question 2: Suppose you make a plan to invest $70,000. You are presented with two alternatives. Which scenario would you rather have?
  a. Know that I'll only be repaid $60,000, for sure.
  b. Take a 50-50 gamble, knowing that I'll get back either $75,000 or $50,000.

Question 3: Choose one of these two outcomes:
  a. An assured gain of $475.
  b. A 25 percent chance of gaining $2,000 and a 75 percent chance of gaining nothing.

Question 4: Choose one of these two outcomes:
  a. An assured loss of $725.
  b. A 75 percent chance of losing $1,000 and a 25 percent chance of losing nothing.

Test Results Analysis

Question 1: People who are loss averse are most likely to select "a," even though "b" offers a larger potential return on the upside.

Question 2: Increased initial endowment aside, this is basically the same question as Question 1. Most people, however, would probably select "b," because most people tend to be loss averse. Loss-averse investors are willing to gamble and risk an even greater loss rather than to admit a loss ("a"). However, this isn't simply a matter of an unconditional penchant for gambling. Most investors (that is, loss-averse investors) prefer the assurance of breaking even over the opportunity to gain a profit in Question 1.

Question 3: The rational response is "b," but loss-averse investors are likely to opt for the assurance of a profit in "a."

Question 4: The rational response is "a." Loss-averse investors are more likely to select "b."

ADVICE

Get-Even-itis.   Beware: Holding losing stocks for too long is harmful to your investment health. One symptom of get-even-itis is that a client's decision making regarding some investments seems to be dependent on the original price paid for that investment. One effective remedy is a stop-loss rule. You may, for example, agree to sell a security immediately if it ever incurs a 10 percent loss. However, it's best to consider an investment's normal, expected levels of volatility when devising a stop-loss rule. You don't want to be forced to sell if an investment's price is just exhibiting its customary ups and downs.

Take the Money and Run.   Loss aversion can cause investors to sell winning positions too early, fearing that that their profits will evaporate otherwise. This behavior limits the upside potential of a portfolio and can lead to overtrading (which also reduces returns). Just as stop-loss rules can help to combat get-even-itis, it is often helpful to institute rules for selling appreciating investments. As with stop-loss rules, price-appreciation rules work best when tailored to reflect details related to fundamentals and valuation. The goal is to let gains run. Remember, too, that in a taxable account, you should avoid paying taxes on appreciations as long as possible.

Taking on Excessive Risk.   Loss aversion can cause investors to hold onto losing investments even in companies that are in serious trouble. In such a case, it may be helpful to educate clients about an investment's risk profile—taking time to discuss items like standard deviation, credit rating, buy/sell/hold ratings, and so on. The investor will then, hopefully, make the right decision to protect the overall portfolio and jettison the risky, poorly performing investment.

Unbalanced Portfolios.   Loss aversion can cause investors to hold unbalanced portfolios. Education about the benefits of asset allocation and diversification is critical, yet it may be insufficient if an investor holds a concentrated stock position with emotional strings attached. A useful question in this situation is: "If you didn't own any XYZ stock today, would you still want to pick up as many shares as you own right now?" If and when the answer is "no," some leeway for maneuvering emerges. Tax considerations, such as low cost basis, sometimes factor in; but certain strategies can be employed to manage this cost.

CHAPTER 20

Recency Bias

*The present is never our goal; the past and present are our
means, the future alone is our goal.*
—Blaise Pascal (1623–1662), French mathematician
and philosopher

BIAS DESCRIPTION

Bias Name: Recency Bias
Bias Type: Cognitive

General Description. *Recency bias* is a cognitive predisposition that
causes people to more prominently recall and emphasize recent events
and observations than those that occurred in the near or distant past.
Suppose, for example, that a cruise passenger peering off the observation
deck of a ship spots precisely equal numbers of green boats and blue
boats over the duration of the trip. However, if the green boats pass by
more frequently toward the end of the cruise, with the passing of blue
boats dispersed evenly or concentrated toward the beginning, then recency bias would influence the passenger to recall, following the cruise,
that more green than blue boats sailed by.

Technical Description. In order to best understand the technical description of recency bias, it is helpful to examine human memory recall test-

ing, the two main components of which are *primacy effect* and the *recency effect*.

When studying human memory, psychologists use a paradigm called *free recall*. In a free recall task, a subject is presented a list of to-be-recalled items, one after another. For example, an experimenter might read off a list of 15 words, presenting a new word to the test taker every 5 seconds. When the experimenter has read the entire list, the subject is asked to recall as many of the listed items as possible (e.g., by writing them down). This is known as a free recall task because the subject is free to recall the items in any order that he or she desires.

The results of a free recall task are plotted on something called a *serial position curve*, which is normally U-shaped. The serial position curve is graphed on a basic, coordinate plane, in which the x axis plots the serial position of to-be-remembered items in the list (e.g., the first item, the second item, the third item, and so on). The y axis, meanwhile, indicates the probability of recalling the item, which is based on the average frequency of recall across a number of subjects in a given trial. The serial position curve, once constructed, tends to exhibit both a *recency* and a *primacy* effect.

The *primacy effect* describes the left portion of the U shape, that is, the elevated portion at the beginning of the curve, which precedes the concavity at the middle. The primacy effect dictates that, in a free recall experiment like the one just described, articles presented at the beginning of a list of to-be-remembered items are remembered better than ones presented in the middle of the list. The primacy effect appears to result from subjects recalling items directly from semantic memory—a type of memory that might be thought of as the "hard drive" of a computer brain. The first items inscribed in a given session onto this hard drive are more precisely retained and are easier to access than items inscribed later on.

The *recency effect* describes the right portion of the serial position curve. When the recency effect appears in a free recall experiment, it means that subjects recall items appearing toward the end of the to-be-remembered list better than they remember items appearing in the middle. The effect is named in such a way because the observations comprising the right-hand tail of the serial position curve correspond to the items the subjects heard most recently prior to the recall challenge. Recency bias is the result of subjects recalling items directly from short-term memory. In continuing the computer analogy, if semantic memory represents a portion of your brain's long-term memory, or "hard drive," then short-term memory is like random access memory (RAM), which contains data that your computer can access dynamically during a session, but which it may lose after rebooting. Short-term memory only stores limited quantities of information over limited periods of time. Therefore, while the primacy effect results from the extra-long-term memory rehearsal accorded to primary items on a list, the recency effect occurs because the items the subject heard most recently are more likely to persist in short-term memory than previous, "older" items that have been discarded.

The technical description of recency bias refers to the errors people make when the recency effect prejudices their recollections. Recency bias privileges information recently retained and neglects events and observations not as fresh in the mind.

PRACTICAL APPLICATION

One of the most obvious and most pernicious manifestations of recency bias among investors pertains to their misuse of investment performance records for mutual funds and other types of funds. Investors track managers who produce temporary outsized returns during a one-, two-, or three-year period and then make investment decisions based only on such recent experiences. These investors do not pay heed to the cyclical nature of asset class returns, and so, for them, funds that have performed spectacularly in the very recent past appear unduly attractive. To counteract the effects of this bias, many practitioners wisely use what has become known as the "periodic table of investment returns," an adaptation of scientists' periodic table of chemical elements. See Table 20.1.

As the periodic table of investment returns in Table 20.1 demonstrates, asset class returns are highly variable. For example, an investor susceptible to recency bias might have embraced large cap growth stocks in 1999, having observed that such stocks prospered in 1996, 1997, and 1998. However, in 2000, 2001, and 2002, large cap growth declined dramatically. Many investors failed to heed the lessons of the periodic chart—namely, that it is nearly impossible to predict which asset classes will perform best from one year to the next and that diversification is consequently the most prudent strategy. Practitioners may find this chart useful when walking a new client through the initial asset allocation

TABLE 20.1 Sample of a Periodic Table of Investment Returns

1995	1996	1997	1998	1999	2000	2001	2002	2003
Large-Cap Value 38.35%	Real Estate 37.04%	Large-Cap Value 35.19%	Large-Cap Growth 38.70%	Small-Cap Growth 43.10%	Commodities 31.84%	Small-Cap Value 14.02%	Commodities 25.91%	Small-Cap Growth 48.54%
Large-Cap Growth 37.19%	Commodities 23.16%	Small-Cap Value 31.80%	International Stocks 20.34%	Large-Cap Growth 33.16%	Real Estate 31.04%	Real Estate 12.36%	Long-Term Bonds 16.79%	Small-Cap Value 46.035
Small-Cap Growth 31.04%	Large-Cap Growth 23.11%	Large-Cap Growth 30.48%	Large-Cap Value 15.65%	International Stocks 27.31%	Small-Cap Value 22.80%	Interm-Term Bonds 8.44%	Interm-Term Bonds 10.26%	International Stocks 39.17%
Long-Term Bonds 30.69%	Large-Cap Value 21.64%	Real Estate 19.66%	Long-Term Bonds 13.52%	Commodities 24.35%	Long-Term Bonds 20.27%	Short-Term Bonds 8.30%	Foreign Bonds 7.01%	Large-Cap Value 30.03%
Small-Cap Value 25.74%	Small-Cap Value 21.37%	Long-Term Bonds 15.08%	Foreign Bonds 12.09%	Large-cap Value 7.34%	Interm-Term Bonds 11.63%	Foreign Bonds 6.05%	Short-Term Bonds 5.76%	Large-Cap Growth 29.75%
High-Yield Bonds 20.46%	Foreign Bonds 12.16%	High-Yield Bonds 13.27%	Interm-Term Bonds 8.69%	Cash 4.74%	Foreign Bonds 9.71%	High-Yield Bonds 4.48%	Real Estate 3.60%	High-Yield Bonds 28.15%
Interm-Term Bonds 18.47%	High-Yield Bonds 11.27%	Small-Cap Growth 12.95%	Short-Term Bonds 7.00%	Short-Term Bonds 3.06%	Short-Term Bonds 8.00%	Long-Term Bonds 4.21%	Cash 1.70%	Real Estate 27.75%
Foreign Bonds 18.24%	Small-Cap Growth 11.26%	Foreign Bonds 11.32%	Cash 5.06%	High-Yield Bonds 2.51%	Large-Cap Value 7.02%	Cash 4.09%	High-Yield Bonds -1.89%	Commodities 23.93%
Commodities 15.21%	International Stocks 6.36%	Interm-Term Bonds 9.65%	High-Yield Bonds 2.95%	Foreign Bonds 2.48%	Cash 5.95%	Large-Cap Value -5.59%	Small-Cap Value -11.42%	Interm-Term Bonds 4.10%
Real Estate 12.24%	Cash 5.25%	Short-Term Bonds 6.66%	Small-Cap Growth 1.24%	Interm-Term Bonds -0.82%	High-Yield Bonds -5.12%	Small-Cap Growth -9.23%	Large-Cap Value -15.52%	Long-Term Bonds 2.48%
International Stocks 11.55%	Short-Term Bonds 4.98%	Cash 5.25%	Small-Cap Value -6.43%	Small-Cap Value -1.49%	International Stocks -13.95%	Commodities -19.51%	International Stocks -15.64%	Foreign Bonds 1.98%
Short-Term Bonds 11.00%	Interm-Term Bonds 3.63%	International Stocks 2.06%	Real Estate -17.00%	Real Estate -2.57%	Large-Cap Growth -22.43%	Large-Gap Growth -20.42%	Large-Cap Growth -27.89%	Short-Term Bonds 1.90%
Cash 5.76%	Long-Term Bonds -0.87%	Commodities -3.39%	Commodities -27.03%	Long-Term Bonds -8.74%	Small-Cap Growth -22.44%	International Stocks -21.21%	Small-Cap Growth -30.27%	Cash 1.07%

process, since it provides a tool for emphasizing diversification over return chasing.

Implications for Investors. As many wealth managers know, recency bias ran rampant during the bull market period between 1995 and 1999. Many investors implicitly presumed, as they have during other cyclical peaks, that the market would continue its enormous gains forever. They all but forgot the fact that bear markets can and do occur. Investors, who based decisions on their own subjective short-term memories, hoped that near-term history would continue to repeat itself. Intuitively, they insisted that evidence gathered from recent experience narrowed the range of potential outcomes and thus enabled them to project future returns. All too often, this behavior creates misguided confidence and becomes a catalyst for error.

When studying the market, good investors analyze large data samples to determine probabilities. By doing so, solid conclusions can be scientifically obtained. Recency bias causes investors to place too much emphasis on data recently gathered, rather than examining entire, relevant bodies of information, which often span much more extensive intervals of time. Investors need to be advised to look at underlying value and not just recent performance. If prices have just risen strongly, for example, then assets may be approaching or may have exceeded their fair value. This should imply that there are, perhaps, better investment opportunities elsewhere. Box 20.1 summarizes investment mistakes that can stem from recency bias.

RESEARCH REVIEW

James Montier's February 2003 paper entitled "Irrational Pessimism and the Road to Revulsion"[1] developed a model using recency bias. This is an outstanding real-world application of behavioral finance, as it lets practitioners observe how recency bias, in combination with anchoring bias, creates false intuition regarding market trajectories.

To proxy investors' expectations, Montier draws on two main behavioral biases: (1) anchoring and (2) recency. Recall, from Chapter 6, that *anchoring* is the term used to describe an investor's adherence to some arbitrary benchmark, often such that related calculations become skewed. Recency bias occurs when more recent events tend to remain

1. Recency bias can cause investors to extrapolate patterns and make projections based on historical data samples that are too small to ensure accuracy. Investors who forecast future returns based too extensively on only a recent sample of prior returns are vulnerable to purchasing at price peaks. These investors tend to enter asset classes at the wrong times and end up experiencing losses.

2. Recency bias can cause investors to ignore fundamental *value* and to focus only on recent upward price performance. When a return cycle peaks and recent performance figures are most attractive, human nature is to chase promise of a profit. Asset classes can and do become overvalued. By focusing only on price performance and not on valuation, investors risk principal loss when these investments revert to their mean or long-term averages.

3. Recency bias can cause investors to utter the words that many market veterans consider the most deceptive and damning of all: "It's different this time." In 1998 and 1999, for example, the short-term memory of recent gains influenced some investors so strongly as to overrule, in their minds, historical facts regarding rational valuations and the bubbles, peaks, and valleys that naturally occur. If your client ever seems to be yielding to this rationale, then it is time for a reality check.

4. Recency bias can cause investors to ignore proper asset allocation. Professional investors know the value of proper asset allocation, and they rebalance when necessary in order to maintain proper allocations. Recency bias can cause investors to become infatuated with a given asset class that, for example, appears in vogue. They often concentrate their holdings accordingly. Proper asset allocation is crucial to long-term investment success.

BOX 20.1 Recency Bias: Behaviors That Can Cause Investment Mistakes

more prominent in decision making than events that occurred further in the past. Montier uses both of these biases as the basis for his model of investor expectations regarding equity returns. Anchoring is represented in the model via a dependence of expectations on the long-run real return from U.S. equities (i.e., the long-run return of just over 7 percent is given a weight of 0.75 in this model of expectations).

The recency effect is captured by giving the geometric 10-year annual price return a weight of 0.25 in the model. The two models are compared in Figures 20.1 and 20.2. Figure 20.1 shows the absolute level of expectations. The rational model shows that investors should expect no more than 5 percent real returns over the long run. Montier's irrational model shows that investors are looking for a return of over 8 percent annually in the long run.

Figure 20.2 shows the measure of the scope for disappointment. This is calculated as the difference between the irrational and rational models. The graph shows the irrational pessimism that gripped the market in the 1970s and early 1980s.

DIAGNOSTIC TESTING

These questions are designed to detect cognitive errors stemming from recency bias. To complete the test, select the answer choice that best characterizes your response to each item.

Recency Bias Test

Note that while most of the tests in this book are primarily intended to be administered by practitioners to their clients, they can, in general, be self-administered. This test, however, does require that someone other than the respondent administer the rest (i.e., it contains free recall memory exercises, etc.).

Question 1: Suppose you are asked to select a mutual fund for your portfolio based only on the fund's performance record. What is your most likely course of action?
  a. I will look at the one to three-year record of the fund to see how the fund has done recently.
  b. I will look at the five-year track record of the fund, as this time period showcases some elements of recent performance, but also historical performance.
  c. I will look at the ten-year track record, even though it doesn't focus on the fund's most recent performance.

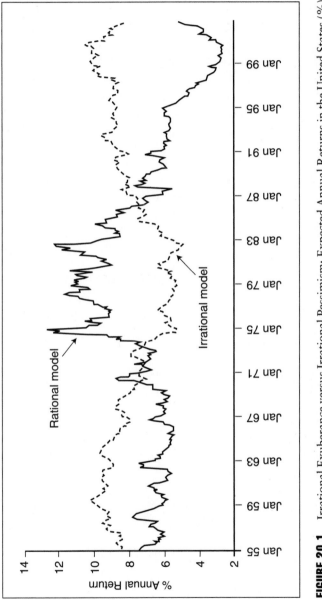

FIGURE 20.1 Irrational Exuberance versus Irrational Pessimism: Expected Annual Returns in the United States (%)

223

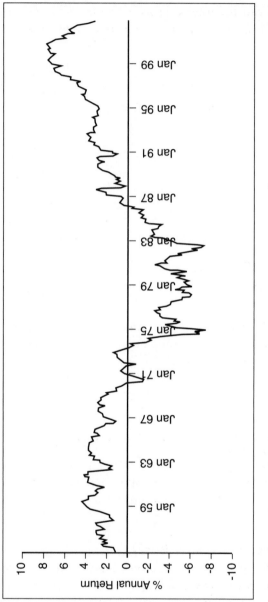

FIGURE 20.2 Scope for Disappointment: Irrational Model Minus Rational Model

Question 2: Read the following list of names to the respondent. Then ask: Did the list contain more male or female names?

1. Sally
2. Mark
3. Amy
4. Annette
5. Jim
6. Barbara
7. Steven
8. David
9. Michael
10. Donna

Test Results Analysis

Question 1: People who select response "a" or "b" are likely subject to recency bias.

Question 2: This list actually contains an equal number of male and female names. The male names, however, are concentrated toward the end of the list. Therefore, people who suffer from recency bias are more likely to recall that the list was dominated by male names.

ADVICE

Box 20.1 listed some errors that investors often commit when they are subject to recency bias. These corresponding strategies can be employed by practitioners who want to attempt to moderate recency bias in their clients.

Sample Size and Extrapolating Trends. Investors afflicted with recency bias often make projections based only on recent data—based on a data sample too narrowly drawn to be accurately informative with regard to future market trends. This behavior is relatively easy to overcome, as investors can often be persuaded by data when it is presented to them. Often, clients simply don't have immediate access to the data they need in order to make good decisions; other times, they lack the patience for undertaking a careful analysis. Education is critical to overcoming this aspect of recency bias.

Price versus Value.   Human nature is to chase "hot money," and investors subject to recency bias often fixate on price performance while neglecting value indicators. Advisors need to demonstrate that out-of-favor, undervalued asset classes can make for very wise investments. The periodic table of investment returns is often a very persuasive visual aid and can help sway the recency-biased client toward a balanced allocation.

"It's Different This Time."   Most practitioners recognize that an uninhibited, spontaneous critique of a client's every investment whim would probably hurt the relationship. Many advisors instead take an "advisory piggy bank" approach, saving up (i.e., holding back) some sentiments with regard to certain clients' ideas about their portfolios. Practitioners of this mind-set rationalize that the number of blatant criticisms (e.g., "How can you be so overconcentrated in XYZ stock?!") that advisory relationships can endure is probably limited. So, they should try to "withdraw from the piggy bank" only on the important occasions. If you're an advisor who utilizes the piggy bank approach and your client utters, "It's different this time," then you may need to make a substantial piggy bank withdrawal. Point to historical evidence until your client understands that it won't be different this time. It never is.

Unbalanced Portfolio.   Proper asset allocation and diversification are crucial to long-term investment success. Educating clients on these principles is essential to helping them reach their financial goals. Do not let your clients become enamored with one certain stock and let that stock dominate a portfolio. The stock could tumble, and your client could lose money. Education is critical to demonstrating why recency bias can be so dangerous. It might, perhaps, go without saying that in these situations, nothing can replace the benefit of objective advice.

CHAPTER 21

Regret Aversion Bias

*I visualized my grief if the stock market went way up and I
wasn't in it—or if it went way down and I was completely in it.
My intention was to minimize my future regret, so I split my
retirement plan contributions 50/50 between bonds and
equities.*

—Harry Markowitz, father of Modern Portfolio Theory

BIAS DESCRIPTION

Bias Name: Regret Aversion Bias
Bias Type: Emotional

General Description. People exhibiting *regret aversion* avoid taking decisive actions because they fear that, in hindsight, whatever course they select will prove less than optimal. Basically, this bias seeks to forestall the pain of regret associated with poor decision making. It is a cognitive phenomenon that often arises in investors, causing them to hold onto losing positions too long in order to avoid admitting errors and realizing losses. Regret aversion also makes people unduly apprehensive about breaking into financial markets that have recently generated losses. When they experience negative investment outcomes, they feel instinctually driven to conserve, to retreat, and to lick their wounds—*not* to press on and snap up potentially undervalued stocks. However, periods of depressed prices often present the greatest buying opportunities.

People suffering from regret aversion bias hesitate most at moments that actually merit aggressive behavior. Regret aversion does not come into play only following a loss; it can also affect a person's response to investment gains. People exhibiting regret aversion can be reluctant, for example, to sell a stock whose value has climbed recently—even if objective indicators attest that it's time to pull out. Instead, regret-averse investors may cling to positions that they ought to sell, pained by the prospect that a stock, once unloaded, might soar even higher.

Technical Description.   An extensive body of literature in experimental psychology suggests that regret does influence decision making under conditions of uncertainty. Regret causes people to challenge past decisions and to question their beliefs. People who are regret averse try to avoid distress arising from two types of mistakes: (1) *errors of commission* and (2) *errors of omission*. Errors of *commission* occur when we take misguided *actions*. Errors of *omission* arise from misguided *inaction*, that is, opportunities overlooked or foregone.

Regret is different from disappointment, because the former implies that the sufferer had some sense of agency in achieving the negative outcome. Also, feelings of regret are more intense when unfavorable outcomes emerge from errors of commission rather than errors of omission. The "Implications for Investors" section uses an example to examine more concretely the distinction between errors of commission and errors of omission in the context of regret aversion bias.

Regret is most palpable and takes the greatest toll on decision making when the outcomes of foregone alternatives are highly "visible" or "accessible." By the same token, regret becomes a less influential factor when consequences of mistakes are less discernible. Some researchers have proposed theories of choice under uncertainty that incorporate regret bias as a partial explanation for observed violations of traditional expected utility theory. Regret theory assumes that agents are rational but base their decisions not only on expected payoffs but also on expected regret. The Allais paradox (Chapter 2), along with other human tendencies that seem to interfere with utility optimization, make sense from the perspective of regret theory. Regret theory bears some similarities to prospect theory (discussed earlier), and many of its predictions are consistent with the empirical observations of human behavior that constitute the building blocks of prospect theory.

PRACTICAL APPLICATION

A hypothetical case illustrates both aspects of regret bias: *error of commission* and *error of omission*. The case shows a regret-averse investor under two sets of circumstances: (1) An investor experienced a loss and regrets his decision to invest. (2) An investor missed an opportunity to invest in something that later appreciated in value and regrets his failure to reap profits.

Suppose that Jim has a chance to invest in Schmoogle, Inc., an initial public offering (IPO) that has generated a great buzz following its recent market debut. Jim thinks that Schmoogle has high potential and contemplates buying in because Schmoogle's price has recently declined by 10 percent due to some recent market weakness. If Jim *invests* in Schmoogle, one of two things will happen: (1) Schmoogle will drop further (Jim made the wrong decision), or (2) Schmoogle will rebound (Jim made the right decision). If Jim *doesn't invest*, one of two things will happen: (1) Schmoogle will rebound (Jim made the right decision), or (2) Schmoogle will drop further (Jim made the wrong decision).

Suppose that Jim does invest and Schmoogle goes down. Jim will have committed an error of commission because he actually *committed the act* of investing and will likely feel regret strongly because he actually lost money.

Now suppose that Jim does not invest and Schmoogle goes up. Jim will have committed an error of omission because he *omitted* the purchase of Schmoogle and lost out. This regret may not be as strong as the regret associated with the error of commission. Why? First, as we learned in Chapter 19, investors dislike losing money more than they do gaining money. Second, in the first possibility, the investor actually committed the act of investing and lost money; in the second possibility, the investor merely did not act and only lost out on the *opportunity* to gain.

Implications for Investors. Regret aversion causes investors to anticipate and fear the pain of regret that comes with incurring a loss or forfeiting a profit. The potential for financial injury isn't the only disincentive that these investors face; they also dread feeling responsible for their own misfortunes (because regret implies culpability, whereas simple disappointment does not). The anxiety surrounding the prospect of an error of commission, or a "wrong move," can make investors timid and can cause them to subjectively and perhaps irrationally favor investments that seem trustworthy (e.g., "good companies"). Suppose that regret-averse Jim is now considering two investments, both with equal projected risk and return. One stock belongs to Large Company, Inc., while the other confers a share in Medium-Size Company, Inc. Even though, mathematically, the expected payoffs of investing in these two companies are identical, Jim will probably feel more comfortable with Large Company. If an investment in Large Company, Inc., fails to pay off, Jim can rationalize that his decision making could not have been too egregiously flawed, because Large Company, Inc., must have had lots of savvy investors. Jim doesn't feel uniquely foolish, and so the culpability component of Jim's regret is reduced. Jim can't rely on the same excuse, however, if an investment in Medium-Size Company fails. Instead of exonerating himself ("Lots of high-profile people made the same mistake that I did—perhaps some market anomaly is at fault?"), Jim may condemn himself ("Why did I do that? I shouldn't have invested in Medium-Size. Only small-time players invested in Medium-Size, Inc. I feel stupid!"), adding to his feelings of regret. It's important to recall here that Large Company and Medium-Size Company stocks were, objectively, equally risky. This underscores the fact that aversion to regret is different from aversion to risk. Box 21.1 reviews six investor mistakes that can stem from regret aversion bias. Remedies for these biases will be reviewed in the Advice section.

RESEARCH REVIEW

Hersh Shefrin and Meir Statman[1] in their paper entitled "Explaining Investor Preference for Cash Dividends" highlighted *regret* as a reason

---

1. Regret aversion can cause investors to be too conservative in their investment choices. Having suffered losses in the past (i.e., having felt pain of a poor decision regarding a risky investment), many people shy away from making new bold investment decisions and accept only low-risk positions. This behavior can lead to long-term underperformance, and can jeopardize investment goals.

2. Regret aversion can cause investors to shy away, unduly, from markets that have recently gone down. Regret-averse individuals fear that if they invest, such a market might subsequently continue its downward trend, prompting them to regret the decision to buy in. Often, however, depressed markets offer bargains, and people can benefit from seizing, decisively, these undervalued investments.

3. Regret aversion can cause investors to hold onto losing positions too long. People don't like to admit when they're wrong, and they will go to great lengths to avoid selling (i.e., confronting the reality of) a losing investment. This behavior, similar to loss aversion, is hazardous to one's wealth.

4. Regret aversion can cause "herding behavior" because, for some investors, buying into an apparent mass consensus can limit the potential for future regret. Needless to say, the demise of the Internet-stock bubble demonstrated that even the most massive herd can stampede in the wrong direction.

5. Regret aversion leads investors to prefer stocks of subjectively designated *good companies*, even when an alternative stock has an equal or a higher expected return. Regret-averse investors may feel that "riskier" companies require bolder decision making; hence, if the investment fails, the consequences reflect more dramatically on an individual's judgment than do the consequences of investing in a "routine," "safe," or "reliable" stock. With increased perception of personal responsibility, of course, comes increased potential for regret. Investing in *good companies* may not permit investors any more return or less return than those companies perceived to be risky.

6. Regret aversion can cause investors to hold onto winning stocks for too long. People fear that by selling a stock that has been doing well, they might miss out on further imminent gains. The danger here is that in finance, as in physics, whatever goes up must come down.

BOX 21.1 Regret Aversion Bias: Behaviors That Can Cause Investment Mistakes that investors prefer stocks that pay dividends. They argued that this is true because by paying dividends, investors can avoid, in some measure, the frustration that is felt when taking an action that leads to a less than desirable outcome. As previously noted, regret is stronger for errors of commission (cases where people suffer because of an action they took) than for errors of omission (cases where people suffer because of an action they failed to take). Suppose that an investor buys stock in Company A, which does not pay a dividend. In order to extract cash flow from this investment consumption, an investor would have to sell some stock. If the stock subsequently goes up in value, the investor feels substantial regret because the error is one of commission; he can readily imagine how not selling the stock would have left him better off. Conversely, suppose the investor invests in Company D, which does pay a dividend. With Company D, the investor would be able to extract cash flow from dividends, and, thus, a rise in the stock price would not have caused so much regret. This time, the error would have been one of omission: To be better off, the investor would have had to reinvest the dividend.

DIAGNOSTIC TESTING

These questions are designed to detect signs of emotional bias stemming from regret aversion. To complete the test, select the answer choice that best characterizes your response to each item.

Regret Aversion Bias Test

Question 1: Suppose that you make an investment in Stock ABC and that over the next 12 months ABC appreciates by 10 percent. You contemplate selling ABC for normal portfolio rebalancing purposes, but then come across an item in the *Wall Street Journal* that sparks new optimism: Could ABC climb even higher? Which answer describes your likeliest response, given ABC's recent performance and this new information?

    a. I think I'll hold off and sell later. I'd really kick myself if I sold now and ABC continued to go up.

    b. I'll probably sell. But I'll still kick myself if ABC appreciates later on.

c. I'll probably sell the stock without any second thoughts—regardless of what happens to ABC's price after the transaction.

Question 2: Suppose that you've decided to acquire 200 shares of LMN Company. You purchase 100 shares now at $30 apiece and strategize to wait a few days before picking up the additional 100. Further suppose that soon after your initial buy, the market takes a comprehensive dip. LMN is now trading at $28, with no change in fundamentals. Which answer most closely matches your thought process in this situation?

a. I will probably wait until the stock begins to go back up before buying the remaining 100 shares. I really don't want to see LMN fall below $28 because I'd regret my initial decision to buy in.

b. I will probably buy the remaining 100 shares. If LMN ends up going below $28, though, I will regret my decision.

c. I will probably buy the remaining 100 shares. Even if LMN falls below $28, I don't think I'll experience a lot of regret.

Question 3: Suppose you have decided to invest $5,000 in the stock market. You have narrowed your choices down to two companies: Big City Company, Inc, and Small Town Company, Inc. According to your calculations, both stocks have equal risk and return payoffs. Big City is a well-followed, eminently established company, whose shareholders include many large pension funds. Small Town has performed well but has not garnered the same kind of public profile as Big City. It has few well-known investors. Which answer most closely matches your thought process in this situation?

a. I will most likely invest in Big City Company because I feel safe taking the same course as so many respected institutional investors. If Big City does decline in value, I know I won't be the only one caught by surprise—and with so many savvy professionals sharing my predicament, I could hardly blame myself for excessively poor judgment.

b. I will most likely invest in Big City Company because if I invested in Small Town Company and my investment failed, I would feel like a fool. Few well-known investors backed Small Town Company, and I would really regret going against their informed consensus only to discover that I was dead wrong.

c. I would feel indifferent between the two investments, since both generated the same expected parameters for risk and return.

Test Result Analysis

Questions 1, 2, and 3: People answering "a" or "b" to any question may harbor susceptibility to regret aversion bias.

ADVICE

This section is organized to address each of the pitfalls of regret aversion bias that are enumerated in Box 21.1.

Investing Too Conservatively. No matter how many times an investor has been "burned" by an ultimately unprofitable investment, risk (in the context of proper diversification) is still a healthy ingredient in any portfolio. Demonstrating to clients the long-term benefits of adding risky assets to a portfolio is essential. Efficient frontier research can be very helpful here. Investing too conservatively doesn't place an investor's assets in any acute danger—by definition, an excess of conservatism denotes a relative absence of risk. However, refusing to assume a risk often means forgoing a potential reward. Investors who swear off risky assets due to regret aversion may see less growth in their portfolios than they could otherwise achieve, and they might not reach their investment goals.

Staying Out of the Market after a Loss. There is no principle more fundamental in securities trading than "buy low, sell high." Nonetheless, many investors' behavior completely ignores this directive. Again, human nature is to chase returns, following "hot" money. Of course, it *is* possible to profit from following market trends . . . the problem is, you never know when the balloon is going to pop and cause, for example, yesterday's coveted security to plummet 40 percent in an afternoon. Disciplined portfolio management is crucial to long-term success. This means buying at times when the market is low and selling at the times when the market is up.

Holding Losing Positions Too Long. An adage on Wall Street is, "The first loss is the best loss." While realizing losses is never enjoyable, the wisdom here is that following an unprofitable decision, it is best to cut those losses and move on. Everyone missteps occasionally—even the world's savviest traders. Hedge funds, for example, can place mistaken bets (remember the Asian financial crisis?) and usually admit to these mistakes, even though this means registering losses of hundreds of millions of dollars. Advise your clients that they shouldn't regret realizing their losses. If people can learn to feel less grief when realizing that they have incurred losses, then the pain of owning up to a loss can be reduced and the effects of regret aversion in such instances can be lessened.

Herding Behavior. If you're a practitioner and you believe that a decision your client has made reflects a herd mentality, then it can help to stop and question the investor's motivations. For example, you might ask your client to pinpoint whether the trade at hand relates to any particular long-term financial goal. Often, investors subject to pack mentalities have a hard time answering this question well. Disconcerted by their own hesitation, many clients at this point will step back and reconsider the consensus of the herd. Others, though, may rationalize: "This is my time to take a risk." This is not, in and of itself, a dangerous statement. Investors are permitted, on occasion, to gamble. They must, however, understand the stakes and the magnitudes of the gambles they undertake. Advisors can help by reminding their clients of the outcomes of some other "flyers" that have been taken in the past, so that, at the very least, a speculative decision can be grounded in an unbiased, historical perspective.

Preference for Good Companies. Investors often think they can save face (especially with their spouses) by buying stock in good companies like GE or Coca-Cola. Such household names have seen their ups and downs, however, just like competitor firms. Don't let clients limit themselves to good companies simply because they fear the regret they might experience if an investment in a lesser-known company doesn't work out. Remember that high-profile brands don't necessarily deliver returns either. GE and Coke are certainly recognizable, but that doesn't mean that either company's stock constitutes a sure thing.

Holding Winners Too Long. It's time to entertain one final Wall Street axiom: "You never get hurt taking a profit." This is not to say that you should not let winners run. However, if you find numerous, objective considerations that favor selling a security and if the only reason *not* to sell is because you fear regretting a missed opportunity should the investment appreciate after you sell it, then it's time to take a step back.

Remember that you may also experience regret when a stock begins to decline after you've held it for too long. Moreover, a helpful approach is to attempt to set aside any emotions that might be impacting the sell decision. Once you feel certain, make a choice—and stick to it. You can always buy in again later on if the stock does indeed represent a good investment opportunity.

Framing Bias

You better cut the pizza in four pieces, because I'm not hungry enough to eat six.

—Yogi Berra

BIAS DESCRIPTION

Bias Name: Framing Bias
Bias Type: Cognitive

General Description.   *Framing bias* notes the tendency of decision makers to respond to various situations differently based on the context in which a choice is presented (framed). In real life, people usually benefit from some flexibility in determining how to address the problems they face. Framing can be explained visually: Take a look at Figure 22.1. Which line is longer?

People subject to framing experience an optical illusion, which leads them to insist that the line on the bottom is longer. The graphic is reproduced, however, in Figure 22.2, this time with vertical marks added in as a guide. Which line is longer?

With the framing effect of the "arrow" detail neutralized, it becomes clear that the line on the top and the line on the bottom are equal in length.

Everyday evidence of framing bias can be found at the grocery store. Many grocers will price items in multiples: "2 for $2" or "3 for $7." This

FIGURE 22.1   Which Line Is Longer?

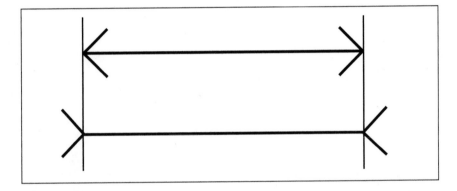

FIGURE 22.2   Which Line Is Longer?

doesn't necessarily imply, however, that any kind of bulk discount is being offered. Have you ever found an item priced at "3 for $7" also available at a unit price of $2.33? This isn't unusual. Shopping represents a rudimentary rational choice problem ("How many oranges should I buy?"), and good salespeople try to frame a solution for a buyer that benefits the store. "Don't buy oranges in units of one," suggests the price policy. "Buy them in multiples of three." This takes advantage of people's susceptibility to framing.

Technical Description. A decision *frame* is the decision maker's subjective conception of the acts, outcomes, and contingencies associated with a particular choice. The frame that a decision maker adopts is controlled partly by the formulation of the problem and partly by the norms, habits, and personal characteristics of the decision maker.

It is often possible to frame a given decision problem in more than one way. Framing effects occur when preferences change as a function of some variation in framing. For example, one prospect can be formulated in two ways: as a gain ("25 percent of patients will be saved if they are provided with medicine XYZ") or as a loss ("75 percent of patients will die without medicine XYZ"). Most people in the first case will adopt a gain frame, which generally leads to risk-averse behavior. In the second case—75 percent of patients will die—most people will adopt a loss frame and thereby become more likely to engage in risk-seeking behavior.

Framing bias also encompasses a subcategorical phenomenon known as *narrow framing*, which occurs when people focus too restrictively on one or two aspects of a situation, excluding other crucial aspects and thus compromising their decision making. For example, take the case of a lawnmower purchase. A consumer working within too narrow a frame of reference might shop for a mower that is fast, while overlooking blade width, fuel economy, and other factors that affect the length of time required to mow a lawn.

PRACTICAL APPLICATION

Decision frames are quite prevalent in the context of investor behavior. Building on the definitions outlined in the preceding section, we can now use our newly acquired insights into framing bias as we consider a typical investor risk tolerance questionnaire. This will demonstrate how framing bias is applied in practice and how advisors should be aware of its effects.

Suppose that an investor completes a risk tolerance questionnaire for the purpose of determining the "risk category" into which he or she falls. The responses the investor selects are highly relevant because the risk category outcome will determine the types of investments that are selected for this individual's portfolio. Ideally, question phrasing and framing—elements uncorrelated with the investor's actual level of risk tolerance—

should not be factors that affect the questionnaire's results. Let's examine some of the material that might appear on a typical risk tolerance questionnaire.

First, suppose that the items on the questionnaire refer to a hypothetical securities portfolio, Portfolio ABC. Over a 10-year period, ABC has historically returned an annual average of 10 percent, with a standard deviation of 15 percent. (Recall that *standard deviation* quantifies the amount of expected variation in an investment's performance from year to year.) Basic statistics dictate that 67 percent of ABCs returns will fall within one standard deviation of the mean, or annual average, return that ABC generates. Similarly, 95 percent of returns will fall within two standard deviations, and 99.7 percent within three standard deviations of the mean. So, if ABC's mean return was 10 percent and its standard deviation was 15 percent, then two-thirds of all returns produced by ABC would equal 10 percent plus-or-minus no more than 15 percent; that is, 67 percent of the time, ABC's return will likely be somewhere between –5 percent and 25 percent. It follows that 95 percent of ABC's returns will fall between –20 percent and 40 percent and that 99.7 percent will fall somewhere between –35 percent and 55 percent.

Now, imagine that one, but not both, of the following questions is to appear on an investor's risk tolerance questionnaire. Both concern Portfolio ABC, and both try to measure an investor's comfort level with ABC, given its average returns, volatility, and so on. However, the two questions frame the situation very differently. As you compare questions 1 and 2, try to imagine how an average investor, probably subject to a few common behavioral biases, might respond to each respective frame. Do you think most investors' answers would be identical in each instance?

1. Based on Table 22.1, which investment portfolio seems like the best fit, bearing in mind your own risk tolerance as well as your desire for long-term return?
   a. Portfolio XYZ.
   b. Portfolio DEF.
   c. Portfolio ABC.
2. Assume that you own Portfolio ABC and that it lost 15 percent of its value over the past year, despite previous years of good performance. This loss is consistent with the performance of similar funds during the past year. What is your reaction to this situation?

TABLE 22.1 Portfolio Selection: Which Portfolio Seems Best?

Portfolio Number	95% Probability Gain/ Loss Range	Long-Term Return
XYZ	2% to 4%	3%
DEF	−6% to 18%	6%
ABC	−20% to 40%	10%

a. Sell all Portfolio ABC shares.
b. Sell some, but not all, Portfolio ABC shares.
c. Continue to hold Portfolio ABC shares.
d. Increase investment in Portfolio ABC.

There is a chance that a person will select similar answers for both questions. However, there is also a significant probability that inconsistent framing will generate inconsistent responses from many investors. Specifically, respondents might reject Portfolio ABC in question 1, yet decide to proceed with ABC in question 2.

In question 1, "95% Probable Gain/Loss Range" refers (in Table 22.1) to an interval of two standard deviations above and below the mean. In 95 percent of all cases, ABC returned 10 percent plus-or-minus 30 percent; its standard deviation is 15 percent.

In Question 2, ABC produced a return that, in two-thirds of all cases, would have been the worst return imaginable: It returned one standard deviation below the mean. However, because question 2 employs one standard deviation rather than two, readers are less likely to consider the one-third of all cases in which ABC could lose more than 5 percent of its value (entering into the 95 percent, rather than the 67 percent, probable gain/loss range).

Like the method employed by grocers (pricing produce in multiples), which subtly suggests some arbitrary, benchmark quantity of oranges for purchase, Question 1 similarly invites people to more intuitively consider the rarer, heavier losses Portfolio ABC could incur if returns breached the 67 percent confidence interval. Here, the implications of framing are important: Inconsistent responses to questions 1 and 2 could make the questionnaire inconsistent and an inaccurate measure of investor risk tolerance (the questionnaire's outcome would be, accordingly, a flawed basis for structuring an allocation). Practitioners need to be acutely aware of how framing can affect the outcome of various investment choices.

Implications for Investors. An individual's willingness to accept risk can be influenced by how questions/scenarios are framed—positively or negatively. Recall, for example, the subjective difference between "25 percent of patients will be saved" and "75 percent of patients will die." The same optimism or pessimism in framing can affect investment decision making. For example, suppose that Mrs. Smith chooses to invest in either Portfolio A or Portfolio B. Further suppose that Portfolios A and B are identical in every respect. Mrs. Smith learns that Portfolio A will offer her a 70 percent chance of attaining her financial goals, whereas Portfolio B offers Mrs. Smith a 30 percent chance of *not* attaining her financial goals. If Mrs. Smith is like most people, she will choose Portfolio A, because its performance prospects were more attractively framed.

Another key point to keep in mind is that framing bias and loss aversion bias can and do work together. When people have suffered losses, they may view losses as the right time to embark on risk-taking behavior; when people have gained, they may feel threatened by options that entail additional risk. For example, an investor who has just suffered a net loss is likely to seek risk with his or her investments. Someone who has gained, however, is more likely to opt for a sure thing.

Box 22.1 reviews four investor mistakes caused by framing bias.

RESEARCH REVIEW

In their 1984 paper entitled "Choices, Values, and Frames," Daniel Kahneman and Amos Tversky[1] studied framing bias in a sample population of physicians, posing the following question to each participating doctor: "Imagine that the U.S. is preparing for the outbreak of an unusual Asian disease, which is expected to kill 600 people. Two alternative programs to combat the disease have been proposed. Assume that the exact scientific estimates of the consequences of the programs are as follows: If program A is adopted, 200 people will be saved. If program B is adopted, there is a one-third probability that 600 people will be saved and a two-thirds probability that no people will be saved. Which of the two programs would you favor?"

1. Depending on how questions are asked, framing bias can cause investors to communicate responses to questions about risk tolerance that are either unduly conservative or unduly aggressive. For example, when questions are worded in the "gain" frame, a risk-averse response is more likely. When questions are worded in the "loss" frame, risk-seeking behavior is the likely response.

2. The optimistic or pessimistic manner in which an investment or asset allocation recommendation is framed can affect people's willingness or lack of willingness to invest. Optimistically worded questions are more likely to garner affirmative responses, and optimistically worded answer choices are more likely to be selected than pessimistically phrased alternatives. Framing contexts are often arbitrary and uncorrelated and therefore shouldn't impact investors' judgments . . . but, they do.

3. *Narrow framing*, a subset of framing bias, can cause even long-term investors to obsess over short-term price fluctuations in a single industry or stock. This behavior works in concert with myopic loss aversion (see Chapter 19): The risk here is that by focusing only on short-term market fluctuations, excessive trading may be the result. This trading behavior has proven to be less than optimal for investors.

4. Framing and loss aversion can work together to explain excessive risk aversion. An investor who has incurred a net loss becomes likelier to select a riskier investment, whereas a net gainer feels predisposed toward less risky alternatives.

BOX 22.1   Framing Bias: Behaviors That Can Cause Investment Mistakes

As previously noted, people answer questions differently based on how the questions are framed—either positively or negatively. Notice that the preceding dilemma is positively framed, focusing on the expected number of "lives saved" in each scenario. When the question was framed in this manner, 72 percent of physicians chose "A," the safe-and-sure strategy: only 28 percent preferred to accept the risks inherent in option "B."

Another statistically identical population of physicians was posed the same basic question. In this trial, however, the scenario was framed negatively: "Imagine that the U.S. is preparing for the outbreak of an unusual Asian disease, which is expected to kill 600 people. Two alternative programs to combat the disease have been proposed. Assume that the exact scientific estimates of the consequences of the programs are as follows: If program C is adopted, 400 people will die. If program D is adopted, there is a one-third probability that nobody will die and a two-thirds probability that 600 people will die. Which of the two programs would you favor?"

As you can see, the two scenarios examine an identical dilemma. Saving 200 of 600 infected people, after all, implies that the remaining 400 of 600 are lost. However, when the question was framed negatively and physicians were concentrating on losses rather than gains, they voted in a dramatically different fashion. In the second trial, 22 percent of the physicians elected the conservative strategy ("400 will die"), and 72 percent felt more comfortable with the more volatile set of possible outcomes. This is almost a perfect, symmetric reversal of the breakdown that prevailed with positive framing.

Advisors need to be aware of how they ask questions. It does matter!

DIAGNOSTIC TESTING

These questions are designed to detect signs of cognitive bias stemming from framing. Instead of one test, however, this section contains two shorter tests designed to be taken in tandem. Would you respond differently to the same dilemma if its framing were altered? Answer the following items and find out.

Framing Bias Mini-Test 1

Question 1: Suppose that you have the opportunity to invest in a fund called MicroTrend. Over the past 10 years, MicroTrend has had an average annual return of 6 percent, with a standard deviation of 10 percent. So if MicroTrend continues to perform consistently, you can expect two-thirds of all returns to fall between –4 percent and 16 percent. How comfortable would you feel about investing in MicroTrend?

a. Comfortable.

b. Somewhat comfortable.

c. Uncomfortable.

Question 2: Suppose that you have the opportunity to invest in a fund called MicroTrend. Over the past 10 years, MicroTrend has had an average annual return of 6 percent, with a standard deviation of 10 percent. So if MicroTrend continues to perform consistently, you can expect 95 percent of all returns to fall between –14 percent and 26 percent. How comfortable would you feel about investing in MicroTrend?

a. Comfortable.

b. Somewhat comfortable.

c. Uncomfortable.

Framing Bias Mini-Test 2

Question 1: Suppose you are preparing for retirement. You need $50,000 annually to live comfortably; but you could take care of basic needs at about $40,000 and could even survive on a minimum of $30,000 if necessary. Further assume that there is no inflation. Now, imagine that you are choosing between two hypothetical investment options. Option 1 guarantees you an income of $40,000 per year—offering you a chance at a risk-free lifestyle. Option 2 offers you a 50 percent chance at $50,000 and a 50 percent chance at receiving $30,000 each year. Which option would you choose?

a. Option 1.

b. Option 2.

Question 2: Suppose you are preparing for retirement. You need $50,000 to live comfortably, but could take care of basic needs at about $40,000, and could even survive on a minimum of $30,000 if necessary. Further assume that there is no inflation. Now, imagine that you are choosing between two hypothetical investment options. Option 1 guarantees you enough income to cover your needs, but it will never provide you a comfortable lifestyle. With Option 2, you have the opportunity for a better lifestyle. With a probability of 50 percent, you might be limited to your bare minimum acceptable income. But, with a corresponding probability of 50 percent, you would enjoy the comfortable lifestyle you desire and an income of $50,000. Which option do you choose?

a. Option 1.
b. Option 2.

Test Results Analysis

Mini-Test 1: People who answer the second question differently from the first are likely subject to framing bias. If you are a practitioner and your client answers in this fashion, then you should remain mindful of the manner in which you present information to the client—because subjective details can have a dramatic impact. Typically, investors susceptible to framing bias choose the riskier strategy in Question 2.

Mini-Test 2: This test can't be interpreted too rigidly because lifestyle preferences are not black and white. However, people subject to framing bias will probably prefer an assured income in Question 1 and a riskier strategy in Question 2. This is because Question 1 is framed in a relatively positive fashion, focusing on the attribute "safe" lifestyle offered from the guarantee in Option 1. The framing in Question 2, however, is less upbeat; it reminds you that neither investment option offers you a reliably pleasurable standard of living. When framing intersects with loss aversion, this type of response pattern is especially likely to result.

ADVICE

Financial markets don't just reflect financial realities. Investors' beliefs, perceptions, and desires exert a tremendous influence on most instruments and indexes. When investor and advisor expectations regarding portfolio performance fail to complement one another, the advisory relationship can deteriorate quickly. So it's important that a practitioner accurately gauge a client's mind-set; this doesn't just mean listening carefully when the client answers important questions. Sometimes, the formulation of the question itself also matters because framing determines reference points and defines expectations. Each investor has the right to express his or her personal financial objectives and should expect investment plans to be created relative to these desires. The advisor needs to ask the right questions and to make sure to understand the client's answers. Assessing investor risk tolerance is a process wherein framing can be particularly influential; so practitioners and clients should make sure to carve out a precise, shared understanding of what constitutes risk and should decide exactly how much risk is tolerable. Ultimately, question framing can and does determine appropriate information elicitation.

This section offers advice on each of the specific investor errors outlined in Box 22.1.

Narrow Framing. Investors engaging in narrow framing may become preoccupied with short-term price oscillations in an isolated stock or industry, or they may favor certain asset classes while remaining oblivious to others. Advisors should encourage clients to keep the big picture in mind: overall wealth accumulation and long-term financial goals. Clients should work on building balanced asset allocations and focus on ensuring that those allocations are helping them meet their financial goals.

Framing and Loss Aversion. Investors who feel that they've been faring poorly will seek out risks, while those pleased with their recent returns tend to play it safe. Advisors should encourage clients to isolate from their ongoing decision making any references to gains or losses incurred in a prior period. Advisors should also try to ask questions that are less likely to elicit biased answers. Finally, an emphasis on education, diversification, and proper portfolio management can help to neutralize these biases.

Unintended Investment Choices Based on Incorrectly Framed Questions. Risk tolerance questionnaires are critical in assessing client goals and selecting appropriate investments. Advisors, therefore, need to be thoroughly familiar with question wording and need to understand—and remain alert for—biases that can be awakened when options are formulated in certain ways. Remember, clear communication ensures the success of the advisory relationship.

Positive and Negative Frames. We've observed the considerable influence that positive and negative framing can exert. The lesson for practitioners is to present facts and choices to clients as neutrally and uniformly as possible. This reduces the likelihood of a biased client response and should help you to help your investors achieve their financial goals.

CHAPTER **23**

Status Quo Bias

Whosoever desires constant success must change his conduct with the times.

— Niccolo Machiavelli (1532)

BIAS DESCRIPTION

Bias Name: Status Quo Bias
Bias Type: Emotional

General Description. *Status quo bias*, a term coined by William Samuelson and Richard Zeckhauser in 1988,[1] is an emotional bias that predisposes people facing an array of choice options to elect whatever option ratifies or extends the existing condition (i.e., the "status quo") in lieu of alternative options that might bring about change. In other words, status quo bias operates in people who prefer for things to stay relatively the same. The scientific principle of *inertia* bears a lot of intuitive similarity to status quo bias; it states that a body at rest shall remain at rest unless acted on by an outside force. A simple real-world example illustrates. In the early 1990s, the states of New Jersey and Pennsylvania reformed their insurance laws and offered new programs. Residents had the opportunity to select one of two automotive insurance packages: (1) a slightly more expensive option that granted policyholders extensive rights to sue one another following an accident, and (2) a less expensive option with more restricted litigation rights. Each insurance plan had a

248

roughly equivalent expected monetary value. In New Jersey, however, the more expensive plan was instituted as the default, and 70 percent of citizens "selected" it. In Pennsylvania, the opposite was true—residents would have to opt out of the default, less-expensive option in order to opt into the more expensive option. In the end, 80 percent of the residents "chose" to pay less.

Technical Description. Status quo bias refers to the finding that an option is more desirable if it is designated as the "status quo" than when it is not.[2] Status quo bias can contribute to the aforementioned inertia principle, but inertia is not as strong as status quo bias. *Inertia* means that an individual is relatively more reluctant to move away from some state identified as the status quo than from any alternative state not identified as the status quo. People less readily abandon a condition when they're told, "Things have always been this way." Status quo bias implies a more intense "anchoring effect."

Status quo bias is often discussed in tandem with other biases, namely *endowment bias* (see Chapter 13) and *loss aversion bias* (see Chapter 19). Status quo bias differs from these two in that it does not depend on framing changes in terms of losses and potential gains.[3] When loss aversion bias and status quo bias cross paths, it is probable that an investor, choosing between two investment alternatives, will stick to the status quo if it seems less likely to trigger a loss—even if the status quo also guarantees a lower return in the long run. Endowment bias implies that ownership of a piece of property imbues that property with some perceived, intangible added value—even if the property doesn't really increase the utility or wealth of the owner. By definition, endowment bias favors the status quo—people don't want to give up their endowments. Loss aversion bias, endowment bias, and status quo bias often combine; and the result is an overall tendency to prefer things to stay as they are, even if the calm comes at a cost.

PRACTICAL APPLICATION

Investors with inherited, concentrated stock positions often exhibit classic status quo bias. Take the case of a hypothetical grandson who hesitates to sell the bank stock he's inherited from his grandfather. Even though his portfolio is underdiversified and could benefit from such an adjustment, the grandson favors the status quo. A number of motives could be at work here. First, the investor may be unaware of the risk associated with holding an excessively concentrated equity position. He may not foresee that if the stock tumbles, he will suffer a significant decrease in wealth. Second, the grandson may experience a personal attachment to the stock, which carries an emotional connection to a previous generation. Third, he may hesitate to sell because of his aversion to the tax consequences, fees/commissions, or other transaction costs associated with unloading the stock.

The advice section of this chapter reviews some strategies for dealing with each of these potential objections—all of which could contribute to status-quo-biased behavior.

Implications for Investors. Box 23.1 reviews four investment mistakes that can stem from status quo bias.

RESEARCH REVIEW

Samuelson and Zeckhauser's paper, "Status Quo Bias in Decision Making,"[4] provides an excellent practical application of status quo bias. It examined a study in which subjects were told that they had each just inherited a large sum of money from an uncle and could choose to invest the money in any one of four possible portfolios. Each portfolio offered a different level of risk and a different rate of return. The scenario was repeated twice; in the first trial, subjects were given only the aforementioned information, with no indication of how the conferring uncle might have invested the money himself. In the second trial, the subjects were informed that the uncle, prior to his death, had invested the sum in a moderate-risk portfolio—one of the four options available to the subjects at present.

As you might expect, the moderate-risk portfolio proved far more popular in the second trial, when it was designated as the status quo, than in the first trial, when all options were equally "new."

This study reinforced the idea that investors tend to prefer upholding the present status. Advisors need to recognize this phenomenon and target their advice accordingly. Status quo bias is strong and, since it is an emotional bias, a lot of skill must be exercised in order to guide clients away from it.

1. Status quo bias can cause investors, by taking no action, to hold investments inappropriate to their own risk/return profiles. This can mean that investors take excessive risks or invest too conservatively.
2. Status quo bias can combine with loss aversion bias. In this scenario, an investor facing an opportunity to reallocate or alter an investment position may choose, instead, to maintain the status quo because the status quo offers the investor a lower probability of realizing a loss. This will be true even if, in the long run, the investor could achieve a higher return by electing an alternative path.
3. Status quo bias causes investors to hold securities with which they feel familiar or of which they are emotionally fond. This behavior can compromise financial goals, however, because a subjective comfort level with a security may not justify holding onto it despite poor performance.
4. Status quo bias can cause investors to hold securities, either inherited or purchased, because of an aversion to transaction costs associated with selling. This behavior can be hazardous to one's wealth because a commission or a tax is frequently a small price to pay for exiting a poorly performing investment or for properly allocating a portfolio.

BOX 23.1   Status Quo Bias: Behaviors That Can Cause Investment Mistakes

DIAGNOSTIC TESTING

These questions are designed to detect signs of cognitive errors stemming from status quo bias. To complete the test, select the answer choice that best characterizes your response to each item.

Status Quo Bias Test

Question 1: Which of the following would you choose?
   a. A 100 percent chance of winning $10,000.

b. An 80 percent chance of winning $13,000, with a 20 percent chance of winning nothing.

Question 2: Your investment portfolio contains a certain high-quality corporate bond. The bond has been providing income for you, and you are happy with it. Your financial advisor analyzes your bond holdings and recommends that you replace the corporate bond with a municipal bond of comparable quality, estimating that you will obtain a better return after capital gains taxes and fees. You aren't familiar with this municipal bond. What is your most likely response?

a. I will sell the corporate and purchase the municipal bond.

b. I will keep things as they are.

Question 3: Suppose that you have inherited a fully liquid investment in a South African gold mine from your eccentric Uncle Jim. You discuss the asset with your financial advisor, and she concludes that your portfolio already contains enough gold and commodities. More important, Uncle Jim's bequest isn't a diversified asset. Your advisor recommends selling it. What is your most likely course of action?

a. I will sell, as recommended by my financial advisor.

b. I will hold onto the gold mine interest, because I don't like to sell or modify things that people pass away and leave to me.

Test Results Analysis

Question 1: This question presents a classic intersection of status quo bias and loss aversion bias; most people exhibit a little of each and, accordingly, select "a." The unbiased option is "b," which has a higher expected value than "a."

Question 2: People who select "b" are likelier to suffer from status quo bias than people who select "a." Option "a" probably offers higher returns, but option "b" is, alas, the status quo.

Question 3. In this situation, most people would behave as depicted in "b," even when lacking any cogent rationale for holding the asset. Option "b" suggests status quo bias; "a" does not.

ADVICE

This section offers advice on each of the specific investor errors outlined in Box 23.1.

Holding Inappropriate Assets.   Education is essential to overcoming this aspect of status quo bias. As previously noted, status quo bias is exceptionally strong and difficult to overcome. Demonstrating the downside risks associated with holding inappropriate assets is often an effective tactic and may motivate people to change their behavior. Another persuasive approach is to demonstrate, based on a single stock position, what could happen to overall wealth levels if the market goes south and then to explicitly link wealth changes with probable lifestyle changes.

Status Quo Bias and Loss Aversion Bias.   Doing nothing is much easier than making a decision. This is especially true when a decision might bring about emotional pain, for example, the decision to sell a losing investment may register the impact of a loss. Sometimes, however, inaction can compromise long-run returns. When clients hesitate to implement changes, advisors should carefully analyze whether adhering to the status quo will affect attainment of financial goals. If you discover that your client's biased behavior will indeed impact his or her wealth down the road, then education is critical. Explain to clients the common cognitive and emotional oversights they may be committing and demonstrate the benefits of decisive action.

Status Quo Bias and Emotional Attachment.   Emotions are perhaps the least legitimate concerns in asset management. When financial goals are in jeopardy, it can be too risky to sit back and adhere to an affective whim. Advisors need to demonstrate how emotions need to be managed. "Emotional intelligence," a well-publicized topic in popular psychology, offers many insights to this end. Do a little reading, and you may find yourself better equipped to help your clients work through their emotional attachments.

Status Quo Bias and Fear of Transaction Costs.   Taxes and fees are legitimate concerns when it comes to altering an allocation status quo. However, more often than not, these concerns pale in comparison to the other potential implications of holding, or exiting, a poorly performing security. If you are an advisor, run through some financial calculations with your client. Then, be ready to be persuasive in communicating the advantages of diversification and proper asset allocation.

Case Studies

CHAPTER 24

Case Studies

Things do not change; we change.

—Henry David Thoreau

Congratulations! If you've gotten this far in the book, you should have developed your practical understanding of behavioral finance micro along the way. In this chapter, we'll draw on all our discussions so far regarding specific behavioral biases and examine three fictional advisor-client case studies. Although each situation will inspire a distinct diagnosis and game plan, all three discussions will focus on the same fundamental questions:

1. How might the client's biases affect the asset allocation decision?
2. Should the advisor try to moderate the impact of these biases or adapt to them?
3. What is the *best practical allocation* for each investor?

Before you begin this chapter, it is recommended you read Chapter 3 if you have not already done so. Chapter 3 provides a good overview of the methodology that underlies these case studies.

All three case studies will assume the same format, which is intended to simulate the approach that practitioners take with clients:

1. An introductory description of the case.
2. Identification of behavioral finance biases.

3. Likely effects of biases in making asset allocation decisions.
4. Decision to moderate or adapt to each bias.
5. The recommended behaviorally adjusted asset allocation—best practical allocation.

For each case study, assume that the year is 2001. Capital markets have cleared their highs (for stocks) and lows (for bonds), but they haven't yet reached the extremes of that market cycle. For simplicity's sake, all allocations will be divided between stocks, bonds, and cash.

Obviously, every advisory relationship is unique, and there is no absolute, definitive way to diagnose and counteract client biases. Moreover, all possible investor types are not presented here. As an advisor, you should read this chapter while keeping in mind how you might handle similar situations in your own practice. You should focus most on applying the methodological *process*—diagnosis, effects assessment, response determination, best practical allocation—outlined.

CASE A: MRS. ADIRONDACK

Mrs. Adirondack (hereafter "Mrs. A") is a single, 70-year-old retiree living a modest lifestyle. Her only income is generated by her investment portfolio, which totals $1 million. Mrs. A was referred to you by your Aunt Sally's friend Mabel, and you've known her for about three years. Your advisory relationship reveals that Mrs. A's primary investment goal is for her assets to sufficiently support her for the rest of her life. She does not, under any circumstances, want to lose money, because she recalls that her relatives lost money in the crash of 1929. You have noticed that Mrs. A is also stubborn and inflexible in her thinking, especially on the topic of financial markets.

Analysis

One day, you reflect on your relationship with Mrs. A and realize that, despite your recommendations to the contrary, she has never once altered her portfolio. Mrs. A owns only municipal and government bonds, and you are concerned that inflation will eventually cause her to outlive her assets. You suspect her discomfort at the prospect of re-allocating her portfolio is due to one or more behavioral biases, and you ask Mrs. A if she is willing to take a 30-minute diagnostic test to examine her investor personality. Mrs. A refuses, but she ultimately agrees to a 10-minute test. To save time, you flip through this book and administer only the questions pertaining to the biases that you most suspect Mrs. A displays: loss aversion, anchoring, and status quo. Mrs. A's responses confirm your instincts. She demonstrates:

■ *Loss aversion bia*s (the tendency to feel the pain of losses more acutely than the pleasure of gains).
■ *Anchoring and adjustment bias* (the tendency to automatically rely on present market levels as neutral benchmarks for predicting future market trends).
■ *Status quo bias* (the desire to keep things as they are).

As part of your allocation review, you also administer a risk tolerance questionnaire to Mrs. A. Her score helps you generate a mean-variance optimized portfolio recommendation: 70 percent bonds, 20 percent stocks, 10 percent cash. So, now that you know Mrs. A can theoretically tolerate a riskier portfolio than the one she carries, you become more convinced than ever that behavioral biases are interfering. Your job is now to answer these three questions:

1. What effect do Mrs. A's biases have on the asset allocation decision?
2. Should you moderate or adapt to her biases?
3. What is the best practical allocation for Mrs. A?

Effects of Biases

Mrs. Adirondack's biases are very consistent and lead to a clear allocation preference. Because Mrs. A does not tolerate risk (loss aversion) and does not like change (status quo), she would naturally prefer the safe, secure asset allocation (100 percent bonds) that she now possesses. Also, since the market has dropped recently, Mrs. A will likely make faulty conclusions regarding current and expected prices (anchoring and adjustment) and will therefore feel wary of any exposure to equities. Thus, if you, as her advisor, presented her with a recommended allocation of 100 percent bonds, she would be likely to immediately agree to that recommendation. However, you need to bear in mind Mrs. A's bias toward such an allocation.

Moderate or Adapt?

You're concerned that Mrs. A might outlive her assets if she adheres to her present allocation, and your financial planning software confirms your fears. Mrs. A's level of wealth, while adequate at present, isn't substantial enough to afford her the (dubious) luxury of an unbalanced allocation of funds in the long run. So, if you *adapt* to her biases—consent to stick with 100 percent bonds—then Mrs. A's only critical, financial goal becomes jeopardized. However, Mrs. A's biases are principally emotional (status quo, loss aversion) and typically cannot be corrected with advice and information. This will complicate things if you attempt to *moderate* her biases.

Now that you know that Mrs. A's wealth level isn't excessive and that her biases are principally emotional, you have all the information that you need in order to "plot" her case on the chart in Figure 24.1. As you can see, Mrs. A's case yields a blended recommendation: you should *moderate and adapt* to her biases.

This course of action, which might appear contradictory, is really

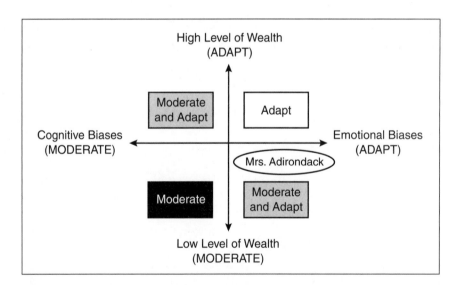

FIGURE 24.1 Illustration of Mrs. Adirondack's Case Study Information
Reprinted with permission by the Financial Planning Association, *Journal of Financial Planning*, March 2005, Pompian and Longo, "Incorporating Behavioral Finance into Your Practice." For more information on the Financial Planning Association, please visit www.fpanet.org or call 1-800-322-4237.

more about compromise. A complete moderation of Mrs. A's biases would imply a mean-variance optimized breakdown: 70 percent bonds, 20 percent equities, 10 percent cash. A complete adaptation, meanwhile, would preserve the allocation of 100 percent bonds. *Moderating and adapting* means negotiating some middle ground. Taking into consideration Mrs. A's wealth level and bias profile, you now begin to draft a best practical allocation.

Best Practical Allocation Decision

You decide that an allocation of *75 percent bonds, 15 percent stocks, and 10 percent cash* would approximate the mean-variance optimizer while also offering some concessions to Mrs. A's conservatism. The first thing you do is to check your financial planning software to ensure that Mrs. A, if she adopts this allocation, will not outlive her money. Indeed, the software calculates that the new allocation suffices. Next, you run your behaviorally modified portfolio through the *Behavioral Asset Allocation Adjustment Factor Model* (BAAAF) and verify that the adjustment factor doesn't exceed 20 percent (see Chapter 3 for guidelines). Indeed, you've only corrected Mrs. A's portfolio by 10 percent, so you are happy with that result. You present your recommendation to Mrs. Adirondack, and you administer a continuing program of investor education on the risk of outliving one's assets. (See Table 24.1.)

TABLE 24.1 Behavioral Asset Allocation Adjustment Factor Model Output for Mrs. Adirondack

	Mean-Variance Output Recommendation	Behaviorally Adjusted Allocation Recommendation	Variance	Change in Percent (Absolute Value)	Change in Percent (Weighted Value)
Equities	20	15	5	25%	5%
Fixed income	70	75	−5	7%	5%
Cash	10	10	0	0%	0%
	100	100	Bias Adjustment Factor =		10%

Reprinted with permission by the Financial Planning Association, *Journal of Financial Planning*, March 2005, Pompian and Longo, "Incorporating Behavioral Finance into Your Practice." For more information on the Financial Planning Association, please visit www.fpanet.org or call 1-800-322-4237.

CASE B: MR. BOULDER

Mr. Boulder (hereafter "Mr. B") is a single 50-year-old, hard-charging pharmaceutical executive earning $250,000 per year. He lives extravagantly and occasionally overspends, but he has saved approximately $1.5 million. Mr. B had a mild heart attack last year but now has a clean bill of health. His primary financial goal is to retire comfortably at 65 and to donate $3 million to his alma mater (he cannot obtain adequate life insurance to cover the gift). You have been working with Mr. Boulder for less than a year. You've drafted a financial plan but have yet to modify Mr. B's preexisting allocation (nearly 100 percent equities). However, you have developed a good working relationship with Mr. B, who listens intently and seems receptive to your recommendations. You believe that Mr. Boulder is a well-grounded person and is self-aware, but you also believe that he has some behavioral issues to deal with.

Analysis

At the outset of your relationship, you outlined a more conservative, mean-variance optimized allocation (see Table 24.2) as an objective in Mr. B's financial plan; however, you are worried that Mr. B may not fully buy into the idea. Your concern is that a severe downward market fluctuation may cut into Mr. B's daily living expenses, including possible

TABLE 24.2 Behavioral Asset Allocation Adjustment Factor Model Output for Mr. Boulder

	Mean-Variance Output Recommendation	Behaviorally Adjusted Allocation Recommendation	Variance	Change in Percent (Absolute Value)	Change in Percent (Weighted Value)
Equities	70	75	−5	7%	5%
Fixed income	25	15	10	40%	10%
Cash	5	10	−5	100%	5%
	100	100	Bias Adjustment Factor =		20%

Reprinted with permission by the Financial Planning Association, *Journal of Financial Planning*, March 2005, Pompian and Longo, "Incorporating Behavioral Finance into Your Practice." For more information on the Financial Planning Association, please visit www.fpanet.org or call 1-800-322-4237.

health expenses. Your financial planning software tells you that with a less aggressive portfolio, Mr. B can still meet his primary financial objectives. However, Mr. B thinks that he is a very good investor, and you are worried that such a change might cause him to regret not being more aggressive. He agrees to complete a comprehensive behavioral bias questionnaire, and his results show susceptibility to:

- *Overconfidence bias* (the tendency to overestimate one's investment savvy).
- *Regret aversion bias* (the tendency to avoid making a decision for fear that the decision may cause regret later on).
- *Self-control bias* (the tendency to spend today rather than save for tomorrow).

The mean-variance optimized allocation you initially calculated for Mr. B was 70 percent stocks, 25 percent bonds, 5 percent cash—Mr. B's risk tolerance better suits a more balanced portfolio. You also have obtained confirmation of the specific behavioral biases that are probably causing the distortion in Mr. B's portfolio. Your job is now to answer these questions:

1. What effect do Mr. B's biases have on the asset allocation decision?
2. Should you moderate or adapt to his biases?
3. What is the best practical allocation for Mr. B?

Effect of Biases

Mr. Boulder's biases clearly incline him toward an allocation dominated by equities. His overconfidence raises his comfort level with stocks, perhaps excessively. He is also likely to regret missing out on any equities surge that he isn't in a position to fully exploit. But Mr. B has a high need for current income to fuel his "spend today" mentality (self-control bias). Therefore, even though his biases favor equity over fixed income, they also imply a need for fixed-income investments: In the event of a market downturn, Mr. B might have to rely on bonds to supplement his lifestyle.

Moderate or Adapt?

Considering his overall level of wealth, Mr. Boulder does not run a serious standard-of-living risk with his present allocation, even in the event of a major market downturn, given his high level of salary. His behavioral biases are also principally emotional (regret aversion, self-control). Referring to the diagram in Figure 24.2, you decide to *adapt* your recommendation.

It's important to note that adapting doesn't mean setting aside all behavioral considerations. You'll create a portfolio more aggressive than the mean-variance optimizer suggests, and this will help Mr. B to adhere comfortably to his allocation. However, at the same time, you'll run a cash flow analysis to ensure that your plan won't leave Mr. B's living expenses at risk if the market turns sour. You will also advise him to keep a comfortable cash reserve.

Best Practical Allocation Decision

In Table 24.2 recall that Mr. B's mean-variance-optimized allocation was 70 percent stocks, 25 percent bonds, 5 percent cash. Using guidelines presented in Chapter 3, you devise a best practical allocation of *75 percent*

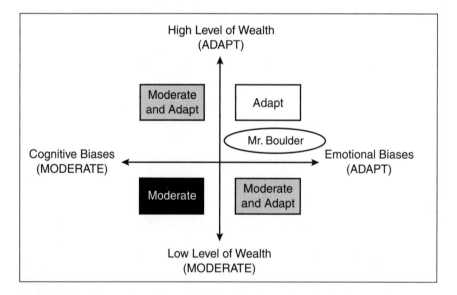

FIGURE 24.2 Illustration of Mr. Boulder's Case Study Information
Reprinted with permission by the Financial Planning Association, *Journal of Financial Planning*, March 2005, Pompian and Longo, "Incorporating Behavioral Finance into Your Practice." For more information on the Financial Planning Association, please visit www.fpanet.org or call 1-800-322-4237.

stocks, 15 percent bonds, 10 percent cash. Your financial planning software verifies that the new allocation should offer adequate living funds for Mr. B, even if the market falls. In accordance with the *Behavioral Asset Allocation Adjustment Factor Model*, you also confirm that your adjustment hasn't exceeded 20 percent (see Chapter 3 for guidelines). Satisfied, you present your recommendation to Mr. B, explaining how you arrived at that particular allocation.

CASE C: THE CATSKILL FAMILY

The Catskill family includes a financially well-informed couple, both aged 36, and two children aged 4 and 6. The family is financially sound but suffered badly during the tech meltdown in 2000. The couple's total income is $120,000, which, like the family itself, is not expected to grow significantly. The Catskills have managed to save $150,000, which they hope might serve as a financial foundation from which to send their children to college and, later, to fund a comfortable retirement. You have been working with the Catskills for five years. You update a financial plan for them annually and recommend an asset allocation. Last year, you suggested the allocation that the mean-variance optimizer generated: 70 percent equities, 25 percent bonds, 5 percent cash. At that time, the Catskills, however, chose to be more aggressive. This year, when you recommended the same mean-variance optimized allocation, the couple actually desired a more conservative position, requesting 50 percent equities, 45 percent bonds, 5 percent cash.

Analysis

You have noticed this pattern before and believe that the Catskills are trend followers. Susceptible to short-lived market fads, the Catskills also tend to move in and out of asset classes in an effort to control their financial destiny. Predictably, however, they have not been too successful with their investments. This couple is typically not receptive when you advise them to "stay the course." Currently, they have the idea that they should be in risk-averse investments (bonds), which have come into fashion following the tech meltdown. You decide to administer a behavioral bias test (for simplicity's sake, imagine that the Catskills complete the test jointly and share the same behavioral profile). You find that the Catskills suffer from:

■ *Illusion of control bias* (the superstition that they can control, or at least influence, outcomes beyond their control).

■ *Recency bias* (mentally emphasizing more recent events unduly with respect to less recent events).

■ *Availability bias* (the tendency to believe that what is easily recalled is more likely to happen).

As stated, the Catskills' mean-variance optimized portfolio recommendation is 70 percent stocks, 25 percent bonds, and 5 percent cash. Given the biases they exhibit, you consider these three questions:

1. What effect do the Catskills' biases have on the asset allocation decision?
2. Should you moderate or adapt to their biases?
3. What is the best practical allocation for the Catskills?

Effect of Biases

The observed combination of biases suggests a clear allocation preference. Availability bias and recency bias leave the Catskills preoccupied, in this case, with the demise of the past decade's tech equity bubble. The trauma they still associate with that event prejudices them toward more conservative investments. Bonds also suit the Catskills' illusions of control. The couple perceives that they will fare better with more direct command of their portfolio and that fixed-income securities are handier and more predictable than equities. So, the bias questionnaire has provided you with insight on why the Catskills have swung toward such a conservative allocation. However, the situation still merits further consideration.

Moderate or Adapt?

Illusion of control bias, recency bias, and availability bias are all cognitive biases—suggesting that they can be moderated with a campaign of information. Furthermore, your financial planning software suggests that an insufficient equity allocation, given the Catskills' modest level of wealth, might fail to cover college and retirement. Thinking along the lines of the chart in Figure 24.3, you decide to *moderate* the Catskills' biases, with the objective of increasing their equities allocation.

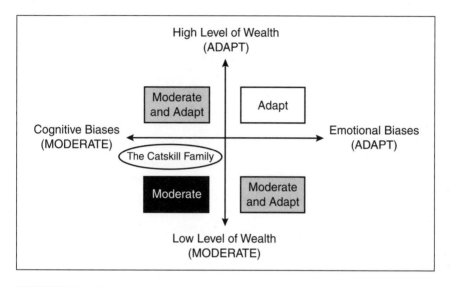

FIGURE 24.3 Illustration of Catskill Family Case Study Information
Reprinted with permission by the Financial Planning Association, *Journal of Financial Planning*, March 2005, Pompian and Longo, "Incorporating Behavioral Finance into Your Practice." For more information on the Financial Planning Association, please visit www.fpanet.org or call 1-800-322-4237.

Best Practical Allocation Decision

The mean-variance optimizer's recommended allocation was 70 percent stocks, 25 percent bonds, 5 percent cash. The Catskills had previously contemplated dropping their equities allocation to 50 percent, but you realized that they were probably unwittingly influenced by cognitive biases when they made this request. You also calculated that their conservative, specified allocation would present a standard-of-living risk. Because the Catskills' biases can perhaps be curbed by an educational discussion, and because you don't want to jeopardize their long-term financial goals, you stand firm and recommend the mean-variance optimized output: *70 percent stocks, 25 percent bonds, 5 percent cash*. Because you haven't adapted this allocation by way of any behavioral adjustments, the *Behavioral Asset Allocation Adjustment Factor Model* is not required.

SUMMARY

Figure 24.4 illustrates the outcomes of the three case studies, plotted on a common set of axes for easy reference.

As an advisor, you may encounter cases resembling any or all of the scenarios entertained here. Or you may happen on less-common cocktails of cognitive and emotional biases. Whatever scenario you encounter, it is hoped that this chapter laid out a useful template methodology that you can expand and tailor in response to almost any client situation. In general, bias type determines the feasibility of and wealth levels determine the exigency of moderating (versus adapting to) a client. Sometimes, the mean-variance output will be correct; other times the use of the *Behavioral Asset Allocation Adjustment Factor Model* is the appropriate course of action.

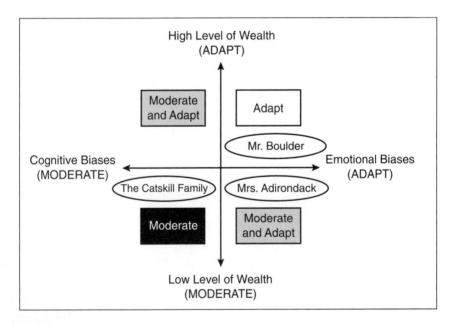

FIGURE 24.4 Illustration of Outcomes of Individual Investor Case Studies
Reprinted with permission by the Financial Planning Association, *Journal of Financial Planning*, March 2005, Pompian and Longo, "Incorporating Behavioral Finance into Your Practice." For more information on the Financial Planning Association, please visit www.fpanet.org or call 1-800-322-4237.

part Four

Special Topics in Practical Application of Behavioral Finance

Gender, Personality Type, and Investor Behavior

No theory of the universe can be satisfactory which does not adequately account for the phenomena of life, especially in that richest form which finds expression in human personality.

—B. H. Streeter

In the Fall 2004 *Journal of Wealth Management,* John Longo and I published a paper entitled "A New Paradigm for Practical Application of Behavioral Finance: Creating Investment Programs Based on Personality Type and Gender to Produce Better Investment Outcomes."[1] This chapter will revisit crucial elements of that paper, which asks: "Do gender and personality type influence investor susceptibility to the biases identified in the behavioral finance literature? If so, can this information benefit wealth managers and clients?"

In the preface of this book, I recalled that this paper and these questions were the genesis of my own professional interest in behavioral finance. Basically, as a wealth management advisor, I had begun to suspect a link between personality type and investment behavior. To 100 random investors of different ages and genders, John and I administered two tests: (1) a detailed Myers-Briggs Type Indicator® personality assessment, and (2) a behavioral finance bias questionnaire. Our results showed some statistically significant links between personality type, gender, and investor behavior. What follows is an abbreviated version of the paper, with my comments interspersed throughout the text.

BACKGROUND

Much of economic and financial theory is based on the assumption that individuals act perfectly rationally and appraise all available information when making economic decisions. Specifically, investors should gravitate toward the most desirable combination of expected return and risk—located at the tangency point along the investor's personal indifference curve—which represents maximum utility given available investment opportunities. Recently, however, numerous papers have called into question economic theory's most basic assumption. Having documented many examples of irrational behavior and repeated errors in judgment, behavioral finance has prompted disillusionment with *Homo economicus*, or "rational economic man." No longer can advisors take for granted an investor's ability to execute the elegant Markowitz portfolio selection model.

In most cases, investors are unaware of their predisposition for error. And, more often than not, an irrational investor is a dissatisfied investor, because biases usually undermine financial goals. If investors come to understand themselves better and attempt to correct these biases, they can do what so many have found so difficult: adhere to a disciplined investment plan.

Psychographic Models Used in Behavioral Finance

Psychographic models classify individuals according to certain characteristics, tendencies, or behaviors. We believe that by segmenting individuals by personality type and gender and correlating these variables with specific investor biases, we can lay the groundwork for applying many of the biases that behavioral finance literature explores (e.g., Khaneman and Tversky[2]). If certain groups of investors prove susceptible to certain biases, then practitioners can recognize behavioral tendencies before investment decisions are made and, likely, produce better investment outcomes.

Two studies—Barnewall,[3] and Bailard, Biehl, and Kaiser (BB&K)[4]— apply useful models of investor psychographics. However, both studies predate significant findings in the behavioral finance literature, including important biases discovered in recent years. Further, we believe that the models Barnewall and BB&K applied cannot describe a wide range of investors; the psychographic model used in our study, the Myers-Briggs Type Indicator® (MBTI), is superior.

The Barnewall model—one of the first and most used—distinguished investors by their passivity or activity in creating wealth.[5] Although it usefully described certain individual investors, it has crucial limitations. Investors aren't just differentiable according to how they've arrived at their wealth. They are, after all, human beings and possess unique, complicated, intellectual and emotional attribute arrays. Moreover, investors are gendered. It might seem regressive to suggest that gender identity preordains financial decision making, and we certainly don't go that far. However, our data does strongly insinuate that when it comes to investing, men and women reason differently. Barnewall didn't take any of these factors into account. The modern investment era demands a better model.

The BB&K model featured some of the principles of the Barnewall model; but, by classifying investor personalities according to level of confidence and method of action, it introduced additional segmentation.[6] Like the Barnewall model, the BB&K model is useful in working with certain clients and may explain in general terms why a person is predisposed to certain investor behaviors. However, the BB&K model neither scientifically described personality type nor links investor behaviors with recently identified investor biases, limiting its utility. As noted, neither study had the benefit of the behavioral finance literature that informs this paper.

Gender and Behavioral Finance

Several studies have examined the link between gender and behavioral finance biases; of these, Barber and Odean[7] is perhaps the most important and comprehensive. The study concluded that men are more subject than women are to the overconfidence bias reflected in trading behavior. The researchers found that, over a six-year period, men on average traded 45 percent more than women. And single men on average traded 67 percent more than single women.

The present study is still more comprehensive, gender testing for many of the other behavioral biases documented in the behavioral finance literature. The data suggest that men and women are markedly different in their susceptibility to behavioral biases. While Barnewall, BB&K, and Barber and Odean have done important work—constructing a founding paradigm for the hands-on deployment of behavioral finance insights—it's time to take the next step.

A New Paradigm for Practical Application of Behavioral Finance: Creating Investment Programs Based on Personality Type and Gender to Produce Better Investment Outcomes

We believe the next phase in the practical application of behavioral finance is to correlate established investor biases with the psychographic and gender profiles of specific investors, as planning with these correlations in mind would yield better investment outcomes. Anticipating this new phase, we try to ascertain if specific gender or personality profiles correlate with susceptibility to any of the biases identified in behavioral finance literature. If so, could investors and advisors benefit from recognizing such a correlation? By tabulating and cross-referencing both an MBTI and a behavioral finance bias questionnaire, we hope to initiate a new paradigm for the practical application of behavioral finance. Table 25.1 summarizes the similarities and differences between the "old [application] paradigm," summarized thus far, and the "new paradigm" our work aims to create.

Myers-Briggs Type Indicator® and Behavioral Bias Testing

Developed and refined over more than 50 years, the MBTI instrument test is the most popular psychographic model in industry use today. Approximately 2 million people take the MBTI each year, and the MBTI is considered the most widely used personality test in history. The MBTI describes 16 personality types based on an assessment of four aspects of human personality:

1. How one interacts with the world and where one directs one's energy (Extraverted or Introverted—E vs. I).
2. What kind of information one naturally notices (Sensing or Intuitive—S vs. N).
3. How one makes decisions (Thinking or Feeling—T vs. F).
4. Whether one prefers to live in a structured or a spontaneous way (Judging or Perceiving—J vs. P).

TABLE 25.1 Paradigms in the Practical Application of Behavioral Finance

Measure	Old Paradigm	New Paradigm
Correlate behavioral finance biases with psychographic measures	No	Yes
Number of aspects of personality tested	2 or 4	8
Rigorous test to determine personality type	No	Yes
Statistical testing to identify and measure biases	Limited	Yes
Gender-based bias testing	Limited	Yes

One's personality type can be designated by a four-letter classification. For example, an introverted, sensing, thinking, judging person is labeled an ISTJ. The sixteen personality types are ISTJ, ISFJ, INFJ, INTJ, ISTP, ISFP, INFP, INTP, ESTP, ESFP, ENFP, ENTP, ESTJ, ESFJ, ENFJ, and ENTJ.

Our questionnaire drew largely on the work of Kahneman and Riepe.[8] In their paper "Aspects of Investor Psychology: Beliefs, Preferences, and Biases Investment Advisors Should Know About," they categorized behavioral biases as biases of judgment, errors of preference, and living with the consequences of decisions. By way of review, *biases of judgment* include overconfidence, optimism, hindsight, and overreaction to chance events. *Errors of preference* include nonlinear weighting of probabilities; people value changes, not states; value of gains and losses function; the shape and attractiveness of gambles; purchase price as a reference point; narrow framing; repeated gambles and risk policies; and short and long views. *Living with the consequences of decisions* includes regrets of errors and omissions and regret and risk taking.

Study Description and Key Results

During the summer of 2002, one hundred investors were administered an MBTI personality test and a behavioral finance bias questionnaire. All responses were anonymous, but participants were requested to list their gender (98 percent populated) and age range (95 percent populated). We first evaluated each respondent's personality type and then tabulated answers to investor bias questions. We answered the question, "Did respondents of opposing personality extremes (and male and female respondents) reveal different investor biases?" For example, did Extroverts respond to a particular question differently from Introverts?

The study yielded many statistically significant insights. Broadly, our findings showed that many personality types and both genders are differentially disposed to numerous behavioral finance biases. Figure 25.1, "Type and Gender-Based Risk Tolerance Scales," illustrates the most widely applicable results of our study. These easy-to-use continuums were developed after determining that susceptibility to the *over-*

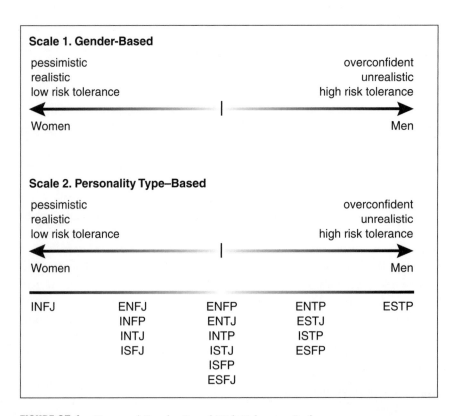

FIGURE 25.1   Type and Gender-Based Risk Tolerance Scales

confidence and *optimism* biases distinguishes both personality type and gender. Specifically, a male ESTP subtype is considered the most-risk-tolerant investor, while a female INFJ is considered the least-risk-tolerant.

These results suggest many useful applications. Chiefly, personality type and gender can be used to create an investment program that will compensate for behavioral biases. For example, introverted, intuitive, feeling, judging people (INFJs) and women tolerate significantly less risk than their type and gender counterparts. A conservative investment plan should be crafted for these individuals—even if a standard risk tolerance questionnaire indicates otherwise—so that this investor class can weather market movements over the long term.

PUTTING IT ALL TOGETHER: IMPLICATIONS FOR PRACTITIONERS

Investment advisors are urged to consider client gender and personality type in assessing risk tolerance prior to executing an investment program. We suggest this four-step method:

Step One: Ask your client to take a personality type test. Completing and evaluating a lengthy MBTI test may not be an option for some advisors and their clients. Conveniently, there are many comprehensive yet easily administered personality tests available. Table 25.2 presents an abbreviated identification methodology adapted from Paul Tieger's 1995 book *Do What You Are: Discover the Perfect Career for You through the Secrets of Personality Type.*[9]

Step Two: Evaluate responses to determine personality type. In subcategories where responses are mixed, just pick whichever side seems to predominate. Remember, too, that each component trait should be envisioned less as a determination between binary outcomes ("you're introverted *or* extraverted") and more as a subsidiary continuum on which preferences can be plotted ("you're *more* introverted than extraverted").

Step Three: Assess risk tolerance using the "Type and Gender-Based Risk Tolerance Scales." Using the scales in Figure 25.1, assess the client. Consider incorporating other aspects of the client's profile into the assessment, such as investor-life-cycle-stage, and other often-used

TABLE 25.2   Simplified Personality Assessment

Extroverts	Introverts
Like being the center of attention	Avoid being the center of attention
Talk more than listen	Listen more than talk
Communicate with enthusiasm	Keep their enthusiasm to themselves

Circle E	or	I

Sensors	Intuitives
Trust what is certain and concrete	Trust inspiration and inference
Value realism and common sense	Value imagination and innovation
Tend to be specific and literal; give detailed descriptions	Tend to be general and figurative; use metaphors and analogies

Circle: S	or	N

Thinkers	Feelers
Step back; apply impersonal analysis to problems.	Step forward; consider effect of actions on others
Value logic, justice, and fairness; one standard for all	Value empathy and harmony; see the exception to the rule
Naturally see flaws and tend to be critical	Naturally like to please others; show appreciation easily

Circle: T	or	F

Judgers	Perceivers
Are happiest after decisions are made	Are happiest leaving their options open
Have a work ethic; work first, then play	Have a play ethic; play first, then work
Prefer to know what they are getting into	Like adapting to new situations

Circle: J	or	P

qualitative measures. Quantitative risk tolerance measures can also be helpful, but they should serve as cross-verifying tools, not isolated indicators (a misguided practice that prevails today).

Step Four: Execute investment program. Once a final assessment has been made from Step 3, the advisor can create an asset allocation and execute an investment program designed to mitigate behavioral biases. Table 25.3 depicts a broad asset allocation framework based on the following assumptions and empirical findings from our study:

1. Women are 33 percent more risk averse than men.
2. The most risk-tolerant gender/personality combination should be 100 percent in equity-based investments.
3. The most risk-averse gender/personality combination should be 100 percent in fixed income–based investments.
4. There is an equal distance between personality clusters (e.g., the distance between the ENFJ . . . ISJF custer is equal to the distance between the ENIP . . . ESFP cluster). Clusters are partitioned by shading in Table 25.3.

Suggestions for Further Research

Given our sample of one hundred individuals, we could not examine—with any degree of statistical significance—behavioral biases for each of the 16 personality types delineated by the MBTI. A research team would need more than one thousand completed questionnaires and personality tests to produce results of significant statistical power. Perhaps a financial institution or other large organization has the resources and incentive to conduct such a large-scale test.

Examining how an individual's responses change over time represents a second avenue for future research. Researchers might ask, "Does age, income, previous investment outcomes, or bull and bear market backdrops influence investor biases; or are biases rooted, relatively static personality traits?" Additionally, researchers might examine whether investor types (e.g., individuals, institutions, growth managers, value managers, small cap managers, fixed-income managers, and international managers) are, like personality types, differentially susceptible to biases.

Note: In terms of additional statistically significant results from our study, beyond those related to the overconfidence and optimism biases, we found the following: Intuitives are more likely to cut losses right away, while Sensing types are more likely to buy and hold and are twice as risk averse as Intuitives are; Introverts are more subject to errors of preference and care about the path of their wealth (i.e., dislike market

TABLE 25.3 Gender-Based and Personality-Based Asset Allocation Model

Personality Type	Suggested Male Asset Allocation	Suggested Female Asset Allocation
INFJ	33.3% equity, 66.6% fixed income	1005 fixed income
ENFJ	50% equity, 50% fixed income	16.6% equity, 83.3% fixed income
INFP	50% equity, 50% fixed income	16.6% equity, 83.3% fixed income
INTJ	50% equity, 50% fixed income	16.6% equity, 83.3% fixed income
ISFJ	50% equity, 50% fixed income	16.6% equity, 83.3% fixed income
ENFP	66.6% equity, 33.3% fixed income	33.3% equity, 66.6% fixed income
ENTJ	66.6% equity, 33.3% fixed income	33.3% equity, 66.6% fixed income
INTP	66.6% equity, 33.3% fixed income	33.3% equity, 66.6% fixed income
ISTJ	66.6% equity, 33.3% fixed income	33.3% equity, 66.6% fixed income
ISFP	66.6% equity, 33.3% fixed income	33.3% equity, 66.6% fixed income
ESFJ	66.6% equity, 33.3% fixed income	33.3% equity, 66.6% fixed income
ENTP	83.3% equity, 16.6% fixed income	50% equity, 50% fixed income
ESTJ	83.3% equity, 16.6% fixed income	50% equity, 50% fixed income
ISTP	83.3% equity, 16.6% fixed income	50% equity, 50% fixed income
ESFP	83.3% equity, 16.6% fixed income	50% equity, 50% fixed income
ESTP	100% equity	66.6% equity, 33.3% fixed income

Reprinted with permission from Institutional Investor, Inc. It originally appeared in the Fall 2004 issue of *Journal of Wealth Management*. It is illegal to make unauthorized copies. For more information please visit www.iijournals.com. All rights reserved.

drawdowns) to a greater extent than Extraverts do; Judging types are one-third more risk averse than Perceiving types are; women are more susceptible to the hot-hand fallacy than men are; men look at their portfolios more often than women do; men are more likely to cut losses immediately, whereas women are more likely to buy and hold; women are one-third more risk averse than men are.

CHAPTER 26

Investor Personality Types

If we don't see a failure as a challenge to modify our approach, but rather as a problem with ourselves as a personality defect, we will immediately feel overwhelmed.

—Anthony Robbins

By now, we've looked at investor behavioral classifications ranging from the foundational Bailard, Biehl, and Kaiser (BB&K) and Barnewall (Chapter 2) to the elaborate Myers-Briggs (Chapter 25). We will briefly review some of these previous discussions before turning toward the main focus of this chapter, *investor personality types*. I will introduce a scheme of my own design that (I hope) offers the same detailed, descriptive flexibility as the Myers-Briggs Type Indicator®. The investor personality test can be used for a quick overview of the type of investor your client is. If you don't have the time or inclination to go through the more elaborate measures outlined in this book, this investor personality section can be used.

REVIEW: THE FIRST INVESTOR TYPOLOGIES

Bailard, Biehl, and Kaiser Five-Way Model

The BB&K model classified investor personalities along two axes: *level of confidence* (vertical axis) and *method of action* (horizontal axis). Thomas

Bailard, David Biehl, and Ronald Kaiser provide a graphic representation of their model (Figure 26.1). The first subclassification that the model incorporates deals with how confidently an investor approaches life in general—including issues unrelated to money. When negotiating a wide variety of life choices, are individuals rigidly self-assured, or do they suffer from misgivings and anxiety? The second element of the BB&K model asks whether investors are methodical, careful, and analytical in their approach to life or whether they are emotional, intuitive, and impetuous. These two elements can be thought of as two axes of individual psychology; one axis is called "confident-anxious," and the other is called "careful-impetuous."

Box 26.1, which is the same as Box 2.1, includes BB&K's descriptions of each of the five investor personality types that the model generates. Bailard, Biehl, and Kaiser also suggest approaches to advising each type of client.

Barnewall Two-Way Model

Marilyn MacGruder Barnewall's psychographic investor model distinguishes between two relatively simple investor types: passive investors

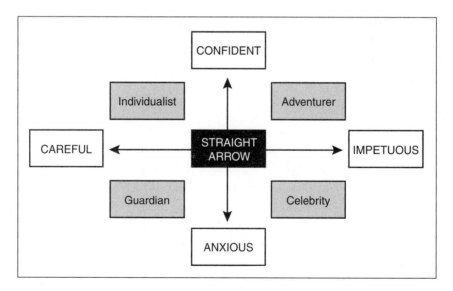

FIGURE 26.1 Representation of the BB&K Model

The **Adventurer**—People who are willing to put it all on one bet and go for it because they have confidence. They are difficult to advise, because they have their own ideas about investing. They are willing to take risks, and they are volatile clients from an investment counsel point of view.

The **Celebrity**—These people like to be where the action is. They are afraid of being left out. They really do not have their own ideas about investments. They may have their own ideas about other things in life, but not investing. As a result they are the best prey for maximum broker turnover.

The **Individualist**—These people tend to go their own way and are typified by the small business person or an independent professional, such as a lawyer, CPA, or engineer. These are people who are trying to make their own decisions in life, carefully going about things, having a certain degree of confidence about them, but also being careful, methodical, and analytical. These are clients whom everyone is looking for—rational investors with whom the portfolio manager can talk sense.

The **Guardian**—Typically as people get older and begin considering retirement, they approach this personality profile. They are careful and a little bit worried about their money. They recognize that they face a limited earning time span and have to preserve their assets. They are definitely not interested in volatility or excitement. Guardians lack confidence in their ability to forecast the future or to understand where to put money, so they look for guidance.

The **Straight Arrow**—These people are so well balanced, they cannot be placed in any specific quadrant, so they fall near the center. On average this group of clients is the average investor, a relatively balanced composite of each of the other four investor types, and by implication a group willing to be exposed to medium amounts of risk.

BOX 26.1   Descriptions of the BB&K Investor Personalities
Source: Thomas Bailard, David Biehl, and Ronald Kaiser. *Personal Money Management*, 5th ed. (Chicago: Science Research Associates, 1986).

and active investors. *Passive investors* are those investors who gained their wealth passively. They may have inherited capital or, as Barnewall suggests, worked as executives or professionals in very large firms. Passive investors have not become wealthy by gambling their own assets, and they demonstrate a need for security that exceeds their tolerance for risk. Corporate managers, lawyers, CPAs, medical and dental nonsurgeons, individuals with inherited wealth, small business owners who inherited their businesses, politicians, bankers, and journalists are other clients whom Barnewall classifies as typically passive investors.

Active investors are those individuals who have risked their own capital in order to earn their wealth. Their tolerance for risk is higher than their need for security. Correspondingly, active investors prefer to maintain control of their own investments. If they become involved in aggressive investments that they perceive as beyond control, active investors' risk tolerance drops quickly. Barnewall notes that, typically, entrepreneurs, small business owners who have built their own businesses, and professionals who head their own firms are all likely to display active investor behavior. Her analysis indicates that a quick, biographic glance at a client could provide important context for portfolio design.

RECENT DEVELOPMENTS IN INVESTOR PERSONALITY TYPES

Both the BB&K and Barnewell models emerged in the mid-1980s, and some notable advancements in investor personality taxonomy have occurred since then. The most significant development has been a move toward identifying specific *investor personality types*. Some large financial firms have conducted studies that classified people as *reluctant investors, competitive investors, analytical investors*, and so on. Individual practitioners have also drafted schemes to sort out motifs in investor behavior. Academic and other research has unearthed some interesting correlations between psychological traits and financial behavior. For example, some personality types have little time or patience for managing money, some start investing too late, and some show more discipline than others. Most modern classification schemes group investors into specific personality "buckets." John Smith might be labeled a "passive" investor or Jane Smith a "Celebrity."

I have taken a different approach to investor personality type analysis in an attempt to escape from inflexible "either-or" dichotomies. Channeling the format of the Myers-Briggs test, the following analysis incorporates three parallel scales, each with opposing "trait" poles, and identifies eight possible trait combinations that can result (analogously to Myers-Briggs's sixteen). A diagnostic test for determining investor personality type is presented, and advice is offered on how to deal with the various behaviors of the eight investor personality types (IPT).

The Eight Investor Personality Types

I identify three investor personality dimensions:

1. Idealist (I) versus Pragmatist (P)
2. Framer (F) versus Integrator (N)
3. Reflector (T) versus Realist (R)

Figure 26.2 offers a visual depiction of these three continuums.

Thus, there are eight possible investor personality types: IFT, IFR, INT, INR, PFT, PFR, PNT, and PNR. We will first review each investor personality type *dimension* and then refer to a diagnostic test, the results of which will correspond to a particular dimension that is designed to determine where an investor falls on a specific behavioral scale ("Are you more idealistic or pragmatic?"). We'll discuss scoring methods for investor personality diagnostics and summarize important investment considerations for each of the eight possible types.

Idealism/Pragmatism (I/P). People who fall at the "idealist" end of the I/P spectrum overestimate their investing abilities, display too much opti-

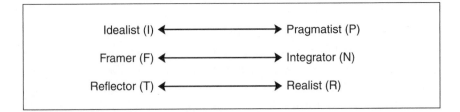

Idealist (I) ←————————→ Pragmatist (P)

Framer (F) ←————————→ Integrator (N)

Reflector (T) ←————————→ Realist (R)

FIGURE 26.2   Investor Personality Type Continuums

mism about the capital markets, and don't seek out information that contradicts their views. They hopefully discern patterns where none exist and believe that their above-average market acumen gives them an exaggerated degree of control over the outcomes of their investments. Often disinclined toward thorough research, they can fall prey to speculative market fads. Idealists can be subject to the following biases: overconfidence, optimism, availability, self-attribution, illusion of control, confirmation, recency, and representativeness.

"Pragmatists" display a realistic grasp of their own skills and limitations as investors. They are not too overconfident about the capital markets and demonstrate a healthy dose of skepticism regarding their investing abilities. They understand that investing is a probabilistic undertaking and do research to confirm their beliefs. Pragmatists are investors who are typically not susceptible to the aforementioned biases.

Framing/Integration (F/N). "Framers" tend to evaluate each of their investments through a particularistic lens and don't consider how each investment fits into an overall portfolio plan. They are too rigid in their mental approach to analyzing problems and do not contemplate exogeneities. The framer's portfolio appears to comprise disassociated "pots" of money, rather than a composite of complementary, interrelated investments. Framers also subconsciously "anchor" their estimates of market or security price levels, clinging to arbitrary purchase points which leads to bias in future calculations.

"Integrators" are characterized by an ability to contemplate broader contexts and externalities. They correctly view their portfolios as systems whose components can interact and balance one another. Integrators understand the performance correlations between various financial instruments and structure their portfolios accordingly. They are flexible in their approach to market and security price levels.

Framers may be susceptible to these biases: anchoring, conservatism, mental accounting, framing, and ambiguity. Integrators are investors who are typically not susceptible to the aforementioned biases.

Reflecting/Realism (T/R). "Reflectors" ("Ts") have trouble living with the consequences of their decisions and have difficulty taking action to rectify their behaviors. They justify and rationalize incorrect actions and hesitate to own up to decisions that have not worked out beneficially.

They also suffer from decision paralysis because they dread the sensation of regret, should they perchance miscalculate.

"Realists" have less trouble coming to terms with the consequences of their choices. They don't tend to scramble for excuses in order to justify incorrect actions, and they assume responsibility for their mistakes. Realists also have an easier time than reflectors with decision making under pressure because they don't experience regret as acutely and, therefore, don't dread it ahead of time.

Reflectors may be susceptible to these biases: cognitive dissonance, loss aversion, endowment, self-control, regret, status quo, and hindsight. Realists are investors who are typically not susceptible to the aforementioned biases.

DIAGNOSTIC TESTING

This section contains 15 diagnostic questions, with a separate set of five questions corresponding to each of the three dimensions of an investor's personality profile. When you finish the three tests, see Test Results Analysis to determine your investor personality type.

Test 1: Idealism vs. Pragmatism

These questions help determine whether an investor is an *idealist* or *pragmatist* (I or P).

Question 1: How much control do you believe you have in picking investments that will outperform the market?
   a. Absolutely no control.
   b. Little if any control.
   c. Some control.
   d. A fair amount of control.
   (Idealist = "c" or "d"; Pragmatist = "a" or "b")

Question 2: For how many consecutive years would a mutual fund manager need to outperform the market before you would consider that manager to be a skilled investor?
   a. 2 years.
   b. 3–4 years.
   c. 5 years.

d. More than 5 years.
(Idealist = "a" or "b"; Pragmatist = "c" or "d")

Question 3: When you are researching an investment, which is more important: relevant news and events of a very recent period *or* relevant news and events in the long-established past?

a. I generally place more weight on events in the recent past and give less emphasis to the distant past.

b. I generally place more weight on events in the distant past and give less emphasis to the recent past.

c. I generally place equal weight on events in the recent past and events in the distant past.

(Idealist = "a" or "b"; Pragmatist = "c")

Question 4: Relative to other investors, how good an investor are you?

a. Below average

b. Average

c. Above average

(Idealist = "c"; Pragmatist = "a" or "b").

Question 5: How easy do you think it was to predict the collapse of the tech stock bubble in March of 2000?

a. Easy.

b. Somewhat easy.

c. Somewhat difficult.

d. Difficult.

(Idealist = "a" or "b"; Pragmatist = "c" or "d"

Test 2: Framing versus Integration

These questions relate to whether an investor is a *framer* or an *integrator* (F or N).

Question 1: You purchase a stock for $20, based on a recommendation from a source that you usually trust. The stock subsequently drops to $15. Assume there is a 50 percent chance that it will now go up $5 and a 50 percent chance it will go down another $5. What do you do?

a. I hold the stock.

b. I sell the stock.

(Framer = "a"; Integrator = "b")

Question 2: Imagine yourself in each of the following situations. Which do you think would make you happier?

a. You lose $10 due to a hole in your pocket, but later you find $20 in the street.

b. You find $10 in the street.

c. I would be equally happy in Example a) and Example b).

(Framer = "a" or "b"; Integrator = "c")

Question 3: Some news is released that might have a negative impact on the price of a stock you hold. How do you typically react?

a. I usually wait for the market to communicate the significance of the information and then decide what to do.

b. I sometimes wait for the market to communicate the significance of the information, but other times I will immediately decide what to do.

c. I always act decisively and immediately decide what to do.

(Framer = "a" or "b"; Integrator = "c")

Question 4: Suppose that you are at a warehouse store, where you intend to purchase a flat screen TV. The model you've selected is priced at $750, and you are about to pay. However, at the last minute, you notice a discarded advertising flier featuring the same TV at a price of $720. You retrieve the ad, examine it more closely, and discover that the offer is still valid. To receive the discount, you'll need to drive to a competing electronics outlet about 10 minutes away. Will you get into your car and travel to the other store, in order to take advantage of the lower price?

a. Yes.

b. No.

(Answer after Question 5.)

Question 5: Suppose you go to a warehouse store to buy a mahogany table. The table that you want costs $4,000, and you decide that you are willing to pay. While you are waiting, you strike up a conversation with another store patron, who reveals that she's seen the same table available for $3,950 at a competing local furniture store about 10 minutes away. Will you get into your car and drive to the other store to obtain the lower price?

a. Yes.

b. No.

Answers to Questions 4 and 5. Most people would probably drive an extra 10 minutes to save $30 on the TV, but wouldn't go to the same trouble to save $50 on the table. While the scenario in question 5 actually nets more savings, a typical mental accounting scheme doesn't envision things this way. People who go out of their way to receive a discount in Question 4 but not in Question 5 are Framers. Those who don't are Integrators.

Test 3: Reflecting versus Realism

These questions relate to whether an investor is a *reflector* or a *realist* (T or R).

Question 1: Suppose you purchased a stock (after following your normal research process) that underperformed its expectations. In the absence of any other information, which statement would you view as more accurate?
a. This sounds like a case of bad luck.
b. This sounds like a case in which I made a mistake.
(Reflector = "a"; Realist = "b")

Question 2: Imagine yourself in each of the following situations. Which "hurts" more?
a. You purchased a stock, and it later fell in price.
b. You did research on a stock and intended to buy it, but never did. Later, it went up in price.
c. Neither scenario is particularly painful. I don't regret mistakes; I view them as a normal part of the investment process.
(Reflector = "a" or "b"; Realist = "c")

Question 3: Suppose that a colleague tells you about a new public company and recommends the stock. You do some research, and you agree that it's a good idea to invest. Shortly after you buy in, the stock appreciates by 20 percent, then falls by 50 percent. You later learn that the coworker sold the stock at its short-lived peak, while you still held your shares. Which statement best descries your reaction?
a. I would be angry, because my friend did not tell me when to sell.
b. I would not be angry, because I should have known when to sell.
(Reflector = "a"; Realist = "b")

Question 4: Was it difficult to predict the rise and subsequent fall of technology stocks at the turn of the millennium?

a. No, it was easy.

b. It was somewhat easy.

c. It was somewhat difficult.

d. It was difficult.

(Reflector = "a" or "b"; Realist = "c" or "d")

Question 5: Your investment portfolio contains a certain high-quality corporate bond. The bond has been providing income for you, and you are happy with it. Your financial advisor analyzes your bond holdings and recommends that you replace the corporate bond with a municipal bond of comparable quality, estimating that you will obtain a better return after capital gains taxes and fees. You aren't familiar with this municipal bond. What is your most likely response?

a. I will sell the corporate bond and purchase the municipal bond.

b. I will keep things as they are.

(Reflector = "b"; Realist = "a")

Scoring Guidelines

To identify the dominant trait on any of the three scales, tally your responses; for example, three out of five "Idealist" answers indicates idealism rather than pragmatism in Test 1. Ultimately, a complete set of responses will produce a three-letter acronym, which indicates some trait combination. In the IPT List, find the acronym that corresponds to your quiz diagnosis. Advice on the three continuums is offered in the next section.

IPT List

1. Investor Personality Type: IFT (Idealist, Framer, Reflector)
   Rating: Needs Improvement.
2. Investor Personality Type: IFR (Idealist, Framer, Realist)
   Rating: Needs Improvement.
3. Investor Personality Type: INT (Idealist, Integrator, Reflector)
   Rating: Needs Improvement.
4. Investor Personality Type: PFT (Pragmatist, Framer, Reflector)
   Rating: Needs Improvement.
5. Investor Personality Type: INR (Idealist, Integrator, Realist)
   Rating: Good.

6. Investor Personality Type: PFR (Pragmatist, Framer, Realist)
   Rating: Good.
7. Investor Personality Type: PNT (Pragmatist, Integrator, Reflector)
   Rating: Good.
8. Investor Personality Type: PNR (Pragmatist, Integrator, Realist)
   Rating: Excellent.

ADVICE

This advice is offered on each of the three investor personality continuums listed at the beginning of the chapter (i.e., I/P, F/N, T/R). If you found your acronym to be an IFT—that is, you were susceptible to all three negative aspects of the three continuums (Idealist, Framer, Reflector)—you need to heed the advice of each of the next three advice sections. If you were, say, an IFR—that is, you were subject to two of the three negative aspects of the three continuums (Idealist, Framer)—then you need to heed advice in the I and F sections but not in the T section. The other personality types follow the same scheme.

I/P. When you answered Test 1 and your score indicated that you were an "Idealist," advice specifically regarding Idealist behavior is this: Idealists need to make sure that they do fundamental research on their investments and ask hard questions before making an investment decision. Seek out information that may be contrary to your beliefs. Be more skeptical about an investment's performance prospects. Don't overestimate your own market savvy—you don't have as much control as you think you do over the outcome of your investments. In fact, even the most accomplished investors cannot control the markets. Things can and do go wrong. You will be a better investor for it!

F/N. When you answered Test 2 and your score indicated that you were a "Framer," advice specifically regarding Framer behavior is this: Keep a broader frame of mind (i.e., the bigger portfolio picture) when making investment decisions. Don't view your investments in unique accounts unless that helps you achieve your investment goals. If you do view your investments in unique accounts, try to make sure that these investments are not correlated with each other. Try to maintain an aggregate view of your portfolio, and don't evaluate an investment or potential investment in isolation from that view. Learn to be more flexible when estimating the value or the direction of market or securities prices. Be aware that investing can be an ambiguous undertaking and that seeking professional guidance is essential to reaching long-term financial goals.

T/R. When you answered Test 3 and your score indicated that you were a "Reflector," advice specifically regarding Reflector behavior is this: When you make a mistake, acknowledge it, and then apply the lesson learned to the next investment experience. Don't rationalize your behavior or make excuses. Instead, recall the rationale behind the decision you made—write down reasons, if necessary. When an investment doesn't perform, revisit your basis for purchasing it. Don't dwell on losses; they will occur. The best action to take is to sell and to redeploy the assets to a better use. Learning from your errors is the only way to become better at investing.

If your investor personality type was a PNR (Pragmatist, Integrator, Realist), congratulations! Based on the answers to these questions, your investor personality doesn't predispose you toward behavioral biases. Diligently heed your PNR instincts, and you should fare well.

CHAPTER 27

Neuroeconomics: The Next Frontier for Explaining Investor Behavior

Science does not know its debt to imagination.

—Ralph Waldo Emerson

An emerging field of study called *neuroeconomics* could offer tremendous insights for private-client investment practitioners. To study the neural basis of economic decision making,[1] neuroeconomics combines tools from *neuroscience*, such as functional Magnetic Resonance Imaging (MRI), Transcranial Cortex Stimulation (TCS), and Electrophysiology; from *psychology*, such as eye tracking and psychophysiology; and from *experimental economics*. In more practical terms, neuroeconomics is a discipline that attempts to bridge the gap between brain science and economic theory in order to better understand the choices people make regarding their money. How, for example, does emotion affect financial decision making? What about risk? Does risk affect people's judgment? How do people perceive uncertainty? Questions like these interest asset managers as well as neuroeconomists.

The most prominent work in the field during the time of this writing is Paul Glimcher's *Decisions, Uncertainty, and the Brain: The Science of Neuroeconomics.*[2] A New York University neuroscientist, Glimcher focuses his research on "the neural events that underlie behavioral decision making. Our approach to this problem consolidates mathematical economic approaches to decision making with traditional neurobiological tools. By using these tools in our physiological analyses of the brain stem, cortex, and the basal ganglia, we hope to develop a coherent view of how the brain makes decisions."[3]

Colin Camerer (California Institute of Technology), George Loewenstein (Carnegie Mellon University), and Drazen Prelec (Massachusetts Institute of Technology) also demonstrate important links between neuroscience and economics in their March 2005 paper, "Neuroeconomics: How Neuroscience Can Inform Economics."[4] Stanford University has contributed credibility and resources to neuroeconomics by dedicating a research laboratory to the nascent field; the Stanford lab has been an important hub for neuroeconomics discourse and experiments. In addition, Jason Zweig, of *Money* magazine, published some influential articles at the turn of the millennium, which keenly observed links between brain activity and investor behavior.

This chapter adopts a neuroeconomics focus, summarizing some important discoveries and hypotheses and suggesting potential implications for practitioners. We'll proceed by exploring, one by one, the neurobiological features most likely to associate with economic decision making. As we describe each brain function, we'll outline consequences for investors, and we'll offer advice for counteracting biased behavior where it arises.

The subtopics we review are: *dopamine, serotonin, amygdala, prefrontal cortex,* and *nucleus accumbens/anterior cingulate.*

OVERVIEW OF BRAIN ACTIVITIES

Dopamine

Background. *Dopamine* is a chemical that is naturally produced in the body. In the brain, dopamine functions as a neurotransmitter and is commonly associated with the neural *pleasure system*. Released in response to, or in expectation of, pleasurable stimuli, dopamine reinforces the inclination to engage in certain activities. Moreover, when a pleasurable result occurs that was unlikely or unexpected, *more* dopamine is released than when an anticipated prize simply arrives. If an expected reward falls through, however, dopamine emission stops completely. This plunges you into a kind of depression. The net effect is that people love the prospect of a one-in-a-million victory—even more so than a predictable windfall of equal magnitude—and feel, to a similarly inordinate extent, let down when a "dependable" prospect disappoints.

Implications for Investors. Dopamine is very important in finance because of its strong influence on risk-taking behavior. The desired effects of dopamine encourage people to go to Las Vegas, to play bingo, to invest in growth stocks, and to hold underdiversified portfolios in pursuit of great gains. If you hear, for example, that your neighbor just reaped a 200 percent return on Google, you might feel an urgent rush to call your broker and "get in." Even if you don't consider yourself a big risk taker, your brain is designed to want to win big. Dopamine makes winning big feel better than just winning—and the prospect of its euphoric effect prevents people from focusing on how small the odds of winning big actually are.

Dopamine has a distressing aspect, however, of which investors need to be aware. Once your brain is conditioned to predict a gain, something unexpectedly harsh happens when that expectation falls flat. While dopamine is active during the prediction phase, the dopamine flow stops immediately if, for example, a gain turns into a loss. This is not unlike the sensation of tearing open a highly anticipated holiday gift, certain you've received that special item you've had your eye on all year, only to discover, beneath the foil, a proverbial lump of coal. In this context, it is not so difficult to imagine how dopamine might indeed play a role in the market's overreaction to short-term earnings disappointments. It is likely that dopamine also contributes to individual behavioral biases—such as overconfidence, optimism, and others—that cause people to take long-shot risks. Finally, dopamine almost assuredly helps to account for greed.

Advice. Simply being aware of dopamine's effect is critically important. The next time you feel an urge to take on odds that objectively seem to be stacked against you, ask yourself if dopamine might be having an effect. Wanting to win is natural, but wanting to win really big is a craving that you may not realistically be able to satisfy. Take a step back, assess the risks, and reflect on why you are taking the action and how you will feel if it doesn't pay off.

Serotonin

Background. Medically, *serotonin* is a neurotransmitter synthesized in the central nervous system and digestive tract. In practical terms, serotonin plays an important role in the biochemistry of depression and anxiety, which influences human sexuality and appetite. A reduction of serotonin in the body is often linked to emotional and behavioral problems, such as anxiety, depression, impulsiveness, and irritability.

Implications for Investors.   Unfulfilled expectations, such as those that result from investment losses, depress brain serotonin levels. These emotional states are biological, protective mechanisms. Anxiety and depression can sometimes paralyze investors, encumbering them against assuming risks. At other times, investors can become impulsive and rely on unproven, erratic investment strategies (usually overtrading) in an attempt to recoup a loss and overcome a depressed state. As stated earlier, loss-averse investors weigh losses twice as heavily as commensurate gains. This fact, along with the statistically proven perils of too-frequent trading, suggests that moving repeatedly in and out of investments is an inherently self-destructive activity. Loss aversion may indeed be a direct result of depressed serotonin levels.

Advice.   Understanding how serotonin works is crucial to understanding why we are loss averse. Susceptibility to "get-even-itis" is, after all, quite widespread. As stated in Chapter 19, loss aversion can cause investors to hold losing investments too long; and a good way to prevent this behavior is to institute a stop-loss rule. A fixed stop-loss rule to sell, for example, after a 10 percent loss is common. This will help to keep the effects of serotonin loss at bay. Loss aversion can also cause investors to "take the money and run," selling winning positions too early out of fear that their luck won't last. Rules that govern the selling of investments should take into account fundamentals, valuation, and so on—not just price.

Amygdala

Background.   Located in the brain's medial temporal lobe, the almond-shaped *amygdala* plays a key role in primary emotions, such as fear and pleasure. Anxiety, autism, depression, narcolepsy, post-traumatic stress disorder, phobias. and schizophrenia are linked to abnormal functioning of the amygdala. It is the amygdala that prepares you for a "fight or flight" response during a sudden event or trauma.

Implications for Investors.   When investors panic as the market drops, the amygdala is probably responsible. An old adage claims that fear and greed are the main drivers of the market. Fear, indeed, has been deeply ingrained within human consciousness since the dawn of time and still has a huge effect today. Many a practitioner has received a frantic phone call from a nervous client during a sharp market downturn. This is an instance, however, in which fear works against an investor rather than acting as a survival instinct; a market trough is always the worst circumstance in which to sell. Instead, it is the time *to add* to undervalued positions. Many traders will tell you that they make the most money in times of panic—when Wall Street's amygdalas are the most active.

Advice.   Managing fear is a challenging but essential part of investing. Sir John Templeton said it best with the statement that investors should "buy when pessimism is at its maximum, sell when optimism is at its maximum." The difficulty with executing this advice is that pessimism (fear) is a powerful force when the markets are heading south. Try to remove the emotional reaction that fear produces, and look at valuation objectively. Oftentimes, as with many recent fear-producing events such as the 9/11 attacks or the Gulf wars, the markets are traumatized due to fear of the unknown. After each postcatastrophic sell-off, the markets have rebounded and then some. If you can keep your head even as those around you do not, then you will undoubtedly find success as an investor.

Prefrontal Cortex

Background.   The *prefrontal cortex* of the brain is involved in planning complex cognitive behaviors, as well as in social behavior and the expression of personality. The prefrontal cortex is found in the cortical regions of the frontal lobe, which are anterior to the primary and the association motor cortexes. The prefrontal cortex allows people to store memories, to draw general conclusions from particular data, to forecast the consequences of actions, and to compare current and past experiences. These functions, in turn, all help people to reach balanced judgments. You can also think of the prefrontal cortex as the brain's "network operations center" for decision making.

Implications for Investors.   Logically, if investors are making cognitive errors, the implication is that the prefrontal cortex does not have the proper data it needs to make balanced, informed decisions. In other words, when investors fall prey to biased behaviors, a lack of information is often to blame. Most of the chapters in this book dealing with specific behavioral biases have stressed the extent to which people can benefit by continuously educating themselves about their investments. The other important implication with regard to prefrontal cortex is that if any damage occurs to this area of the brain, through accidents or the natural aging process, investors can become very myopic in their reasoning. Studies have shown that people suffering from damaged cortexes demonstrate more immediate, less premeditated thinking and aren't as competent at long-range planning. Advisors need to be aware of this fact when helping injured and elderly people.

Advice.   Education is the key to combating cognitive biases. Practitioners who keep their clients carefully informed are helping to ensure healthy, long-term business relationships. Investors who want to limit their own cognitive errors can, along the same lines, seek out guidance via an advisor or self-education. Keeping the prefrontal cortex armed with the information it needs to make good decisions can mean the difference between making money and losing money.

Nucleus Accumbens/Anterior Cingulate

Background.   This discussion encompasses two organs: (1) the *nucleus accumbens* is a collection of neurons located where the head of the caudate and the anterior portion of the putamen meet just lateral to the septum pellucidum (basically, it is located behind your eyes). This area of the brain plays an important role in reward, pleasure, and addictive behaviors. (2) The *anterior cingulate*, the frontal part of the cingulate cortex, plays a role in a wide variety of autonomic functions, such as regulating heart rate and blood pressure, and is vital to cognitive functions, such as reward anticipation and decision making.

Together, the nucleus accumbens and anterior cingulate help people to recognize patterns and choose between alternatives. When activities take place around you, these two organs "light up" and begin to search for patterns in your environment. Millions of years ago, this primal instinct worked to humans' advantage; it helped them to monitor phenomena like weather, food distribution, and predator behavior. Today, if you're like most people, you probably aren't even aware of your brain's constant pattern seeking. But, the nucleus accumbens and anterior cingulate are as active as ever.

Implications for Investors. The most obvious implication for investors is that because the brain is searching for patterns, it may convince the cerebral cortex (the network operations center) that a pattern exists when, in fact, one does not exist. For example, in the 1990s, many companies reported on a very regular basis that they had exceeded their quarterly earnings estimates—if only by a few pennies. (It is now known that there may have been some "earnings management" taking place—but that is another story.) Each time, stock prices would jump in response to the news. When the brain sees a pattern—"This company has surpassed its earnings forecasts three quarters in a row!"—it often extrapolates and assumes that this pattern will continue into the future. Without proper objective thinking, investors falling into this trap will get burned when an earnings shortfall inevitably occurs. Wall Street traders are notorious for punishing companies that miss their earnings estimates, and people who previously bought up shares in these ill-fated companies can lose lots of money. This brain behavior may explain why value stocks, whose earnings rarely conform to any pattern, perform well over the long term. Because people are less likely to perceive patterns in companies that have inconsistent earnings, they may not be as quick to pick up on these companies as good investments.

Advice. Like your respiration or heartbeat, pattern seeking is persistent and innate; you can't consciously curb an instinct so deeply wired by eons of evolution. However, you can make sure to base your decision making only on those trends you've *rationally* distinguished through diligent research (not rules of thumb or intuition). Be wary of investments that have enjoyed spectacular earnings runs. Remember Cisco in the 1990s? Cisco, which helps to build and manage networking infrastructures, displayed consistently stellar earnings for many years in a row. When the Internet boom stopped, however, Cisco's stock took a horrific tumble. Studies have shown that Cisco is not alone and that, in general, stocks with consecutive stellar runs suffer not-so-stellar declines when they miss their earnings forecasts.

Notes

Chapter 1

1. The Federal Reserve Board, http://www.federalreserve.gov/boarddocs/speeches/1996/19961205.htm.
2. Robert Shiller, *Irrational Exuberance* (New Haven, CT: Yale University Press, 2000).
3. Owen A. Lamont and Richard H. Thaler, "Can the Market Add and Subtract? Mispricing in Tech Stock Carve-Outs," *Journal of Political Economy* 111, no. 2 (2003): 227–68.
4. This paper can be found on Meir Statman's home page at http://lsb. scu.edu/finance/faculty/Statman/Default.htm.
5. Nobel Prize web site: http://nobelprize.org/economics/laureates/2002/.
6. Jon E. Hilsenrath, "Belief in Efficient Valuation Yields Ground to Role of Irrational Investors: Mr. Thaler Takes on Mr. Fama," *Wall Street Journal,* October 18, 2004.
7. Ibid.
8. Meir Statman, "Behavioral Finance: Past Battles and Future Engagements," *Financial Analysts Journal* (November/December 1999).
9. Eugene Fama and Kenneth French, "The Cross-Section of Expected Stock Returns," *Journal of Finance* (1992).
10. Dream Value Management web site: http://www.dreman.com/.
11. James O'Shaughnessy, *What Works on Wall Street* (New York: McGraw-Hill Professional, 2005).
12. Dream Value Management web site: http://www.dreman.com/.
13. Robert Haugen and Philippe Jorion, "The January Effect: Still There after All These Years," *Financial Analysts Journal* (January-February 1996).
14. Russell Investment Group web site: http://www.russell.com/us/education_center/.
15. Chris R. Hensel and William T. Ziemba, "Investment Results from Exploiting Turn-of-the-Month Effects," *Journal of Portfolio Management* (Spring 1996).

Chapter 2

1. Adam Smith, *The Theory of Moral Sentiments* (1759).
2. Jeremy Bentham, *An Introduction to the Principles of Morals and Legislation* (1789).
3. John Maynard Keynes, *The General Theory of Employment* (New York: Harcourt, Brace, 1936).
4. A. E. Roth, "On the Early History of Experimental Economics," *Journal of the History of Economic Thought* 15 (Fall 1993): 184–209.

5. Ibid.

6. Ibid.

7. Ibid.

8. Donald Broadbent, *Perception and Communication* (New York: Pergamon Press, 1958).

9. H. Raiffa, *Decision Analysis: Introductory Lectures on Choices under Uncertainty* (Reading, MA: Addison-Wesley, 1968).

10. Daniel Kahneman and Mark Riepe, "Aspects of Investor Psychology: Beliefs, Preferences, and Biases Investment Advisors Should Know About," *Journal of Portfolio Management* 24 (1998): 52–65.

11. Daniel Kahneman, Paul Slovic, and Amos Tversky (eds.), *Judgment under Uncertainty: Heuristics and Biases* (New York: Cambridge University Press, 1982).

12. This paper can be found at http://www.garfield.library.upenn.edu/classics 1983/A1983QG78800001.pdf.

13. Daniel Kahneman and Amos Tversky, "Prospect Theory: An Analysis of Decisions under Risk," *Econometrica* 47 (1979): 313–27.

14. Ibid.

15. Daniel Kahneman and Mark Riepe, "Aspects of Investor Psychology: Beliefs, Preferences, and Biases Investment Advisors Should Know About," *Journal of Portfolio Management* 24 (1998): 52–65.

16. Ibid.

17. M. Barnewall, "Psychological Characteristics of the Individual Investor," in *Asset Allocation for the Individual Investor*, ed. William Droms (Charlottesville, VA: Institute of Chartered Financial Analysts, 1987).

18. Thomas Bailard, David Biehl, and Ronald Kaiser, *Personal Money Management*, 5th ed. (Chicago: Science Research Associates, 1986).

19. Ibid.

Chapter 3

1. Michael Pompian and John Longo, "Incorporating Behavioral Finance into Your Practice," *Journal of Financial Planning* (March 2005): 58–63.

2. Richard D. Glass, "Investment Education or Advice? That's the Wrong Question to Ask," *Employee Benefits Journal* 25, no. 2 (June 2000) (International Foundation of Employee Benefits).

3. Daniel Kahneman and Mark Riepe, "Aspects of Investor Psychology: Beliefs, Preferences, and Biases Investment Advisors Should Know About," *Journal of Portfolio Management* 24 (1998): 52–65.

Chapter 4

1. Roger G. Clarke and Meir Statman, "The DJIA Crossed 652,230," *Journal of Portfolio Management (*Winter 2000).

2. S. Lichtenstein, B. Fischoff, and L. D. Phillips, "Calibration of Probabilities: The State of the Art to 1980," in *Judgment under Uncertainty: Heuristics and Biases,* ed. David Kahneman, Paul Slovic, and Amos Tversky, (New York: Cambridge University Press, 1982), 306–334.

3. Brad M. Barber and Terrance Odean, "Boys Will Be Boys: Gender, Over-confidence, and Common Stock Investment," *Quarterly Journal of Economics* 116, no. 1 (February 2001): 261–92.
4. Terrance Odean, "Do Investors Trade Too Much?" *American Economic Review,* 1999, 1279–98.
5. Ibid.
6. Ibid.
7. Barber and Odean, "Boys Will Be Boys."

Chapter 5
1. Daniel Kahneman, Paul Slovic, and Amos Tversky (eds.), *Judgment under Uncertainty: Heuristics and Biases* (New York: Cambridge University Press, 1982).
2. Kenneth L. Fisher and Meir Statman, "A Behavioral Framework for Time Diversification," *Financial Analysts Journal* (May/June 1999).
3. See Morningstar web site: www.morningstar.com.
4. See Dalbar, Inc., web site: www.dalbar.com.

Chapter 6
1. G. Northcraft and M. Neale, "Experts, Amateurs, and Real Estate: An Anchoring-and-Adjustment Perspective on Property Pricing Decisions," *Organizational Behavior and Human Decision Processes* 39 (1987): 84–97.

Chapter 7
1. L. Festinger, *A Theory of Cognitive Dissonance* (Stanford, CA: Stanford University Press, 1957).
2. See www.money.cnn.com/1998/06/12/mutualfunds/q_worstfunds.
3. W. N. Goetzmann and N. Peles, "Cognitive Dissonance and Mutual Fund Investors," *Journal of Financial Research* 10 (Summer 1997): 145–58.
4. Ibid.

Chapter 8
1. Daniel Kahneman, Paul Slovic, and Amos Tversky (eds.), *Judgment under Uncertainty: Heuristics and Biases* (New York: Cambridge University Press, 1982).
2. Pedro Santa-Clara and Rossen Valkanov, "The Presidential Puzzle: Political Cycles and the Stock Market," *Journal of Finance* (October 2003).
3. Brad M. Barber and Terrance Odean, "All That Glitters: The Effect of Attention and News on the Buying Behavior of Individual and Institutional Investors (working paper, University of California-Berkeley, 2002).
4. See Paul Slovic, Baruch Fischoff, and Sarah Lichtenstein, "Facts versus Fiction: Understanding Public Fears," in *Judgment under Uncertainty: Heuristics and Biases,* ed. Daniel Kahneman, Paul Slovic, and Amos Tversky (New York: Cambridge University Press, 1982), 463–91.
5. S. Gadarowski, "Financial Press Coverage and Expected Stock Returns" (working paper, Cornell University, 2001).

Chapter 9
1. Dana S. Dunn, "Demonstrating a Self-Serving Bias," *Teaching of Psychology* 16 (1989): 21–22.
2. Simon Gervais and Terrance Odean, "Learning to Be Overconfident," *Review of Financial Studies* 14, no. 1: 1–27.
3. Ibid.

Chapter 10
1. Ellen Langer, "The Illusion of Control," *Journal of Personality and Social Psychology* 32 (1975): 311–328.
2. Andrea Breinholt and Lynnette A. Dalrymple, "The Illusion of Control: What's Luck Got to Do with It?" *The Myriad: Westminster College Undergraduate Academic Journal,* Summer 2004.
3. Ibid.
4. Terrance Odean, "Do Investors Trade Too Much?" *American Economic Review,* 1999, 1279–98.
5. Gerlinde Fellner, "Illusion of Control as a Source of Poor Diversification: An Experimental Approach," published by Max Planck Institute for Research into Economic Systems in Jena, Germany, May 2004.
6. Ibid.

Chapter 11
1. Ward Edwards, "Conservatism in Human Information Processing," in *Formal Representation of Human Judgment,* ed. B. Kleinmutz (New York: John Wiley & Sons, 1968).
2. David Hirshleifer, "Investor Psychology and Asset Pricing" (working paper, Fisher College of Business, The Ohio State University, 2001).
3. James Montier, *Behavioural Finance: Insights into Irrational Minds and Markets* (West Sussex, England: John Wiley & Sons, 2002).
4. James Montier, "Equity Research" (research report, Dresdner Kleinwort Wasserstein, 2002).
5. Nicholas Barberis, Robert W. Vishny, and Andrei Shleifer, "A Model of Investor Sentiment," *Capital Ideas* [University of Chicago] 1, no. 2 (Winter 1998).
6. Werner F. M. De Bondt and Richard Thaler, "Does the Stock Market Overreact?" *Journal of Finance* 40, no. 3 (July 1985): 793–805.
7. Barberis, Vishny, and Shleifer, "A Model of Investor Sentiment."
8. Ibid.
9. Ibid.

Chapter 12
1. Leonard J. Savage, *The Foundations of Statistics,* 2nd rev. ed. (New York: Dover, 1972).
2. Daniel Ellsberg, "Risk, Ambiguity, and the Savage Axioms," *Quarterly*

Journal of Economics 75 (November 1961): 4, 643–69. © 1961 by the President and Fellows of Harvard College. Reprinted with permission by MIT Press Journals.

3. Chip Heath and Amos Tversky, "Preferences and Beliefs: Ambiguity and the Competence in Choice under Uncertainty," *Journal of Risk and Uncertainty* 4 (1991): 5–28.
4. John R. Graham, Campbell R. Harvey, and Hai Huang, "Investor Competence, Trading Frequency, and Home Bias" (working paper, Duke University, 2003).
5. P. Maenhout, "Robust Portfolio Rules and Asset Pricing" (working paper, Harvard University 1999).
6. Graham, Harvey, and Huang, "Investor Competence, Trading Frequency, and Home Bias."
7. Ibid.

Chapter 13

1. Daniel Kahneman, J. L. Knetsch, and Richard H. Thaler, "The Endowment Effect, Loss Aversion, and Status Quo Bias: Anomalies," *Journal of Economic Perspectives* 5, no. 1 (1991): 193–206.
2. J. L. Knetsch, "The Endowment Effect and Evidence of Nonreversible Indifference Curves," *American Economic Review* 79 (5): 1277–84.
3. Ibid.
4. W. Samuelson and R. Zeckhauser, "Status Quo Bias in Decisions Making," *Journal of Risk and Uncertainty* 1, no. 1: 7–59. With kind permission of Springer Science and Business Media.
5. John A. List, "Does Market Experience Eliminate Market Anomalies?" *Quarterly Journal of Economics* 118 (February 2003): 41–71.
6. Ibid. © 2003 by the President and Fellows of Harvard College and the Massachusetts Institute of Technology. Reprinted with permission by MIT Press Journals.

Chapter 14

1. Richard H. Thaler and Hersh M. Shefrin, "The Behavioral Life-Cycle Hypothesis," *Economic Inquiry* (1988).
2. Richard H. Thaler and Shlomo Benartzi, "Save More Tomorrow: Using Behavioral Economics to Increase Employee Saving," *Journal of Political Economy* 112, no. 1: S164–87.
3. Annamaria Lusardi, "Explaining Why So Many Households Do Not Save" (working paper, Irving Harris Graduate School for Public Policy Studies, University of Chicago, 2000).
4. Annamaria Lusardi, "Information, Expectations, and Savings for Retirement," in *Behavioral Dimensions of Retirement Economics*, ed. H. Aaron (Washington, D.C.: Brookings Institution and Russell Sage Foundation, 1999), 81–155.

Chapter 15

1. Daniel Lovallo and Daniel Kahneman, "Delusions of Success. How Optimism Undermines Executives' Decisions," *Harvard Business Review* 81, no. 7: 56–63, 117.
2. Susan Stabile (St. John's University School of Law), transcript of U.S. Senate Committee on Governmental Affairs Enron Hearings, February 5, 2002.
3. Paul Farrell, "Investors Are Their Own Worst Enemy. Nobel Laureate Says Optimism Sabotages Performance," CBS Marketwatch.com, July 22, 2003, http://cbs.marketwatch.com/news/story.asp.
4. See Dalbar, Inc., web site: www.dalbar.com.
5. Torben Lütje and Lukas Menkhoff, "What Drives Home Bias? Evidence from Fund Managers' Views" (working paper, University of Hannover, January 6, 2004).
6. Robert J. Shiller, F. Kon-Ya, and Y. Tsutsui, "Why Did the Nikkei Crash? Expanding the Scope of Expectations Data Collection," *Review of Economics and Statistics* 78 (1996): 156–64.

Chapter 16

1. Richard H. Thaler, "Towards a Positive Theory of Consumer Choice," *Journal of Economic Behavior and Organization* 1 (1980): 39–60.
2. Richard H. Thaler, "Mental Accounting Matters," *Journal of Behavioral Decision Making* 12, no. 3: 183–206.
3. Amos Tversky and Daniel Kahneman, "Rational Choice and the Framing of Decisions," *Journal of Business* 59 (1986): S251-S278.
4. Drazen Prelec and Duncan Simester, "Always Leave Home without It: A Further Investigation of the Credit Card Effect on Willingness to Pay," *Marketing Letters* 12, no. 1: 5–12.
5. Tversky and Kahneman, "Rational Choice."
6. Ming Hang, Nicholas Barberis, and Tano Santos, "Prospect Theory and Asset Prices," *Quarterly Journal of Economics* (February 2001).
7. Lucy F. Ackert , Narat Charupat, Bryan K. Church, and Richard Deaves, "An Experimental Examination of the House Money Effect in a Multi-Period Setting" (working paper, Federal Reserve of Atlanta, September 2003).
8. Daniel Nevins, "Goals-Based Investing: Integrating Traditional and Behavioral Finance," *Journal of Wealth Management* (Spring 2004): 8–23.
9. Jean L. P. Brunel, "Revisiting the Asset Allocation Challenge through a Behavioral Finance Lens," *Journal of Wealth Management* (Fall 2003): 10–20.

Chapter 17

1. T. Gilovich, *How We Know What Isn't So: The Fallibility of Human Reason in Everyday Life* (New York: Free Press, 1993).
2. Meir Statman and Kenneth L. Fisher, "Cognitive Biases and Market Forecasts," *Journal of Portfolio Management* (Fall 2000).
3. Robert J. Prechter, *At the Crest of the Tidal Wave: A Forecast for the Great Bear Market* (New York: John Wiley & Sons, 1997).

Chapter 18

1. B. Fischoff, "Hindsight/Foresight: The Effect of Outcome Knowledge on Judgment under Uncertainty," *Journal of Experimental Psychology: Human Perception and Performance* 1, no, 3: 288–99.
2. Richard Posner, "Rational Choice, Behavioral Economics, and the Law," *Stanford Law Review* 50 (1998): 1551–75.
3. Michael Cooper, Roberto Gutierrez, and William Marcum, "On the Predictability of Stock Returns in Real Time," *Journal of Business* 78, no. 2 (April 2005).
4. Ibid.

Chapter 19

1. Daniel Kahneman and Amos Tversky, "Prospect Theory: An Analysis of Decision under Risk," *Econometrica* 47 (1979): 263–291.
2. Hersh Shefrin and Meir Statman, "The Disposition to Sell Winners Too Early and Ride Losers Too Long: Theory and Evidence," *Journal of Finance* 40 (1985): 77–90.
3. Rajnish Mehra and Edward C. Prescott, "The Equity Premium: A Puzzle," *Journal of Monetary Economics* 15 (March 1985): 145–61.
4. Shlomo Benartzi and Richard H. Thaler, "Myopic Loss Aversion and the Equity Premium Puzzle," *Quarterly Journal of Economics* (February 1995): 73–92. See http://gsbwww.uchicago.edu/fac/richard.thaler/research/myopic .pdf.
5. Ibid.

Chapter 20

1. James Montier, "Irrational Pessimism and the Road to Revulsion" (research report, Dresdner Kleinwort Wasserstein, February 2003).

Chapter 21

1. Hersh Shefrin and Meir Statman, "Explaining Investor Preference for Cash Dividends," *Journal of Financial Economics* 13 (June 1984). Reprinted in *Advances in Behavioral Finance*, ed. Richard H. Thaler (New York: Russell Sage Foundation, 1993).

Chapter 22

1. Daniel Kahneman and Amos Tversky, "Choices, Values, and Frames," *American Psychologist* 39 (1984): 341–50. Reprinted as Chapter 1 in *Choices, Values, and Frames*, ed. Daniel Kahneman and Amos Tversky (New York: Cambridge University Press and the Russell Sage Foundation, 2000).

Chapter 23

1. W. Samuelson and R. J. Zeckhauser, "Status Quo Bias in Decision Making," *Journal of Risk and Uncertainty* 1, no. 1 (1988): 7–59.

2. Daniel Kahneman, J. L. Knetch, and Richard H. Thaler, "The Endowment Effect, Loss Aversion, and Status Quo Bias: Anomalies," *Journal of Economic Perspectives* 5, no. 1 (1991): 193–206.
3. Samuelson and Zeckhauser, "Status Quo."
4. Ibid.

Chapter 25

1. Michael Pompian and John Longo, "A New Paradigm for Practical Application of Behavioral Finance: Creating Investment Programs Based on Personality Type and Gender to Produce Better Investment Outcomes," *Journal of Wealth Management* (Fall 2004).
2. Daniel Kahneman and Amos Tversky, "Prospect Theory: An Analysis of Decision under Risk," *Econometrica* 47 (1979): 263–91.
3. M. Barnewall, "Psychological Characteristics of the Individual Investor," in *Asset Allocation for the Individual Investor,* ed. William Droms (Charlottesville, VA: Institute of Chartered Financial Analysts, 1987).
4. Thomas Bailard, David Biehl, and Ronald Kaiser, *Personal Money Management*, 5th ed. (Chicago: Science Research Associates, 1986).
5. Barnewall, "Psychological Characteristics."
6. Bailard, Biehl, and Kaiser, *Personal Money Management.*
7. Brad M. Barber and Terrance Odean, "Boys Will Be Boys: Gender, Overconfidence, and Common Stock Investment," *Quarterly Journal of Economics* 116, no. 1 (February 2001): 261–92. © 2001 by the President and Fellows of Harvard College and the Massachusetts Institute of Technology. Reprinted with permission by MIT Press Journals.
8. D. Kahneman and M. Riepe, "Aspects of Investor Psychology," *Journal of Portfolio Management* (Summer 1998): 52–64.
9. P. Tieger and B. Barron-Tieger, *Do What You Are: Discover the Perfect Career for You through the Secrets of Personality Type* (New York: Little, Brown, 1995).

Chapter 27

1. Antonio Rangel, "Neuroeconomics at Stanford" (Stanford University), http://neuroeconlab.stanford.edu/necon_stanford.htm.
2. Paul W. Glimcher, *Decisions, Uncertainty, and the Brain: The Science of Neuroeconomics* (Cambridge, MA: MIT Press, 2003).
3. Paul W. Glimcher, "Planning and Action in the Oculomotor System" (New York University), http://www.cns.nyu.edu/corefaculty/Glimcher.php.
4. Colin Camerer, George Loewenstein, and Drazen Prelec, "Neuroeconomics: How Neuroscience Can Inform Economics," *Journal of Economic Literature* 43 (2005): 9.

Index

Michael M. Pompian is the Director of the Private Wealth Practice at Hammond Associates, an investment consulting firm serving institutional and private wealth clients. Pompian earned an MBA from Tulane University and a BS in Management from the University of New Hampshire. He holds the Chartered Financial Analyst (CFA) designation and is a Certified Financial Planner (CFP) and a Certified Trust Financial Advisor (CTFA). Prior to joining Hammond Associates, Pompian was a Wealth Management Advisor with Merrill Lynch and PNC Private Bank. Prior to these positions, he was an investment advisor to a family office in Dallas, Texas. He is a member of the CFA Institute (CFAI) and the New York Society of Securities Analysts (NYSSA) and is on the board of trustees for several nonprofit organizations. Pompian has written and published several articles on the subject of behavioral finance in the *Journal of Wealth Management* and the *Journal of Financial Planning* and is a frequent speaker on the topic of behavioral finance. He is married with two sons and lives in Bedminster, New Jersey. He can be reached at mpompian@hammondassociates.com.